# COMPUTER SECURITY
## Readings from
## *Security Management*
## Magazine

# COMPUTER SECURITY
# Readings from
# *Security Management*
# Magazine

Edited by

**Shari Mendelson Gallery**

**Butterworths**

Boston London Durban Singapore Sydney Toronto Wellington

Individual chapters reprinted with permission of American Society for Industrial Security, from *Security Management*.

**Library of Congress Cataloging-in-Publication Data**

Computer security.

    Includes bibliographies and index.
    1. Computers—Access control.   2. Electronic data processing departments—Security measures.
I. Gallery, Shari Mendelson.  II. Security management.
QA76.9.A25C655   1987     005.8     86-18867
ISBN 0-409-90084-2

Butterworth Publishers
80 Montvale Avenue
Stoneham, MA 02180

10 9 8 7 6 5 4 3 2 1

Printed in the United States of America

# CONTENTS

ASIS                                                                      xiii

Introduction                                                               xv

PART   I. COMPUTERS—A SOURCE OF SECURITY CONCERN                            1

1.     "Why Haven't You Done Something About EDP Security?"
       *Roger D. Wilson and Martin E. Silverman*                            3
       Managers must concern themselves with computer security
       because computer security is a business management prob-
       lem, not a technical problem. Eight features of a comprehen-
       sive EDP security program are discussed.

2.     Before Disaster Strikes, Fortify Your Computer
       *Henry M. Kluepfel*                                                   9
       The proliferation of computer use and the known examples
       of computer abuse provide clear evidence that computer
       crime is potentially devastating. Research findings point the
       way of prevention; new ways of doing business in a comput-
       erized environment are needed.

3.     Computer Security Belongs in the Security Department
       *Henry J. Beattie*                                                   19
       The common practice of assigning responsibility for EDP se-
       curity to EDP staff is a mistake. Educating security staff
       about computers is far easier and more effective than train-
       ing highly mobile DP personnel in the many relevant facets
       of security.

4.     Are You Computer Wise?
       *Frederick G. Tompkins, CPP*                                         23
       Computer security is multidisciplinary and requires that a re-
       sponsible manager be trained extensively in both security
       and computers. A recommended course of study is presented
       for security pros who need DP expertise, and another is set
       forth for DPers who need security know-how.

5.   The Gap between *Computer* People and *Security* People
     *Dennis F. Poindexter*                                          27
     A number of factors contribute to the gap; getting people to
     recognize the differences in perspective is one step toward
     needed cooperation. A team approach to computer security
     is increasingly logical in light of the complexity of the field.

6.   Automated Information Systems: The Same Rules Don't
     Apply
     *James A. Schweitzer, CDP*                                      35
     Automated information systems differ from paper-based
     ones; they lack the physical entities upon which traditional
     safeguards rely. New information characteristics need new
     procedures for security, auditability, and control.

PART  II. EVALUATING THE RISKS                                       39

7.   Judging Your Computer Liability
     *Robert F. Johnson, CPP*                                        41
     While the concept of the duty to safeguard has not specifi-
     cally been stated in law with regard to computers, analogies
     in product liability and malpractice suits can be seen. Regu-
     latory developments impose a duty, and various financial
     and securities agreements put forth safeguarding require-
     ments. Knowing responsibilities as well as rights is impor-
     tant for computer security.

8.   Put Information Assets on the Balance Sheet
     *Dr. Alan G. Merten, Patrice Delaney, Beth Pomerantz, and
     Paula Kelly*                                                    51
     Attaching appropriate value to assets is basic to making
     good security decisions; showing information assets on the
     organizational balance sheet forces increased awareness of
     the need to expand and update controls. How to value intan-
     gible assets is explained. The exercise can be useful for allo-
     cating control resouces, but must be repeated since
     organizations are dynamic.

9.   The Basics of EDP Risk Assessment
     *James R. Wade*                                                 57
     To decide (and justify) what to do to protect computer facili-
     ties, an EDP risk assessment is often advocated. Generally a
     systems approach is used, looking at communications, per-
     sonnel, documents and media, procedures, and the environ-
     ment of the DP center. Step-by-step guidance through the
     process is given.

10. Computing Security Risk Analysis: Is it Worth it?
*James A. Schweitzer, CDP* 83
Traditional risk analysis has flaws and is expensive; a program of business information security can be a good alternative.

11. The Hidden Risk in Risk Analysis
*Howard R. Keough, CPP* 87
Assembling the cost information and assets inventory necessary for a comprehensive risk analysis can be a prohibitive
task.

PART III. FOCUSING PROTECTION EFFORTS 91

12. Selective Protection
*Frank T. Roedell* 93
Focus protection efforts on the most valuable and creative
work and seek support from top management and product
management. Develop a plan for protecting those assets,
then promote it to gain support.

13. Information Security Strategy
*Donald J. Coppotelli* 97
What happens when data processing functions are spread
across many organizational divisions? GE turned to a task
force to set up corporate-wide security standards and standard risk assessment methodology to evaluate the cost effectiveness of security measures.

14. Effectively Securing Business Communications
*James A. Schweitzer, CDP* 101
Business communications frequently involve computers, and
all business communications activities have implications for
information security. Recognizing the various processes
within which each of these activities falls can aid in the determination of proper protection measures.

15. Protecting Information Outside the Office
*M. L. Proctor* 105
The portability of computers introduces another security concern as employees transport hardware and sensitive information outside the traditional work environment.

16. Don't Forget to Debrief
*M. L. Proctor* 109
When an employee has worked with sensitive information, a

lot of vital information can walk out the door when that employee departs. A security debriefing should be standard practice.

17. Data Security—Key to Protecting Your Store's Assets
    *Charles Jackson*                                                      113
    Development of controls must be an integral part of any
    computer-based system. This has proven particularly important in the retailing industry.


PART IV. IDENTIFYING THE THREAT                                           121

18. Who Are the Computer Criminals?
    *Jay Becker*                                                          123
    An analysis of cases in the National Center for Computer
    Crime Data's files discounts two of the most common ideas
    of who computer criminals really are. Becker outlines seven
    points of view, on the part of the offenders, that show up
    most frequently.

19. Computer Abuse Research Update
    *Donn B. Parker*                                                      131
    The Computer Abuse Research Project looked at possible relationships between the proliferation of computers and increasing reports of computer crime. This 1980 update
    examined findings as of 1979.


PART V. MANAGING EDP AND INFORMATION SECURITY                             145

20. Some Basic Bytes on Keeping Computer Security Thieves
    Out of Your System
    *Arion N. Pattakos, CPP*                                              147
    Minimize losses and maximize availability of data, equipment and processing capability by establishing in-depth security safeguards that follow an overall security posture
    appropriate to the operational uses and value of a particular
    computer system.

21. Insurance Against a Data Disaster
    *Bernard Balter*                                                      155
    Off-site data storage is a widely recommended insurance
    measure; site selection criteria are outlined.

22.  Quick, Efficient Recovery of the DP Function: A Critical
     Security Responsibility
     *Michael Sobol*                                                   159
     EDP auditors and security professionals share the responsi-
     bility for contingency plans to maintain continued processing
     capabilities in the event of disruption of normal processing
     functions. This responsibility has been dictated by several
     government and professional standards.

23.  How Changes in Computing Practices Affect Security
     *James A. Schweitzer, CDP*                                        167
     Most companies lack policies on time-sharing, remote pro-
     cessing, and distributed computing environments. A review
     of current practices that are weak and recommended protec-
     tive measures.

24.  Will Computer Security Keep Pace?
     *Carl R. Armstrong, CCP*                                          181
     Except for government installations, automated system secu-
     rity for mainframe computers is spotty; smaller operating
     systems tend to have even less security support. Despite im-
     provements in security software, most advances have been
     made in security hardware for computers.

25.  Remote Controls for Computer Data: Data Processing Firms
     Offer Security Packages
     *Mary Alice Crawford*                                             187
     Many firms rely on service bureaus for data processing; se-
     curity provisions by these firms should be among the selec-
     tion criteria.

26.  Computational Cryptography Is an EDP Security Aid
     *William E. Perry and Herbert S. Bright*                          191
     What are potential uses of cryptography for computer secu-
     rity, and what is its proper role in the DP security program?

PART  VI. PHYSICAL SECURITY ISSUES                                     201

27.  Seven Fallacies Confuse Computer Fire Safety
     *Robert V. Jacobson, CPP*                                         203
     Fire safety, an important computer security consideration,
     continues to be confused by some commonly accepted mis-
     information.

28.    Security in the Trenches
       *Charles H. Norris, Jr., PE*                                    211
       Open-plan offices offer flexibility and savings, but introduce
       security weaknesses. Changes at the design stage can offset
       some of these shortcomings.

29.    Scanning the Site for Computer Installations
       *Richard H. Bessenhoffer*                                       215
       Features that make a site desirable often also make it vulner-
       able. Factors to be considered are explained from a security
       perspective.

30.    Controlling Physical Access from a Central Location
       *Brian B. Austin*                                               221
       Electronic access controls are useful tools for data process-
       ing security. A look at some of the sources of such controls
       and evaluation criteria are presented.

31.    What's New in Computer Security Accessories
       *Sandy Evans*                                                   233
       Four categories of hardware accessories are examined: en-
       cryption devices, call-back systems, identification devices,
       and physical anti-theft devices.

32.    Destruction of Input and Output Materials
       *Megan Jaegerman*                                               239
       Protecting the contents of a computer system can be point-
       less if the sources of information that go into it and the data
       that come out of it are not controlled with equal care. Op-
       tions for disposing of input and output materials are exam-
       ined.

33.    Conservation and the Destruction of Classified Waste
       Material
       *Gerald A. Straccia*                                            247
       The Department of Defense encourages destruction of classi-
       fied waste. One company found it could do so by recycling
       the resulting waste materials, to good end, both economi-
       cally and environmentally.

PART   VII. SOFTWARE CONTROLS                                          251

34.    How to Select and Implement a Data Security Product
       *Robert E. Johnson*                                             253
       The selection of a data security product complicates the

choice and implementation of a computer system. The process should begin before a need is perceived. Who should be involved and how such products should be integrated into existing controls are examined. Some products available for IBM mainframes are reviewed.

35.    A Technical Approach to Computer Access Control
       *Eugene F. Troy, Stuart W. Katzke, and Dennis D. Steinauer*    267
       Access control encompasses defining rules governing access privileges, implementing technical mechanisms to enforce these rules, and establishing administrative practices and procedures for effective and secure operation.

36.    A Model for Screening Computer Users
       *Charles Goodroe*    275
       An example of a computer system access program is presented and the logic and functions in the control process are described step by step.

PART    VIII. IF A CRIME IS SUSPECTED . . .    287

37.    The Role of the Questioned Document Examiner in Computer Crime Investigations
       *Dr. David A. Crown*    289
       If a computer crime is suspected, establishing acceptable evidence may prove difficult. A series of steps for using a questioned document examiner to aid in the effort is set forth.

Index    293

# ASIS

The American Society for Industrial Security is a worldwide organization of management specialists dedicated to protecting corporate and institutional assets. Founded in 1955, the Society is comprised of directors, managers, and supervisors responsible for security and asset protection programs in government, public institutions, and every field of business.

For large and small organizations from New York to New Delhi, ASIS members develop and administer programs to thwart every conceivable crime—from pirating trade secrets to shoplifting. They are also responsible for minimizing losses from natural and man-caused disasters.

ASIS disseminates information and tailors instructional programs to meet the rapidly expanding responsibilities of security professionals. Through more than 179 chapters in the US and abroad, and through frequent educational programs and publications, ASIS enables members to keep posted on developments in security and to share their specialized knowledge and skills.

ASIS has standing committees whose efforts focus on security functions common to most types of organizations such as physical security, disaster planning, computer security, proprietary information, fire prevention, and terrorism. A second group of committees concentrates on security concerns of specific types of organizations, such as government installations, retailers, financial institutions, health care facilities, and energy firms.

## Security Management

*Security Management* is a monthly magazine published by the American Society for Industrial Security (ASIS). Written for the benefit of practicing security professionals, *Security Management* (*SM*) covers all aspects of the diverse field of security. Every kind of organization—from large defense contract manufacturers to hotel and motel chains to transportation companies—has assets that need protection. In some cases the assets are costly physical equipment, in other cases the assets take the form of critical information or the specialized knowledge of a top executive. Each month *SM* presents articles that help security managers, in all kinds of organizations, learn ways to better protect their employers' assets.

# INTRODUCTION

Whether you view the spread of computers as a good development or a bad one, computers are becoming a fact of life in modern society. They are rapidly being adopted in nearly every type of business as well as in many schools and homes. This spread carries implications for just about every discipline; security is no exception. Not every security job is affected, but the security of any organization where computers are introduced is.

For that reason, whenever computers are introduced into an organization's operations, whether the first computer is being brought on line or equipment is being added or replaced, the impact on the organization's security should be examined. All too often security is forgotten amidst the excitement about new equipment and improved capabilities. But just as computers have proven to be an enormous boon to the processing and storage of business information, so too have they proven a powerful tool for those who would use or alter information to their own, less-than-honest ends. Because computers enable more information to be handled more quickly, they seem to magnify the opportunity for serious damage, whether it is due to errors or intentional acts of abuse.

Computers frequently represent sizable equipment investments, which automatically should make them a security concern. Further, all computer equipment is easily damaged, making it a common target for disgruntled employees, and in the case of personal computers, the equipment can be literally carried out the door. The fact that computers often become such an integral part of day-to-day operations makes having them out of commission due to theft or damage quite costly to an organization, sometimes enormously so. This characteristic alone qualifies computers as important assets to be protected.

Of course, software and data alteration or manipulation can have a similar deleterious effect, sometimes with greater potential for damage, so software and data accessibility also deserve security attention. But from whom? Does the responsibility belong to data processing personnel? Or does it fall within the sphere of security staff? Or somewhere else? The issue is much debated, but the most effective answer is doubtless that computer security must be a shared responsibility and effort.

Where and how does the computer security effort start? What must be taken into consideration once the need for computer security has been recognized? What threats must be guarded against? Who are the most likely perpetrators of these threats? These and related questions are the focus of this book.

As a compilation of articles that have been published in a single, multi-faceted magazine, this volume is by no means a comprehensive guide to computer security.

Because the articles were originally presented over an extended span of time, some repeat introductory information to set the stage for the ideas subsequently set forth. One article, "Controlling Physical Access from a Central Location," has been abridged to eliminate dated information that would not be helpful to the reader.

The reader is also cautioned to keep in mind that legislative, regulatory, and judicial developments not covered within the scope of this book may affect computer security activities. Therefore this book should not be relied upon as the final authority for any legal points. The reader is advised to seek further legal guidance as appropriate.

Just as no aspect of computers remains static for long, security for them is also a continually developing field. Consequently, it is encumbent upon anyone charged with responsibility for computer security to monitor current sources of information on the subject as they become available. *Security Management* regularly carries articles about computer security. Numerous other periodicals in the security field, the data processing field, and other management disciplines, such as auditing and risk management, frequently address the subject as well. In addition, educational programs offered by the American Society for Industrial Security and other organizations are also good sources for learning more about current computer security techniques. The reader is encouraged to take advantage of these resources.

# PART I

## Computers—A Source of Security Concern

Short of Rumplestiltskin, you would be hard-pressed to find anyone who is unaware of the explosion of computer technology in our world. Relatively few types of business remain that have not integrated computers into some aspect of their operations. As organizations come to rely on computers for increasing numbers of functions, managers are faced with the fact that this reliance opens new security vulnerabilities and enlarges some old ones. From this realization must come preventive action or management is falling short of its responsibilities.

The articles in Part I present convincing evidence of the importance of computer security and offer guidance for the development of computer security programs. Who should shoulder the responsibility and what training is appropriate for these individuals are suggested. Observations about how automated information systems differ from traditional, paper-based ones lend insight into why, as one author puts it, ''new ways of doing business in a computerized environment are needed.''

1

# CHAPTER 1

## "Why Haven't You Done Something About EDP Security?"

Roger D. Wilson
Martin E. Silverman
Consultants
Coopers & Lybrand

Spurred by publicity about hackers and their antics, publications as different as the *New York Times* and *Datamation* have recently made computer security a hot topic on their pages. Some have criticized computer hackers for their lack of ethics, while others have praised them for their creativity and curiosity.

Regardless of how we feel about the hackers, their activities and the publicity have clearly demonstrated the vulnerability of the data processing resource. As business becomes more and more dependent on electronic data processing (EDP), it is equally clear that senior managers must concern themselves with computer security. Management must become familiar with the problem and with the issues that will affect their companies.

Management must first recognize two basic facts:

1. *EDP security is not a technical problem* and thus not the sole responsibility of the EDP director. EDP security is a business management problem relating to the protection of a vital corporate asset as valuable as the physical means of producing a product or the intellectual and decision-making capabilities of management itself. That asset is corporate data: the key to knowing your company, your clients, your market, and your strategies for survival.

Reprinted with the permission of the American Society for Industrial Security, from *Security Management*, March 1985 p 69.

2.   *EDP security can no longer be applied after the fact* to a newly developed computer application or system. EDP security must be planned, engineered, and monitored from the design stage of systems development through an application's obsolescence.

## UNDERSTANDING THE REALITIES

Even before hacking incidents began to come to light, the subject of EDP security was being discussed with increasing frequency in publications directed at senior management. The reasons for this concern were and are very simple:

- Modern American business has become almost totally dependent on the availability of data processing resources.
- The amount of money being spent on these resources has increased to a level that makes it leap off the pages of corporate financial statements, demanding examination.
- The evolution of minicomputers and microcomputers and recent advancements in word processing and telecommunications capabilities have spread dependence on data processing throughout the corporation.
- Senior management is continuously exhorted to experiment with decision support, executive support, and financial modeling systems that are user-friendly and require no programming knowledge.

In the executive-oriented microcomputer arena alone, data that used to require three signatures and four passwords to view is being distributed for individualized "what-if" analysis. This important data is being left on floppy disks on unattended desks in scores of offices across the nation. Other data, entered directly by secretaries, analysts of all varieties, and executives themselves, without benefit of standards and edit procedures, are being used to generate management decisions that are accepted because they are "supported by the computer."

As a result of these and other factors, management's desire for comprehensive EDP security has been intensified. However, management must realize EDP security can no longer be handled as a technological add-on controlled by the central EDP resource. Instead, it must become an integral part of the corporate way of doing business.

It is the responsibility of EDP management to develop an overall security program and to educate employees in its use and importance. However, senior management must take the necessary first steps if the emphasis of the security program is to change from protecting solely the central DP facility to protecting all computerized information in the company.

## CORRECTING THE PROBLEM: A PLACE TO START

It is imperative that all concerned with developing an EDP security program understand it is not a one-shot deal. Rather, such a program must be comprehensive, going far beyond a good lock for the computer room door or a regular schedule for changing passwords. If EDP security is to be meaningful, it will require changes in the way systems are developed, hardware and software are acquired, and new computer-related products are planned. It will affect daily operating procedures, not necessarily negatively, and will require the support of management at all levels if security is to be effective.

The architect of an EDP security program proposal must remember that few corporations will be prepared to completely overhaul their operations overnight. Any security proposal must be evolutionary in nature, with long-term objectives clearly distinguished from short-term goals. This method will not only enable an organization to grow into its new environment, but will also enable the EDP or security manager to sell the program in manageable pieces that do not place extraordinary demands on the corporate budget and bottom line.

While your program may be constructed somewhat differently, the following eight segments can be used to describe the features required in a comprehensive EDP security program:

1.  *Administrative security.* This component deals with issues such as organizational structure (responsibilities, controls, checks and balances), personnel policies, standards and procedures, and insurance of various types. Clearly, an EDP security program cannot be isolated in a data-processing vacuum; it must become one of the corporate programs, subject to the same review and maintenance processes as other programs of company-wide importance.

2.  *Physical security.* Included in this segment of the security program are the measures used to protect a company's computer equipment and its support facilities and environments from natural or created hazards and to inhibit and/or detect and report on access by unauthorized personnel. While this is the most commonly thought of aspect of EDP security, the growth of distributed processing environments and the burgeoning popularity of the user-friendly microcomputer should cause us to refocus attention on this "already secure" area.

3.  *Data security.* Data is the primary resource and product of the EDP department and one of the most important assets of the corporation. Data security measures are directed at ensuring the computerized assets of the corporation (customer data, market data, executive support data, personnel data, etc.) are protected against interception, disclosure, theft, manipulation, loss, and both accidental and deliberate destruction. Areas of concern are data center operations, file handling, library procedures, off-site backup validation, report and document handling, input/output control procedures, and restrictions placed on remote on-line operations.

4.  *Documentation security.* While often overlooked, court records prove that access to systems documentation (even "old" versions) can give an outsider full access to your data-processing system. Standards and procedures relating to the security of this material as well as standards and procedures relating to its development, use, and distribution must be part of a comprehensive EDP security program.

5.  *Data communications security.* The proliferation of terminals throughout computerized companies and the dramatic growth of microcomputers is far from

over. This growth has been at least matched by the growth of support software that enables these boxes to talk to one another as well as to central corporate computers. The result is a growing exposure that must be addressed. The majority of publicized security breaches reported over the last few years all reveal that data was obtained or system resources utilized through illegal communications access. The combination of internal control procedures and physical devices necessary to prevent such system compromises are the subject of this security module.

6.   *Software integrity*. Operating software and applications software tend to be forgotten once they are installed and functioning properly; yet, tampering with either can wreak havoc. This module deals with the development and maintenance of procedures designed to ensure no unauthorized modification of operating or application systems has taken place.

7.   *Applications security*. While each of the above modules deals with security issues on a corporate basis, a set of procedures and processes must be put in place to ensure each individual application meets the corporate guidelines, and security controls specific to an individual application are in place and regularly tested.

8.   *Contingency planning*. Even the most comprehensive EDP security program cannot provide 100 percent assurance that your computer complex is protected against all eventualities. As our dependence on computers for daily business viability grows, it is of increasing importance that a contingency plan be developed. In fact, for banks, it is specifically cited as a requirement in a circular issued by the comptroller of the currency. A contingency plan is a documented set of actions, resources, and procedures that will be used to recover and maintain vital computing functions in the event facilities are rendered partially or totally inoperable for an extended period of time.

The development of a contingency plan is not simple; it cannot be cut and pasted from a generalized recovery cookbook, nor can its development be delegated to outsiders. Such a plan must reflect management's thinking about its markets, customers, and competitors, and how they must be supported in the event of a prolonged outage of computer support services. These thoughts and decisions must then be used to determine a hierarchy of applications: critical, necessary, and desirable. This determination, as well as the recovery strategies to deal with each of these applications, must come from within the organization, primarily from the user community.

Once this ordering of priorities has been accomplished, the user community and the data-processing organization can cooperate in the development of procedures that will allow the applications to function during a recovery period. Joint planning and cooperative execution of the recovery plan makes the result a business resumption plan, rather than a technical data center relocation exercise.

As you can see from the descriptions, there are really two time frames covered by a comprehensive EDP security program: the day-to-day and the catastrophic. While many managers easily disregard the latter with cavalier comments such as "It won't happen to me" or "I can recover when it happens," it is simply corporate Russian roulette to allow this perception to persist. The assumption that, after a disaster, you can recreate your data-processing resource to a level sufficient to support critical business functions does not reflect prudent management.

A decision on the part of the data-processing manager to ignore contingency planning places the entire organization in significant jeopardy. While it is easier to envision the need for this planning for banks and brokerage firms, which rely on data-processing support to deliver their products and services, it requires little imagination to extend this view to manufacturing and other service organizations. Once your system is down, if your "contingency plan" has your data-processing department relying only on the best efforts of computer manufacturers for recovery, and data-processing resources are unavailable for a prolonged period, you have not planned at all.

## THE FIRST STEPS

So where do we go from here? Clearly, EDP security is a necessity whose time has come. Clearly, management must take the lead. The steps are evident:

- Management must learn all it can about security, and use all the help available.
- Security and EDP managers must educate their managers and company computer users about the need for security measures.
- Management must make the development of an EDP security program a formal project supported by the board of directors and accepted by the EDP manager.
- Realistic interim goals for achieving satisfactory, company-wide computer security must be set.
- The EDP manager should be encouraged to join professional support organizations that will keep him or her up on developments in computer security.

For those with an existing security program, put it under a microscope. Are you sure actual practice follows established standards and procedures? Get an independent assessment of your status. Broadcast the realities of your security program's effectiveness throughout the organization, along with a commitment to a reasonable and cost-effective improvement program.

Don't wait until outside groups ask why you haven't done something about EDP security, or why your company is so exposed. Worse yet, don't wait until an actual incident occurs because your system had no protection. The time is right for management action.

# CHAPTER 2

## Before Disaster Strikes, Fortify Your Computer

Henry M. Kluepfel
District Manager
for Corporate Security
A T & T

Computer systems and their data are vulnerable to error, omission, abuse, or all three at a variety of points by a variety of persons, inside and outside the data processing network. Several surveys on the scope of computer abuse and crime, initiated in the wake of computer hackers' antics, underscore this point. For example, a survey conducted by the American Bar Association (ABA) of 283 respondents who represent a broad range of private industry and a substantial number of federal, state, and local government agencies led to the following conclusions:

- Use of computers to steal tangible or intangible assets is viewed as the most serious form of computer crime.
- Annual losses incurred as a result of a computer crime appear to be enormous; losses between $145 million and $730 million were reported by seventy-one respondents.
- 48 percent of the respondents had experienced "known and verifiable amounts of computer crime."

Overwhelmingly, the ABA survey respondents believed that controlling similar incidents in the future could best be addressed by the following measures:

- More comprehensive and effective self-protection by private business.
- Education of users concerning computer security vulnerabilities.
- Deterrents to computer crime and abuse through federal and state legislation specifically aimed at the problem. At present, thirty-one states have enacted such statutes (see Exhibit 2–1).

Reprinted with the permission of the American Society for Industrial Security, from *Security Management*, March 1985, p. 35.

| State | Statute | Year Enacted |
|---|---|---|
| Alaska | Title II, Chapter 81, Section 900 (b) (51) & Title II, Chapter 46 (11.46. 200 & 484 & 990) | 1984 |
| Arizona | Title 13, Criminal Code, Sections 13-2301, 12-2316 | 1978 |
| California | Penal Code, Section 502 | 1980 |
| Connecticut | Public Act 84-206, Laws | 1984 |
| Colorado | Criminal Justice Code, Sections 18-5.5-101, 102 | 1979 |
| | Amended | 1983 |
| Delaware | Amend Chapter 5, Title II, New Section 858 | 1982 |
| Florida | Sections 815.01 to 815.07 | 1978 |
| Georgia | Sections 16-9949a to 16-9954a | 1981 |
| Hawaii | Chapter 208, Section 708 | 1984 |
| Idaho | Title 18, Chapter 22, 18-2201, 2202 | 1984 |
| Illinois | Criminal Code, Sections 16-9, 15-1 | 1979 |
| Iowa | 716A.1 to 716A.16 | 1984 |
| Maryland | Article 27, Section 146. | 1984 |
| Massachusetts | Chapter 147, Sections 1, 2 | 1983 |
| Michigan | Title 28, Sections 28.529 or 752.791 through 797 | 1980 |
| Minnesota | Sections 609.87 to 609.89 | 1982 |
| Missouri | Section 570.085 to 570.086 | 1982 |
| Montana | Chapter 485 Sections 45-2-101 Sub Sections 1, 2 & 3 | 1981 |
| Nevada | Chapter 205 of NRS, amended Section 2 to 10 | 1983 |
| New Mexico | 30-16A-1 to 30-16A-4 | 1979 |
| North Carolina | Sections 14-453 to 14-456 | 1980 |
| Ohio | Sections 2901.01, 2913.01 | 1979 |
| Oklahoma | Title 21, Section 1951 | 1984 |
| Pennsylvania | Title 18, Section 3933 | 1983 |
| Rhode Island | Criminal Offenses 11-52-1, 11-52-4 | 1979 |
| South Carolina | Title 16, Chapter 16, Sections 10, 20 & 30 | 1984 |
| South Dakota | Section 43-43B1 through 7 & Related Section 23A-35A-2 | 1982 |
| Tennessee | Computer Crimes Act of 1983, Section 39-3-1401 | 1983 |
| Utah | Criminal Code 76-6-701 to 76-6-704 | 1979 |
| Virginia | Sections 18.2 - 98.1 | 1978 |
| | Amended | 1984 |
| Wisconsin | Section 943.70 | 1982 |

**Exhibit 2–1.**   States with computer-related crime statutes.

Noting the tremendous increase in the number of computers and computer users in recent years, the ABA survey report noted: "This proliferation of machines and knowledgeable users, along with recent concrete examples of the damage that can be caused by one person with one personal computer, provides disturbing and undeniable evidence that the scope and significance of computer crime and its potentially devastating effects are broad and deep."

Another recent survey of computer crime, conducted by the American Institute of Certified Public Accountants' electronic data processing (EDP) fraud review task force, involved 5,127 banks and 854 insurance companies, which together reported 119 cases of EDP-related fraud. The survey revealed the following facts:

- Clerical employees were the most frequent perpetrators, but management and supervisory-level personnel were responsible for frauds involving larger dollar amounts.
- A common weakness among the reported cases was inadequate separation of employee duties.
- Losses ranged up to several million dollars, but the majority of cases involved $25,000 or less.
- Most cases involved manipulation of input data outside the data processing department.

The task force report on this survey noted a variety of methods used to conduct the frauds, but "few perpetrators used sophisticated techniques; many took advantage of weaknesses in the system of internal accounting controls."

Similar conclusions were reached in a 1982 study of federal computer systems conducted for the President's Council on Integrity and Efficiency (PCIE) by the inspector general of the US Department of Health and Human Services. In answer to the question, "Who are the perpetrators?" the PCIE study revealed the following facts:

- Seventy-five percent of computer criminals acted alone.
- Most were nonsupervisory federal employees.
- Four out of five fraud perpetrators earned $20,000 a year or less, but half the abusers earned over $20,000 a year.
- Most fraud perpetrators (65 percent) were functional users of systems, but most abusers (59 percent) were data processing personnel.
- Most fraud cases (74 percent) received judicial action (and possibly administrative action); most abuse cases (61 percent) received administrative action only.

Conclusions on the adequacy of controls (deterrents to crime and abuse) reached in the PCIE study added much to the analysis of the problems. For example, responses to questions on controls were generally of poor quality:

- One-fifth of those surveyed gave no answers to questions on controls.
- Others often provided illogical or incomplete answers. For example, fraud was found accidentally after three years' time by one respondent, but the same person said adequate controls were in place.

- More than three-fourths of the respondents were unable to say whether their system had been audited or reviewed.
- More than two-thirds of the respondents did not know whether vulnerability to risk assessment programs were in place.

Poor systems controls were implied in the survey findings, since half the cases were found by accident.

These findings document the views of many computer security experts. Says consultant Robert Courtney, "Controls are used to keep honest people honest. . . . Absence of controls many times will be observed as errors by an employee . . . [and] if those errors go without correction or reporting . . . they invite fraud." And according to Donn Parker of SRI International, "Computer crime is a people problem, and it needs people solutions. Technological controls only reduce the likelihood of violation of trust on the part of people, so it's still a people problem."

Perpetrators of computer abuse are those who have the skills, knowledge, access, and motive to carry out the act. As the ABA survey report found, while management cannot control the development or direction of computer skills, it can limit knowledge about the system particulars and control access to computer system resources to deter computer crime and abuse.

## THE MOST FORMIDABLE DANGER

The most formidable danger to a computer system is from authorized employees— those who know its weaknesses and controls and, at some future date, may exploit this vulnerability if they become disgruntled. To further narrow down the people aspect of computer security vulnerabilities, security measures must be aimed at both the users and providers of data processing services.

Three other distinctive features mark computer abuse. Too many times,

- The introduction of computer or minicomputer systems has resulted in the radical restructuring of the processes designed to prevent or disclose dishonesty. The control functions tend to be misunderstood, disabled, destroyed, or ignored.
- The goal in designing and installing new systems is to use available computer technology as much as possible. Typically, this goal is pursued with inadequate resources and insufficient time, and audit trails are created by the system developers and programmers, mainly as an aid to later systems repairs or maintenance.
- Computer systems and programs are generally designed to make it easy to process information—to be people-friendly and fault-tolerant.

We have all heard the term "user friendly," meaning a computer system provides user supports, such as on-line manual distribution, training and prompts, error-checking and correcting utilities, and HELP commands to assist inexperienced users understand the various program functions. Combine these user-friendly system qualities with the

- Inadequate password management
  —Trivial passwords
  —Group passwords
  —Obvious passwords assigned to users
  —Passwords not changed frequently or otherwise restricted
  —Password and password files not protected properly

- Improper application of access or usage controls
  —Multiple ''super users'' or system administration personnel
  —Read, write, and execute controls improperly applied to files, directories, memory, or privileged commands
  —Controls inadequate to ensure transferred or terminated employees no longer have access to databases

- Networking vulnerabilities
  —Each machine dependent upon others to protect passwords
  —Improperly administered log-ons and accounts
  —The originator (host) assumed to be responsible for all access controls

- Improper management and protection of backup files
  —No off-site storage
  —Critical business applications and supporting data

- Inadequate protection of sensitive data
  —Other users can access data
  —System temporary files can access data
  —Destruction procedures inadequate

- Lack of security awareness
  —Void in training and documentation for users/administrators
  —Infrequent audits or security reviews
  —A ''so what'' attitude on the part of the user (''my files aren't supersensitive'')
  —''That's not my job'' attitude on the part of the system administrator

**Exhibit 2–2.**    Attributes of an abuser-friendly computer system.

control deficiencies listed in Exhibit 2–2, and you have the attributes of an abuser-friendly system—awaiting or perhaps already the victim of computer hackers, dishonest employees, or other interlopers.

Abuser friendliness has permeated many systems used for the automated office and its support network. Though the problems of being abuser friendly are generic, the solutions must be specific to the system, the company, and the user community.

The only way to review system security is through effective security and audit oversight. Management must be committed to protecting vital corporate assets—data and computer systems the business relies on for successful operation. As illustrated in Exhibit 2–3, an effective EDP security program requires the involvement of users, data systems managers, programmers, corporate security personnel, and internal auditors. It goes without saying, the proprietary nature of the data in corporate computers mandates each manager be responsible for efficient, comprehensive, and cost-effective measures to guard and control these assets.

## MAKESHIFT MEASURES WON'T WORK

The computer-abuse problem cannot be resolved by makeshift measures. The solution requires a new method for designing, controlling, measuring, and maintaining the integrity of computerized information-handling systems. New ways of doing business in a computerized environment are needed.

Management should also recognize that the time to build in the necessary controls is when a computer system is being developed or an existing one modified. In our experience, it can be up to 100 times more expensive to introduce adequate internal controls after a system has been developed or modified.

Although the technology generally exists to control computer crime and abuse effectively, implementing this technology requires both users and data systems managers to understand the technology, be trained in it, use it, and above all, support it.

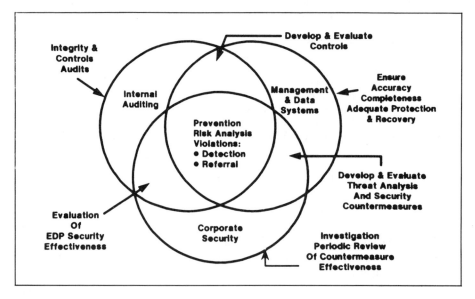

**Exhibit 2–3.** EDP security in and around the computer.

This last statement may appear obvious, yet the absence of one or more of these actions has been associated with most recent computer hacker incidents as well as most other cases of computer abuse.

Since a computer system and its data can be compromised in a variety of ways, computer facilities must be physically and logically secured. The degree of security required should be based on a cost/benefit or risk analysis approach. We assume risk to our corporation's data and computer assets when a vulnerability exists and those assets are threatened. The degree of risk involved depends on both the probability of a threat occurring and the cost of recovering the loss.

The terms ''risk analysis'' and ''cost/benefit analysis'' mean determining the value or adequacy of protective mechanisms, called countermeasures. Obviously it would not be cost-effective to spend more to prevent a harmful event from occurring than the cost of the loss should the event take place. Countermeasures, then, must prevent the harm or minimize its effect while easing the recovery from a harmful event.

## LAYERS OF SECURITY

Security should be implemented in layered rings around an asset to be protected. The outer ring is made up of physical security countermeasures, such as personnel access control systems. The outer ring should allow entry only to authorized employees with a legitimate need to access portions of data during specified times.

Realizing that the absolute effectiveness of physical security measures is virtually impossible (since we can access a computer's information remotely), the next countermeasure layer involves administration. Administrative countermeasures include such procedures as escorting visitors and contract repair personnel to the computer center, and immediately terminating an employee's access to the system and the data processing facility when he or she is discharged or reassigned.

The next ring of protection involves the person/machine interface, called ''personnel subsystems.'' Personnel subsystems countermeasures include such controls as making sure passwords are changed periodically and that they are not printed or displayed (echoed) on the terminal of the party logging on. Since people are the weakest link in any computer security system, the success of any computer security efforts should depend on the integrity of the fewest number of people possible.

Ultimately, the computer should be used to protect itself. The next ring of security is therefore known as computer systems countermeasures. They include designing systems that are not obvious to computer hackers or other interlopers. Likewise, inappropriate attempts to log on and guess passwords should be viewed as an attempted breach of security. Access to computer resources (information files) and transactions (read, write, delete, modify) should be limited to those with proven need for them. Access control systems for the computer must be established, even though operational sacrifices are required.

Effective computer security must include implementation of measures to detect, document, and refer all system violations to the security department. Controls are installed to keep honest people honest. If people see that violations of controls are unnoticed and unchallenged, then illicit acts are not far away.

Although an established security program for corporate data reduces the risk of disrupting computer system resources, it will not entirely eliminate the risk. Therefore, the organization needs effective methods of restoring the availability of the computer system, and its applications, should an emergency situation occur. These contingency plans and disaster recovery methods should be implemented in a manner appropriate to the impact a given disaster would have on the organization (see Exhibit 2–4).

## DISASTER RECOVERY PLAN

Of course, the ability to recover from a disaster is in large measure determined by the adequacy of available resources, but one question remains: "At what cost?" Costs must be measured in terms of available capital, skilled people, inventories, customer

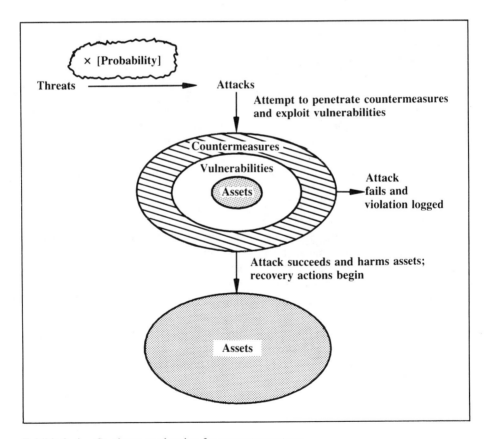

**Exhibit 2–4.**    Contingency planning for computer systems.

service, held orders, lost business, corporate image, and other factors. Therefore, it is imperative the company implement adequately documented, tested, and maintained disaster recovery plans and mechanisms. This step will ensure critical business operations that apply to the computer are quickly and adequately resumed (including programs, functions, and activities that, if lost, would significantly affect the company or the products and services it provides). An effective computer center disaster recovery plan is outlined in Exhibit 2–5.

Contingency planning should not be a panic response to a scare story, but a prudent part of an organization's plans. Moreover, contingency planning should be integrated into the work cycle of all managers whose responsibilities include critical business or operations.

In 1983, for example, the corporate offices of a San Francisco-based national food distributor were contaminated in a toxic chemical spill. As a result, the firm's information resources network was forced to evacuate and temporarily relocate its offices and main computer center for almost a year. Obviously, if the corporation had not completed its disaster recovery plans before the accident, they would not have been able to report, as they did, a loss of only one business day's processing time (not one customer order was lost).

In a catastrophe, it may be virtually impossible to return quickly to the original documents providing the information held within the computer system. As a result, each corporate computer center and minicomputer center that processes or supports critical business applications should have a documented disaster recovery plan. The

An effective computer center disaster recovery plan should do the following:

- Identify critical functions and computer applications.

- Identify the computer hardware and software configurations required to support those applications.

- Identify alternate backup systems.

- Provide for security in the backup situations.

- Assign backup planning and recovery missions, responsibilities, and individual roles.

- Effectively communicate those roles to the responsible parties and their alternates.

- Provide for the availability of data, supplies, equipment, and copies of the plan at the alternate sites.

- Provide for testing of the plan.

**Exhibit 2–5.**    A computer center disaster recovery plan.

plan should be approved by a high level of corporate management. The plan should include the following points:

- Adherence to generally accepted security measures and internal controls for safeguarding the computer system, its data, and the personnel who operate and maintain it. Such a requirement is essential. Not only do physical security and data security countermeasures decrease vulnerabilities, they also insure against a recurrence or the introduction of a second disaster once the recovery plan has been implemented.
- Priorities for critical business or operations applications or systems that must operate during recovery to keep the business running. To assign these priorities, users and systems managers must evaluate the impact a loss of the application would have for given periods such as one hour, one day, one week, one month, three months, a year.
- Written step-by-step instructions outlining the responsibilities and actions to be taken by organizations, departments, teams, and individuals on a daily, weekly, or monthly basis (contingency actions) or after a disaster (recovery actions). These instructions should include responsibilities for and performance of such actions as grandfathering system files and databases; securing off-site storage of critical backup data, supplies, and forms; designating a backup recovery site; and writing agreements that specify availability.
- Testing procedures and drills to ensure the plan is adequate and contingency actions are operating properly.

These elements form the general characteristics of an effective, current, and tested disaster recovery plan. Periodically, the plan should be updated to ensure its integrity, reviewed and approved by the security department, and checked by internal auditing. The results of the review should then be used promptly to reevaluate and update the plan.

As a wise man once said, "Hindsight will always be better than foresight if we do not effectively communicate individual and organizational roles, responsibilities, objectives, and requirements to our employees." Said another, "Show me the real problem, and many times the answer will be obvious."

# CHAPTER 3

## Computer Security Belongs in the Security Department

Henry J. Beattie
Computer Protection Group, Inc.

When it comes to their security departments, chief executive officers and other top line managers continue to make the same mistakes today they were making almost twenty years ago. Over the years many CEOs have come to realize that security departments are as much an integral part of the corporate structure as income-producing divisions and that as such they deserve a distinct budget, increased management support, and more sophisticated responsibilities. However, management still fails to capitalize fully on its security investment.

Recognition of the importance of the security function has taken many years, and it has come mainly as a result of the professionalism displayed by security practitioners. The CPP program has also contributed to this attitude by providing an acknowledged set of standards for the industry. Training programs and seminars have focused attention on the myriad problems that can be handled successfully by a company's security department.

The traditional functions of security—loss prevention, access control, and preemployment screening—are where corporate managers are most likely to observe performance. On those rare occasions when security personnel are consulted about problems not strictly linked to their main responsibilities, corporate managers are usually impressed with their resourcefulness and flexibility. Companies where this has been true are most likely to have enlarged the security department and varied its responsibilities.

In spite of these advances, managers have almost universally persisted in shutting security personnel out of the data processing facility, although a good percentage of their corporate assets lie there. Aside from access control, managers have favored untrained EDP personnel to handle their computer security concerns.

I say untrained because, aside from a few criminal justice or security-oriented colleges, I know of no courses that train computer professionals in computer-based

Reprinted with the permission of the American Society for Industrial Security, from *Security Management*, May 1983, p 90.

fraud prevention, forms control, computer evidence considerations, systems vulnerabilities, risk management, or any of a dozen other subjects that can be grouped under
the broad umbrella of computer security. The very few colleges that do offer such
courses usually don't have a computer science degree program.

As problems with computer security have multiplied, companies have turned to
their accountants (bringing a new branch to the discipline—EDP auditor), their attorneys (a few of whom practice what they call "computer law"), and their programmers and systems analysts. Employees in this last category pose special problems, for
while they usually try to construct programs and systems that will prevent intrusions
or manipulations by outsiders, they themselves are the greatest threat to corporate
assets.

A study published by the US Government Printing Office indicates that, based
on a limited number of interviews, the typical computer criminal can be profiled as a
skilled technologist of about twenty-five who occupies a position of trust.[1] If the author
had tried to describe a programmer/analyst, he could not have done better.

The most elaborately designed (and expensive) software installed to protect a
database is useless unless sufficient safeguards against internal threats are instituted.
The transitory nature of the EDP professional and his seeming lack of corporate loyalty
(don't confuse "computer loyalty" with corporate loyalty) suggest that security controls are best administered, and in some cases devised, by the corporate security
department.

What about the EDP auditor and the attorney? In the case of the auditor, what
sense does it make to allow the same person who has devised the safeguards to test
them and report on their effectiveness? An individual in such a position is bound to
exhibit some bias or filtering effect in any subsequent report. Additionally a recent
court decision indemnified auditors by clearly stating that they are not "detectives"
and cannot be held liable for failing to discover a cleverly constructed fraud.*

Attorneys can be useful at a certain final phase in a computer-based fraud incident.
They also can provide reliable information about guidelines for privacy issues and
personnel matters. However, nothing in their training qualifies them to institute, design,
or administer a security program.[2]

The administration of a computer security program requires an interdisciplinary
approach. Elements of computer technology, law, investigation, and on occasion
criminal prosecution must be brought to bear if an acceptable level of security is to
be maintained. The latter three disciplines more closely resemble security department
responsibilities than data processing activities. Because of this balance, I suggest that
corporate managers make some effort to train security directors in computer technology.

The principles of investigation and security can be brought to bear quite successfully in the data processing department. An FBI study published in July 1979
found that 58 percent of computer crimes can be successfully investigated by personnel
with only an "awareness" level of training. An additional 35 percent can be investigated with a "comprehensive" level of training.[3]

---

*For a complete description of the EDP audit function, see Krause and MacGahan, *Computer Fraud and
Countermeasures*, (Prentice-Hall, 1979), Chapter 8.

The FBI defines the awareness level as five days of training and the comprehensive level as four weeks. The content of these courses, with the exception of references to federal law and unique evidence considerations, consists mainly of an introduction to EDP principles, programming and systems documentation, and computer crime examples. The first two subjects can be covered in in-house seminars developed by corporate DP personnel and local community college curricula. Outside consultants or study material can supply an acceptable level of familiarity with examples of reported computer abuse.

The objective of thus educating security directors is not to create more systems engineers, but to have security professionals who can function competently in the data processing department. This ability will enable them to recognize the need for controls here as well as they do in other parts of their companies.

In addition to access control, management may consider assigning the following DP responsibilities to the security department:

1.  *Personnel screening and monitoring.* The rapid turnover of EDP personnel who have or will have access to corporate assets demands verification of preemployment statements. The practice of promoting people from positions that do not call for rigorous background checks to ones that do without performing a check is common in computer installations and a real security problem.

2.  *Administration of codes and passwords.* Personnel problems aggravate maintenance of passwords, making necessary fixed responsibility for assignment, expiration, and protection of codes and passwords. I doubt a security professional would acquiesce to the common practice of using a birthdate for a password, which highly trained systems analysts have been known to do. Recommendation of such a practice only serves to highlight the point made earlier that "computer people" usually don't have a keen sense of appreciation for security principles.

3.  *Identification and control of sensitive elements of the database.* Computer generated assets are looked at differently by loss prevention personnel, who have come to recognize that almost all corporate assets can be the target of misuse or theft. Monitoring distribution of and access to these elements outside the DP department is particularly suited to the security department.

4.  *Control of the EDP library.* The position of EDP librarian has long been recognized as requiring the least technical skill, but it is through this person that the most sensitive files and programs are accessed. Maintenance of control logs is an important task of this position. With security department presence in this visible position, management's determination to prevent abuse is evident.

5.  *Administration of logs.* Control of all physical logs should rest with the security department. Periodic inspections should be carried out with an eye toward identifying unusual, excessive, or inconsistent activity. Console logs should be obtained on a frequent but random basis with the same objective in mind.

6.  *Distribution and subsequent collection and disposal of sensitive output.* Distribution of sensitive information outside the DP department is particularly suited to the security department. An often overlooked task is the subsequent collection and destruction of sensitive reports. Assigning this task to the security department relieves other employees of this vital yet mundane task.

7. *Forms control.* Most companies have few formal procedures for forms control. A blank form is mistakenly seen in the same light as a blank piece of paper. Even where that form filled out could authorize the transfer of millions of dollars, no attention is paid to the blank forms until some authorization signatures turn out to be forgeries.

8. *Communications security.* Securing a computer system's communications does not automatically mean use of a data encryption method. A much more lethal threat to a computer system is vandalism of an unlocked telephone company junction box located away from the facility.

9. *Control of and access to backup files.* It is useless to mount expensive security control over immediate files if little or no attention is paid to files located off-site.

10. *Backup facilities and disaster planning.* Having engineers plan the necessary configuration of hardware needed for disaster recovery is of utmost importance. However, it is equally important for security personnel to co-plan procedures that will allow them to shift attention from one site to another if necessary.

11. *Membership on the data processing committee.* In organizations large enough to support a DP committee, serious thought should be given to including the security director. He or she may not need to know about every minor request, but if the security department is aware of pending projects, safeguards can be considered at the design stage. As security personnel receive increasingly sophisticated training, it may be possible to have a security professional present at the "structured walkthrough" of a particularly sensitive program. This individual would not provide technical assistance, but would be there to learn where the program is most vulnerable. By its very nature a modular program is most easily attacked and should be the subject of security review.

The assignments just described are by no means the only ones that can be given to the security department. Because a "comprehensive" level of familiarity with computer technology can be achieved in a relatively short time, CEOs should seriously consider training the security managers in DP principles and enhancing the role of security departments in protecting computer assets. Unique assets demand unique approaches to their protection, and the relatively small investment required to train security personnel will be returned many times over.

## REFERENCES

1. *Computer Crime—A Criminal Justice Resource Manual* (Washington, DC: US Government Printing Office, 1979), pp. 53–54.
2. Krause and MacGahan, *Computer Fraud and Countermeasures*, Chapter 8 (New York: Prentice Hall, 1979).
3. "Computer Crime Investigators, a New Training Field," *FBI Law Enforcement Bulletin* (July 1979).

# CHAPTER 4

## Are You Computer Wise?

Frederick G. Tompkins, CPP
Senior Principal Scientist
ORI Inc.

Recently, when looking for some reference material on computer security, I came across the topical index of 1980 *Security Management* articles. The computer security articles included such topics as: "Computer Abuse Update," "The Gap Between Computer People and Security People," and "The Role of the Questioned Document Examiner in Computer Crime Investigations." More recently, articles have been presented dealing with risk analysis and data processing disaster recovery.

Each of these articles, and others on the subject of computer security, attempt to convince us there is a computer security problem or to offer an approach for solving one of the many problems related to computer security. Unfortunately, much of the available literature assumes the reader has enough understanding of both data processing and security to be able to apply proposed solutions or approaches.

Security managers who are new to the field of computer security usually do not have a well-rounded education in both fields. A good educational foundation in data processing is required by the security professional. Conversely, a good educational foundation in security is essential for the data processing professional. Basic education and a practical understanding of the organization's products or services and upper management's requirements will go a long way toward assuring the successful implementation of a reasonable and adequate computer security program.

The bottom line is that computer security is a multidisciplinary field and the security manager or the data processing manager responsible for the computer security program needs more than a one-day course in the complementary discipline.

Both security and data processing professionals are at a disadvantage when they have their first encounter with the field of computer security. The following scenario has been repeated almost every time I have presented a seminar or lecture on computer security. A security manager says to me, "I have just been appointed to be the computer security official for my organization. I know a lot about physical security (or

Reprinted with the permission of the American Society for Industrial Security, from *Security Management*, Sept. 1982, p 69.

computer programming and operations), but can't tell the difference between software and hardware (or HALON and $CO_2$). Where do I go to get some training and what type of courses do I need?''

Except in a few rare cases, a single course will not provide enough background to permit you to function comfortably in the computer security world. Some government educational facilities, such as the Department of Defense Computer Institute in Washington, DC, the Army Logistics Management Center at Ft. Lee, VA, and the Office of Personnel Management, offer one- or two-week courses that provide a good awareness of the problem.

While these organizations and the courses they present serve a useful purpose, they are not able, nor are they intended, to provide the depth of training that is desirable. Some colleges and universities are starting to offer courses in computer security such as those offered at Northern Virginia Community College, George Washington University, and Golden Gate University in San Francisco. However, most of us have probably overlooked a convenient and inexpensive source of education—the local community college.

Most community colleges offer either certificate or two-year programs in security management, law enforcement, computer science, and data processing. Many of us probably received our initial formal education in security or data processing by attending a community college. For those of us who received our basic education through military service or on-the-job training and wanted a college degree, the local area community college provided a convenient transition back into the academic community. The opportunity for evening courses allowed many to remain gainfully employed and pursue an academic program. In retrospect, those of us who attended evening classes quite often received a secondary benefit—exposure to practicing professionals who had the day-to-day experience of applying the theory of the textbooks. I strongly urge you to once again look to the local community college to fill those gaps in education necessary to survive in the field of computer security.

I suggest that security professionals consider a minimum curriculum of four data processing courses: introduction to data processing, computer operations, systems analysis and design, and a programming language such as COBOL.

An introduction to data processing should provide an overview of the various pieces of equipment normally found in a data processing operation, a description of the various data processing personnel duties, and how data is represented electronically in the computer and on the various storage media. It should cover the types of languages used to communicate with computers and the history and future of computers. Probably the most important thing learned in this introductory course is data processing terminology.

A course in computer operations should provide the student with the opportunity to see, touch, and operate an actual computer system. Typically, there is some repetition of the lecture material presented in the introduction to data processing course, but the practical hands-on operating of the equipment gives the security professional a good appreciation for the vulnerability of computers to operations personnel.

Third in the series of courses should be the systems analysis and design course. This should instruct the student in how computer applications software systems are designed. The security professional will probably find that many of the problems of analysis, definition, interview, and design techniques are very similar to techniques used in investigations.

Last in a basic curriculum is a course in programming. COBOL is probably the most widely used in the business world; however, a course in RPG or BASIC is just as beneficial. The objective for the security professional is to develop an understanding of programming practices and the ways in which programmers can exploit applications software.

While this recommended curriculum will not qualify security managers as data processing experts, it should prepare you to understand the world of data processing. A secondary benefit is that you may well develop the knowledge or the skills to apply data processing techniques and the advantages of automation to the security function.

Regarding basic security education for the data processing manager, I would like to caution security managers not to underestimate the need for such education for their data processing personnel. Security is just as much a part of management science as is data processing, and it has certain theoretical foundations peculiar to it. The growth and direction of security theory is dependent upon changes in technology, social structures, and political relationships. It is also affected by civil and criminal law, managerial practices, and the constraints of financial resources.

Security draws upon the support of all branches of engineering, upon architectural and industrial design and the communication arts. The data processor should remember that the function of security is to protect and conserve assets against loss and reduction in value without undue loss to primary resources and operations.

I suggest that the data processing professional consider a minimum curriculum of four security courses: introduction to security, principles of loss prevention, criminal investigation, and physical security.

An introduction to security should provide the historical, philosophical, and legal basis for security. Additionally, the course should cover the role of security and the security individual in modern society; the concept of professionalism; and a survey of the administrative, personnel, and physical aspects of the security field. As with any introductory level course, one of the most important goals for the student is a good understanding of the terminology of the field.

A course in the principles of loss prevention should provide an overview of the functional operations of security, such as theft and risk control, security surveys, and loss prevention management in proprietary and governmental institutions.

The third course in the series should be criminal investigation. This should provide coordinated lecture and laboratory experience in the fundamentals of investigation, techniques of crime scene recording and search, collection and preservation of evidence, and methods used in security investigations.

Last in the basic security curriculum is the physical security course, which should outline the concepts of physical security and how management systems and physical security requirements and standards should be integrated. The study of inanimate aspects of security, including alarm and surveillance devices, and the animate aspects of protection, such as costing, planning, and engineering, should also be included.

To further increase the education of the data processing professional, courses in environmental security, safety and fire prevention, and industrial fire protection might also be considered.

The idea is that a good educational base in the opposite discipline will permit both the data processor and the security practitioner to communicate more effectively. It should also permit both to gain more from the available literature. If both security and data processing managers will make the effort to understand the other profession, and especially take the time to learn the other terminology, a good computer security program should be possible in most organizations.

# CHAPTER 5

## The Gap between *Computer* People and *Security* People

Dennis F. Poindexter
DCASR, Indianapolis

Interest in the security of data processing operations is burgeoning, occasioned, in part, by the proliferation of media coverage of computer-assisted crimes and the misuse of computer equipment. These often sensationalized stories, accompanied by increasing management awareness of the vulnerabilities of the data placed in computer systems, heightened emphasis on privacy concerns, and the rising value of goods reduced to transferable form, have caused many firms to seek greater protection for their computer systems.

As the concern over computer security has grown, the security professional has been hard-pressed to keep pace with the ever-changing, technically complicated environment. One method of trying to upgrade computer system security that is becoming more and more common is the inclusion of data processing professionals on the security staff. Another method is the assignment of technical specialists to augment inspection programs and auditing. This practice has met with reactions ranging from cooperative mutual assistance to diametric opposition. The difference in the level and intensity of cooperation is often found in the ease of communication (or lack thereof) between people in fields who only recently began trying to work together.

A familiar and readily advanced explanation for the difficulty in communications between security professionals and data processing professionals cites the differences in their terminologies. Although specialized terminology aids communication among those in a specific field by reducing the time needed to exchange ideas, it also hinders communication with people outside that field. Still, the disparate language explanation is oversimplified and misleading. The gap between security people and data processing people is more fundamental. Other differences in orientation between members of these two groups are more significant and more divisive than language peculiarities.

Traditionally, the data processing field has relied on the general public's ignorance of data processing functions as a built-in protective device (Parker, 1973).

Reprinted with the permission of the American Society for Industrial Security, from *Security Management*, Oct. 1980, p. 50.

During the early stages of development, keeping people in the dark about data processing was both a logical and a practical approach. Few computers were in use and very few people knew the secrets of the inner workings of the imposing machines. Today, the ignorance tactic is no longer a recognized security measure. Yet substantial numbers of system supervisors and managers are computer professionals who began their training and gained their experience when security by exception was the rule. Many of these people still accept the idea that keeping people ignorant about their systems will protect those systems. This belief is supported by enough truth that it will persist unless, or until, vulnerability is demonstrated by an abuse or other adverse event.

As the people working with computers specialize into hardware, software, and operations, the belief in ignorance as a source of protection is revived. Indeed, being a computer "expert" these days is nearly impossible. The usual "help wanted" ads in any newspaper attest to the demand for a variety of exclusive skills, especially in view of the myriad distinct hardware items and software packages in use. For simplicity, and often for protection of proprietary business interests, these distinct items are carefully guarded. In such an environment, being a generalist is increasingly difficult. Certainly, by necessity, a great deal of overlap occurs between the various aspects of data processing. That the specialization in effect produces its own ignorance is paradoxical. The need for more data processing specialists to assist security is obvious.

In many businesses, security and data processing are mutually exclusive. Even some of the largest corporations have established computer security sections made up solely of data processing personnel. This decision to assign employees with computer backgrounds to security is an expeditious one. Unfortunately, it may not be the best approach to achieving optimum protection of computer-related assets. Security personnel are oriented toward different job objectives than are data processing personnel. This difference in orientation slants the emphasis each specialist puts on the protection task. Limiting responsibility (and authority) for computer security to data processing personnel may lead to an unintentionally narrow understanding of computer security problems.

Even in facilities where the security department is not responsible for data security, consultation and coordination of effort between the security staff and the data processing staff is common. The quality of this cooperation depends upon how well the personnel in one field can relate to those in the other. The importance of this communication link cannot be overlooked.

## A CHANGING THREAT ENVIRONMENT

Technology is changing the threat environment of computer operations by increasing the technical knowledge of more people outside specific facilities. Today, high school sophomores are writing programs and building their own computer hardware, a clear indication of the dramatic increase in the number of technically qualified potential abusers. As a consequence, computer security demands speed in establishing preventive measures, which can only be achieved by cooperation between security personnel and data processing personnel.

The challenge lies in communicating security problems effectively to data processing professionals, and technical DP concerns that affect security effectively to security personnel. The language barrier is only part of this problem. Most people rely on terms familiar to those in their profession, but each of us expects to make a certain adjustment in learning the language of a new office or new associates. The deeper communication gap between security and data processing was once expressed to me by a DP professional replying to a question about the impact of adding a particular type of hardware. He responded, "The answer to your question is easy enough, but I wonder why you asked it."

This example hints at the fundamental difference between security and data processing, which lies to some extent in the amount of previous experience a person has had with security measures. To a greater extent, however, the difficulty lies in the different levels of abstraction used in the two fields—not a matter of either knowledge or language, but of the focus of both.

To illustrate levels of abstraction, S.I. Hayakawa (1964) used the example of Bessie, a cow. On one level, Bessie is a particular aggregation of atoms and molecules; on another level, Bessie is flesh, skin, and bone; on yet another level, Bessie is an object labeled "Bessie"; from another aspect she is specifically a cow; and for those who are so oriented, Bessie is a Holstein. When people with divergent orientations talk about Bessie, part or all of the message may be lost because of their different levels of reference.

Security personnel and data processing personnel bring with them their own levels of abstraction, levels divergent from each other. The diversification of computer technology has yielded a high degree of abstraction in various specialties but not necessarily in data processing as a whole. Security, by far a more generalized field, often has a wide range of technological specialization, but its orientation demands a broader perspective than that of data processing. Thus, in my view, the level of abstraction in security is actually higher, as a rule, than it is in data processing. This differentiation of levels of abstraction is not particularly important, *until* these divergent fields must establish a joint policy and work together under it.

Both sides need to recognize the differences in their perspectives. Unfortunately, getting people to do this is a time-consuming task, and, in many cases, one that is never accomplished. As an example, take the problem of access control. The term is familiar to practitioners in both fields, but the concept is defined differently. For the security specialist, access control may begin with entry controls at the front door and extend to authorizing users by means of a password. The data processing specialist, however, may be inclined to think of access control only as it relates to the data base itself. If a person is denied access by software features, use of a hardware device may not, in the DP specialist's view, qualify as access to the system. This discrepancy can cause untold days of discussion if some commonly agreed upon definitions (or boundaries) of terms are not settled from the start.

Another problem related to levels of abstraction concerns the divergent views of the end objective held by security and DP personnel. The data processing staff is geared toward efficiency of operation. At almost every level of the business, speed and accuracy are stressed, and rightfully so. Computers are incomprehensibly fast if prepared properly, and they can operate with a minimum of human intervention.

The security specialist is also oriented toward efficiency, but the security field itself is not. If security were unnecessary, all phases of business would be affected. Every aspect of security entails certain restrictions that impede efficiency. Security personnel aim for tolerable restraints within management-specified limits. At the same time, data processing personnel are working to eliminate whatever restraints may be hampering their efficiency. While this does not imply that a data processing employee would intentionally subvert security, it does suggest that the DP practitioner is far less oriented toward restraints. This fact should be considered when attempting to initiate policies for computer security.

Hardware maintenance provides a good example of this point. Most organizations cannot hire a maintenance specialist for each type of data processing equipment they use. When a piece of equipment malfunctions, the operators lose productive time and expensive equipment is idle. The maintenance person is needed as soon as possible and must be able to locate and repair the problem quickly. The security staff, in doing its job, does not want to admit just anyone to the premises. Consequently, the repair person must be able to produce adequate identification to assure security he or she has indeed been sent by the maintenance company.

Another security concern arises in an organization that has proprietary information (which may be in the computer) it does not want removed, observed, or destroyed. In this case, maintenance personnel may need an escort. Unfortunately, not just any escort will do. Few people understand what needs to be done to repair computer equipment, yet a reasonably knowledgeable monitor is needed to accompany anyone working on such equipment.

Maintenance personnel often test and replace various components using diagnostic routines and analyzers. Many of these tools can record or remove recorded media, posing a serious danger if critical proprietary or classified defense information is stored in the equipment being repaired. Yet the computer staff is unlikely to be amenable to restrictions that may interfere with getting hardware back in working order. Nonetheless, the organization must make certain concessions to protect its wider interests. Consultants may find more and more restrictions on their activity, in spite of the fact that they are often hired to increase efficiency.

## WORKING FROM DIFFERENT EXPERIENCES

The conflict between the orientation of security personnel and that of data processors is not easily resolved. Both viewpoints are well entrenched and continue to divide the two fields. A well-established principle of interpersonal communications, ''the momentum of set,'' in this instance works against cooperation. The people in the two fields base decisions on different experiences, and input from a source that does not fit the expectations learned from past experiences is likely to be ignored. (G.R. Rogers and others, 1969.) This tendency has serious implications for security.

Security operations are many times cued to particular events that indicate an unusual occurrence and may be a key to an attempted system penetration. Ignoring these keys will encourage further attempts to enter a system and thereby improve the chance of this happening. A simple example will illustrate this point.

In most systems, some type of file protection is used to restrict access. Passwords are a common means of limiting access. In theory, every person eligible to use the system should be able to enter a password in one attempt. Practicality allows for more than one try. After a set number of attempts, software features can be used to lock out the terminal from which the entry is being attempted. In more sophisticated systems, the terminal is identified to the operator console and kept on-line so its activity can be monitored. The trouble with any such system (and most mechanical/electrical entry systems) is that it *usually* works, but not always.

Every time passwords are changed, that well-known "ten percent who never get the word" start showing up. Operators are busy with jobs; hardware goes down; and software doesn't always work as it should. These problems are typical, everyday ones. Unfortunately, people are inclined to make assumptions about familiar occurrences: the terminal on the fourth floor frequently locks people out; Dave calls to say he is locked out and needs to get data for Jim up in Production. The corporate procedure calls for an investigation, but this is the second time today the blasted thing has locked someone out, and . . . the software probably isn't right, maybe all the changes weren't made.

To an experienced security officer, the scenario is all too familiar. With computer systems, the problem is aggravated by continuous systems failures. If everything worked properly we would set up a computer system and never have to worry about it, but that is seldom the case. A good security officer notices things out of the ordinary and follows through with an investigation. A computer operator who took time to do this sort of thing might soon be working elsewhere.

Three factors—level of abstraction, orientation, and the momentum of sets— may be seen as environmental elements working against cooperative effort between DP and security people. If recognizing a problem were all that was needed to solve it, stating the fundamental differences between security personnel and data processing personnel would be sufficient to resolve the conflicts. In practice, however, recognition alone does not take care of the problem.

Some people believe creating a computer security specialist requires a choice between trying to turn a computer specialist into a security expert and training a security specialist to be a computer expert. People with computer backgrounds tend to lean toward the former as the easier task, while security-trained individuals advocate the latter. The conceptual differences between the two fields are sufficient that both kinds of computer security specialists are really needed. Each brings something to the task that the other may not. The technical complexities of the computer field, as has been pointed out, make becoming a computer security expert difficult, if not impossible, for any one person. Consequently, a team approach to the job becomes increasingly important and logical.

In 1974, Donn Parker described the aspects of a computer operation that need to be covered in an audit. Although the auditing function is only a limited part of overall computer security, the problem remains: *"The areas of specialty include physical security, operational security including recovery and backup application analysis and programming, systems programming, and electronic engineering. This implies a team approach to auditing to achieve the necessary depth of expertise in these diverse areas."*

Another publication, produced by the Rand Corporation states: *"The security problem of specific computer systems must be solved on a case-by-case basis employing the best judgment of a team consisting of systems programmers, technical, hardware, and communications specialists, and security experts."* (Ed. Ware, 1970)

Unfortunately, no one person can be responsible for all aspects of computer security. Even agreeing that more than one person is necessary, and then bringing both security and data processing together, is not enough.

The tendency to become defensive about your position is natural when people from different fields and backgrounds come together. Yet the important task of policy development leaves no room for provincialism. Computer specialists are often viewed with high regard; security specialists, except in rare instances, find their efforts receive less emphasis. Security people are often expected to fulfill their assignments with less money and lower status than are computer personnel. This existing difference in status can foster proprietary behavior in terms charged with establishing computer security policies. Everyone must recognize that policy will be based on the input of a variety of sources, all of which need to be logically considered. When high-stakes corporate interests are at issue, cooperation on all sides is essential.

Such cooperation requires mutual belief in the value of other participants' views. The individual overseeing computer security must ensure that the organization's interests are given priority over whatever differences exist between subgroups such as security and computer personnel. While focusing efforts on organizational objectives may be easy enough initially, over a period of months security restrictions that cut efficiency can take a heavy toll on data processing operations. Similarly, the technical details of computer systems can stymie the best security professional. Compromising the computer security program is often easier than facing the fact that acknowledged differences of view take time and frank discussion to resolve.

## MANAGEMENT'S RESPONSIBILITY

Management's responsibility in resolving these conflicts lies in defining what level of restraint is acceptable and what information must be protected. The former is a complex task that must be guided by the nature of the threat to the data base. Agreeing to agree may be the most useful first step toward tackling the job. Security has resources to identify many of the known threats and general types of corporate information being protected. Data processing can relate this information to what is being stored in the computer system and make realistic assessments as to which of the threats could be most easily carried out.

Data processing management sometimes neglects to establish which information requires backing up. They leave such decisions to systems managers, who may not understand that the information essential to restoring the computer system may not be critical to restoring the business operation. In the same way, protecting all information at the same level is putting the most important information on the same footing as the least important. Just as the capability of backup systems has limits, so does the capacity to protect volumes of information. Once the question of how much *can* be protected and how much *must* be protected is resolved, more technical discussions can begin.

This is the stage at which the problems of abstraction, orientation, and set become prevalent. It is also the point at which language poses a legitimate problem. The weight of the burden falls largely on security personnel, but data processing personnel must also realize that "computer security" is two words. Security has a set of terms not easily understood, and DP specialists have just as much responsibility to try to understand them as security personnel do to master the basics of computer jargon.

From a security view, the objective of security is to prevent crime. Barring that, detecting a crime is the next best thing. Computer security has changed the latter goal. The problem of data theft is much like that of someone photographing important papers and then returning them to their proper place. Evidence is seldom left so the loss goes unnoticed and no alarm is raised. The objective of computer security must be to make the possibility of gaining unauthorized access to particular data as difficult as possible. Many organizations are getting better at accomplishing this objective, but success is coming only through extensive cooperation between people conceptually attuned to both security and data processing.

## BIBLIOGRAPHY

Festinger, L. *A Theory of Cognitive Dissonance*. Harper and Row, 1957.

Hayakawa, S. I. *Language in Thought and Action*. Harcourt Brace Jovanovich, 1964.

Parker, Donn B. "Computer Security: Some Easy Things to Do." *Computer Decisions*. Hayden Publishing Company, January 1974.

Parker, Donn B., Susan Nycum, and S. Oura. *Computer Abuse*. Stanford Research Institute, November 1973.

Rogers, C. R. "A Theory of Therapy, Personality, and Interpersonal Relationships as Developed in the Client-centered Framework." *Psychology: The Study of Science*. McGraw-Hill Book Company, 1969. Also, *On Becoming a Person*, Houghton Mifflin, 1961.

Ware, Willis H. (ed.). *Security Controls for Computer Systems*. The Rand Corporation, February 1970.

# CHAPTER 6

## Automated Information Systems: The Same Rules Don't Apply

James A. Schweitzer, CDP
Systems Security Technology Manager
Xerox Corporation

When an automated office information system (OIS) replaces a manual, paper-based system, simply transferring existing security, audit, and control measures from one to the other does not work. Traditional safeguards intended to ensure the integrity, correctness, and privacy of information rely heavily on physical entities not present in automated systems.

Consider, for example, a manual accounts payable system that provides for various checks and balances using physical elements—in this case, the original order, the receiving ticket, the invoice, and the payment voucher. Clerical employees lock up the various accounts payable documents in filing cabinets or desks. As long as the physical containers are not damaged, the information can be considered secure, private, and auditable.

In a fully automated system, however, checks and balances may only use electronic representation of these documents. As a result, organizational and procedural precautions traditionally used to ensure integrity, security, and control may be modified, bypassed, or negated. Concern for this vulnerability is seen in legislation on privacy and in recent trends toward redefining what constitutes "due care" in business financial controls.

Office information systems (OIS) convert information to a form that, for purposes of security, control, and auditability, is novel. Time and place constraints inherent in paper-based information systems no longer apply. Information is more portable both in physical (magnetic) form and in electronic form. Access to and modification of information no longer requires physical access to the office facility. Anyone with a terminal is capable of entering the data base surreptitiously without leaving any evidence.

Reprinted with the permission of the American Society for Industrial Security, from *Security Management*, Feb. 1983, p 45.

These new information characteristics need new procedures for security, auditability, and control. Any customized physical and procedural security elements for automated systems require certain built-in precautions.

The essence of information security or privacy in an automated system is the ability to limit access to information on a need-to-know basis. This need to know can be based on authorization by an appointed authority or on a general statement of rights, such as the one found in the fair credit laws. System software then must allow the system user to establish and maintain—based on current needs—logical access controls.[1] Also, the software and its supporting procedures must be reasonably convenient to apply.

Effective access control system software should incorporate three security levels:

1.  User identification or a claim to be a certain person. Usually this claim is made by entering a secret code or password into the system.
2.  User authentication, or proof that the identity claim entered in the first step is valid. Usually this step is supported by some element possessed by the claimant, such as a magnetic card, fingerprint, or voice print. In practice, this level often uses secondary passwords despite their obvious weaknesses.
3.  User authorization, or the limited approval of predetermined actions allowed for the individual who has been identified and authenticated. These authorizations typically come from a systems table established by some policy or law and are based on the need-to-know principle. Authorization may establish ''what may be seen'' or ''what may be done,'' or a combination of these two actions.

When an OIS is part of a communication network, encryption should be provided for sensitive information. In the near future, encryption will probably be the means for implementing network-wide security in office automation systems, providing an effective tool for overall access control and communications security.[2]

The access control system also must be capable of maintaining current tables of each user's right or authorizations and validating identification and authentication tokens.[3] Since the very purpose of office automation is to deal more effectively with variables, the system must be able to accommodate changes in job assignments, new company or department priorities, and different business situations. The system should also allow for human intervention to check the accuracy of day-to-day processing. These checks might include the following:

*   An authoritative method for establishing an individual's right to use the system, based on policy or situational decisions.
*   A controller or security officer who monitors the access control software and resulting logs and records.
*   Formal communications between personnel and security to ensure that official policy is reflected in the system security tables.
*   Processes that permit changes to system tables reflecting new job assignments or modifications and cancellations of authorization.
*   Ways to follow up indications of trouble or attempted penetration.

- Specified intervention at appropriate places or times to establish the integrity and accuracy of the OIS operation.

The procedures must provide adequate records, with pointers to electronic files where needed, to allow review and audit of system activities.

Finally, some physical security measures are needed. These procedures should include:

- Protection for both magnetic media and paper. Facilities should be provided and instructions given to lock up tapes, disks, and cartridges when they are not in use.
- Protection for communication cables that pass through areas not controlled by the user.
- An awareness of those places where information changes form, such as a central printer, copier, or communications center. These locations call for careful planning of security measures to avoid casual observation or theft of sensitive data in its original or copied form.

Once necessary software systems, procedures, and physical controls are put in place, secure operation of an OIS will depend on the good will and motivation of the individual users. Threats to these systems are legitimate—from the casual, sophisticated "hacker" to the intentional misuse of electronic information for criminal or socially disruptive purposes.

As office information systems deliver computing power to individuals at work and at home, protective structures will depend increasingly on the ability of users to follow the rules. Therefore, defining and publishing the responsibilities of those using advanced systems is an important part of ensuring security and privacy. OIS implementation plans should include motivational training to encourage the acceptance of this responsibility by staff members assigned to use the office systems.

Office information systems, manual or automated, must provide for security, privacy, and auditability. Transferring the traditional tasks of office workers to automated systems must be done in such a way that control over information—a vital company asset—is not lost.

## REFERENCES

1. Lance J. Hoffman, *Modern Methods for Computer Security and Privacy*, Chapters 2 and 3 (New York: Prentice-Hall, Inc., 1977).
2. Roger M. Needham and Michael D. Schroeder, *Using Encryption for Authentication in Large Networks of Computers* (Palo Alto, CA: Xerox Palo Alto Research Center, 1978).
3. Grayce M. Booth, *The Distributed System Environment*, Chapter 20 (New York: McGraw-Hill Book Co., 1981).

# PART II

# Evaluating the Risks

Inherent to any decision about what resources should be devoted to protecting any asset is an assessment of the relative importance of that asset. In the case of computers and the information they contain, numerous factors need to be weighed, and in the current litigious climate in the United States, liability issues are not the least of them. Therefore the opening article of Part II addresses the question of organizations' duty to safeguard their computers and computerized information.

A second article recommends assigning book values to information assets to force increased awareness of the need to develop and update security controls relative to these assets. How to assign value to intangible assets is explained.

Deciding what steps to take to protect computer facilities and information assets is a complex task that many experienced sources believe is best approached through an EDP risk assessment. The assessment process is detailed in this section, and several alternative approaches advocated by other security practitioners are presented.

# CHAPTER 7

## Judging Your Computer Liability

Robert F. Johnson, CPP
President/General Manager
First Security Services

Two general categories of legal concern exist for security professionals whose organizations use computers. The first is the organization's legal responsibility to protect the content and use of the computer. The second, which comes into play if protective efforts fail, is the legal recourse available to the organization if a crime is committed against or by means of its computer.

### THE DUTY TO SAFEGUARD—LIABILITY

A question arises as to whether management would be liable, in the case of an occurrence of adverse consequence, for failure to use a computer security method or device that was available on a cost-effective basis and would have been instrumental in preventing that occurrence. [For similar issues relative to non-security devices, see T. J. Hooper, 60 F.2d 737; *Northwest Airlines, Inc. v. Glen L. Martin Company*, 224 F.2d 120.] The standard of care*—in such an instance has not yet been ascertained. While a company is clearly liable if an employee develops or applies a program incompetently or negligently, the extent of a company's responsibility in employing the computer is difficult to determine. [*Chatlos Systems, Inc. v. National Cash Register*

---

Reprinted with the permission of the American Society for Industrial Security, from *Security Management*, Aug. 1982, p 25.

*In this sense, standard of care is the legally requisite level of skill or performance required of a supplier of goods or services. The standard may be firmly established in practice and acceptance or may be ill-defined and subject to subsequent definition in a legal proceeding. Even when a standard is accepted as adequate in a given industry or trade, litigation may result in a determination that the accepted standard was inadequate in light of technological or managerial improvements. This has been held to be particularly so where the improvements were related to the safety of a product or activity and were generally available on a cost-effective basis. (See T.J. Hooper, *Northwest Airlines*, above.)

*Corp.* 479 F.Supp. 738; *IBM v. Catamore Enterprises, Inc.* 548 F.2d 1065; *Triangle Underwriters, Inc. v. Honeywell, Inc.* 604 F.2nd 734.]

The accessibility of computer operations to unauthorized intrusions, malevolent or not, and the severe consequences that may result from such intrusions, are likely to figure in court decisions determining that a company has a professional obligation to secure computers from such violations. Defendants have been found liable for failure to maintain adequate security precautions in other instances. [See e.g., *Garzilli v. Howard Johnson's Motor Lodges Inc.*, 419 F.Supp. 1210, 1212, n.2 (E.D.N.Y. 1976) failure to secure lock on door to motel room.]

For this reason, security measures and auditing procedures designed to identify potential or actual abberations in the computer system are of paramount importance in safeguarding system integrity and protecting against liability claims. Failure to institute these precautions is likely to violate the computer professional's requisite duty of care, and thus would result in liability for harm done, even if the harm is directly attributable to an unauthorized intrusion.

Another prime example of this duty exists on behalf of financial institutions pursuant to the Electronic Funds Transfer Act [15 U.S.C. Section 1693 et. seq., (1979)]. Under the EFT Act, the financial institution provides the customer with an account access. The legislative history of the act indicates that Congress officially adopted a system that provides for limited liability on the part of consumers [S. Rep. No. 915, 95th Cong., 2nd Sess. 6, (1979)]. This provision increases the risks taken by the financial institutions and provides a stimulus to maximize the security of the EFT system.

Congress has recognized that "this is an appropriate assignment of risks since the financial institution has established the EFT system and the ability to tighten its security characteristics." Thus, financial institutions that fail to maintain the highest degree of protection for their computer technology, do so at their own peril.

Assertion of a claim based on alleged inadequacy of safeguards may result in a liability judgment or, at the very least, could cause prolonged and costly litigation. From a management perspective, therefore, victimization by computer-related crime may result in cost and consequences similar to that of alleged or actual liability for the occurrence. The law is indefinite regarding this point, but by analogy to other issues and cases, such as products liability and malpractice, the concept of such liability seems quite probable.

The legal issues of individual privacy also pose a legal motivation for implementing effective computer security measures. Many of the recommendations in the report of the Federal Privacy Protection Study Commission, *Personal Privacy in an Information Society* (1977), specifically relate to safeguards to be taken to protect the privacy and related rights of individuals. Particular emphasis was placed on protections to be afforded computerized data of that nature. Subsequent bills introduced at the state and federal levels have incorporated the safeguard requirements, which would seem inherently to include measures to safeguard computer facilities.

A number of regulatory developments in recent years, as well as recommendations by voluntary standards organizations, illustrate the increasing importance assigned to internal accounting controls adequate to protect organizational assets. The increasing use of computers and telecommunications equipment to record and transmit data substantially increases the risk and potential consequences of acts adversely affecting organizational assets.

In light of these factors, the Securities and Exchange Commission issued for comment a proposed rule requiring a statement of management on internal controls (Ref. 44 Fed. Reg. 885479, May 1979). The proposed rule was subsequently withdrawn in June 1980 (45 Fed. Reg. 40134); however, more such rules can be anticipated mandating control systems, with obvious implications for computer security and audit controls.

Although responsible corporations have for some time acknowledged the obligation to maintain accurate books and records and to have adequate internal controls, the obligation was not explicitly established in public law until passage of the Foreign Corrupt Practices Act (FCPA) of 1977 (15 U.S.C. Sec. 78M). Part of the act pertains to accounting standards applied to all companies that have a class of stock registered in accordance with Section 12 or that are required to file reports pursuant to Section 15(D) of the Securities Act of 1934. This section requires companies to devise and maintain a system of internal accounting controls to provide reasonable assurance that:

- all transactions are executed in accordance with management's general or specific authorization;
- transactions are recorded as necessary to permit preparation of financial statements in conformity with generally accepted accounting principles or any other criteria applicable to such statements and to maintain accountability for assets;
- access to assets is permitted only in accordance with management's general or specific authorization; and
- the recorded accountability for assets is compared with the existing assets at reasonable intervals and appropriate action is taken with respect to any differences.

The phrase "reasonable assurance" is contained in the FCPA in reference to the statement required concerning the effectiveness of internal accounting controls. The concept of reasonableness, as opposed to absolute assurance, was incorporated into the act and subsequently proposed SEC rule in recognition that the interest of shareholders is not well served if the cost of internal accounting controls exceeds the benefits thereof. Obviously the cost-benefit of any particular control or series of controls will be difficult to state precisely; therefore decisions on "reasonable assurance" will necessarily depend on estimates and judgments by management in individual circumstances. Development of a computer security program based on management methods and technologies used by risk managers and by corporate security and computer security professionals will assist senior management in fulfilling the responsibility of providing the required "reasonable assurance."

In addition to this statutory audit requirement, which is limited to subject firms, various forms of financing and security agreements set forth specific requirements for safeguarding and controlling the asset subject to the agreement. Failure to safeguard by means consistent with the current level of state-of-the art administrative procedures and technology may give rise to charges of breach of contract or related action. This general duty to safeguard all assets would, by analogy, apply to computerized assets.

Since July 1978, the New York Stock Exchange has required each company it lists to adopt an audit committee policy. Among the duties of these audit committees is performance of a review of the firm's internal audit controls with both internal audit controls with both internal and independent auditors.

A special advisory committee on internal accounting controls, formed by the American Institute of Certified Public Accountants (AICPA) in 1977, issued a report in 1979 to provide guidance on the development of audit and control systems.

Commenting on the special considerations concerning the audit and control of electronic data processing operations, the report states:

- There is often less documentary evidence of the performance of control procedures in computer systems than in manual systems.
- Information in manual systems can be read by the user without the aid of a machine. Files and records in EDP systems are usually in machine-sensible form and often cannot be read without the use of a computer.
- Information in an EDP system can be more vulnerable to physical disaster, human error, unauthorized manipulation, or mechanical malfunction than information in a manual system. Concentration of data, multiple users, and multiple access are characteristics that may increase the vulnerability of EDP systems.
- Computer processing of individual transactions may require better anticipation of potential problems. Manual systems often rely on human judgment to identify problems as they occur.
- Various functions may be concentrated in an EDP system, thus reducing traditional segregation of duties. A single person may be able to make unauthorized changes (for example, modifying a program, data base, or master file) that negate internal accounting controls or permit improper access to assets. Appropriate segregation of EDP functions may overcome this weakness.
- Additional specialized knowledge may be required to evaluate internal accounting controls in an EDP environment.
- Changes to the system are often more difficult to implement in an EDP system than in a manual system.
- With proper controls in place, EDP systems can provide greater consistency than manual systems because they uniformly subject all transactions to the same controls.

*(A copy of the report is available from the AICPA, 1211 Avenue of the Americas, New York, NY 10036.)*
Information in the report may be helpful in identifying issues related to ascertaining whether a duty was breached, i.e., identifying liability issues. AICPA has also published nine booklets on the topic of audit controls for computer systems.

The obligation to protect EDP assets can also be viewed as part of the general duty of care for officers and directors required under federal securities laws and state corporation laws. Under appropriate circumstances, the reports cited and similar issuances from professional organizations and regulatory bodies could be used to establish the argument that failure of management to ensure adequate audit controls for computerized systems in conformance with accepted standards constitutes failure in the duty of due care.

## IF A CRIME OCCURS

In most known instances, computers are merely tools used in the commission of white collar or economic crimes, and the terms ''computer-related'' or ''computer assisted'' crime are more appropos than ''computer crime.'' Consequently, in dealing with computer-related crime, we are in fact dealing with old crimes in new forms—forms that present special challenges to those involved in the prevention, detection, investigation, and subsequent prosecution or defense of these criminal acts.

Brief examples of how computers can be used by individuals with access to commit fraud include:

- misuse of inventory to direct material to be delivered to a certain address;
- modification of data to cover inventory shortages in collusion with warehouse or other personnel;
- use of an accounts payable system to generate fictitious bills and subsequently retain payment of them;
- acceptance of kickback payments from suppliers or customers for altering accounts receivable records;
- generation of payroll checks to fictitious persons or overpayment to individuals for kickbacks; and
- provision of valuable business information, such as customer records, to competitors for reward.

Although all of these methods existed and were used in the pre-computer world of business, the concentration of the ability to process thousands of transactions in the hands of a few persons increases both the opportunity and the potential impact of computer-related fraud.

Losses due to computer-related crime can take several forms:

- theft by use of the computer;
- fraud induced by use of the computer;
- theft of data, programs, or sensitive information;
- misuse of or unauthorized access to data;
- physical damage to computer resources; and
- denial of or interference with computer services.

Nearly any traditional crime—for instance, embezzlement, employee theft, or payroll fraud—can occur in computer operations, as can schemes specifically related to the computer: misappropriation of computer time, theft of programs, or illegal acquisition of proprietary information, such as computerized or computer-related trade secrets.

The potential for compromise of national security information also exists by means of unauthorized access to classified information in either government or private industry data banks. In the private sector this potential is ostensibly limited by restrictions on use of computers/networks to compile, sort, or process classified information. (See *Industrial Security Manual for Safeguarding Classified Information* DOD 5220.22-M Sec. XIII.)

Given the heightened potential for the use of computers as tools in or targets of crimes, the problem of prosecuting such cases arises. Because computers are an enigma to so many people, the prospect of a computer crime case can be intimidating to the police, prosecutors, defense attorneys, courts, and corporate security personnel. The need for educating such parties about computers is great, as is the need for communication among them.

The Bureau of Justice Statistics of the US Department of Justice has been funding the development of technical assistance materials and programs for the investigation and prosecution of computer-related crimes. Although the primary focus of these efforts is the criminal justice community, they can be expected to benefit the legal and corporate communities as well. Among the results of the effort are two publications, *Computer Crime, Criminal Justice Resource Manual* (Grant #78-SS-AX-0031 Report, Superintendent of Documents, US Government Printing Office) and *Investigation of Computer Related Crime*.

Due to the legislative void regarding computer-related crime, courts have had to go through what has been described as "tortuous mental and statutory gymnastics" to fit a defendant's conduct to the proscription of various alternatively used statutes at the state and federal levels. (This practice has yielded an inability to gauge the extent of computer-related crimes, since prosecution is usually under ordinary statutes.)

The distinctions between computer-related crimes and traditional crimes is best illustrated by a comparison of two major cases: *United States v. Jones*, 553 F2d 351 (4th Cir. 1977), *cert. denied*, 431 US 968 (1977), and *Hancock v. State*, 402 SW 2d 906 (Tex. Crim. App. 1966). In the *Jones* case, the defendant and her brother operated a scheme whereby the defendant was able to receive and cash checks her brother had caused to be issued fraudulently. He did this by creating a false account for the defendant and manipulating accounts payable numbers. By entering false data into the computer, the defendant's brother caused checks to be issued to the defendant instead of to a legitimate creditor. The District Court of Maryland constructed the actions of the defendant as common law forgery and thus within an exclusionary clause of a statute cited in the indictment dismissing the case. [*United States v. Jones*, 414 F.Supp. 964 (D.Md. 1976).] The Circuit Court of Appeals reversed, finding the crime was actually "a case of computer abuse involving the input into a computer facility of allegedly altered accounts payable data." (*United States v. Jones*, 553 F.2d at 353). The case was characterized in testimony before Congress as fraud upon the computer:

(T)he . . . computer was not considered to be an agent of Jones and her cohort, but rather an instrumentality of the corporation. In making this finding, the court held that in effect, the computer was defrauded when the bogus information was submitted to it. Accordingly, the checks were not forgeries but rather were obtained by fraud within the meaning of the statute.

Therefore, *Jones* may be classified as a computer-related crime, and not a traditional offense, although prosecuted under a conventional federal statute. In contrast, the *Hancock* case involved the traditional crime of felony theft. The defendant in that case stole software consisting of 59 computer programs and offered to sell them by way of an agent to a competitor of his employer. The Texas court held that the subject computer programs were property with a value in excess of the $50 threshold amount required under the terms of the relevant state statute.

While computer systems are often the objects of traditional crimes such as arson or sabotage, in other instances manipulation of computer-controlled processes, such as heat detection or air-conditioning controls, may effect destruction. A traditional crime, e.g., arson, may be accomplished by means of computer technology, and thus would be properly classified as a computer-related crime.

Perhaps the most apparent illustration of the special nature of a crime in which computer system provides the essential characteristic is in electronic fund transfers. The medium of computer technology gives rise to a particular type of computer crime, most notably the employment of the EFT system to unauthorized ends. The unfailing accuracy many people ascribe to computers, plus their unwillingness or inability to comprehend the nature of how computers function, have created an aura of mystery and credibility about computer science. This has in turn led to crimes of fraud or false pretenses dependent upon false data presumed to be derived from legitimate computations.

Complicating the issue of what constitutes a computer crime are the characteristics of computerized information and programs. While most courts have not yet had to confront the tangible/intangible property characteristics of software and data, a few have struggled to define the elements of criminal prosecutions involving computers.

The problem of whether a computer program was tangible or intangible property arose initially in a 1972 decision in California, *Ward v. Superior Court* [3 C.L.S.R. 206 (Cal. Super. 1972)]. The defendant, by use of a data phone hookup and his knowledge of certain computer codes, tapped the computer of a competitor and gained access to a valuable program. The statute under which he was indicted made criminal the theft of any article representing a trade secret. The court found that what the defendant had received by his tap was nothing more than electronic impulses transmitted by the computer. The court deemed these impulses to be not tangible and thus not an "article" within the ambit of the statute. Nevertheless, the court did find the defendant's making a copy of the program afterwards constituted copying a trade secret once he had gained access to it. (*Ward* at 208–209.) [Regarding trade secrets, see M.G.L. Ch. 266, Sec. 30(4) and Sec. 60(a), and M.G.L. Ch. 93, Sec. 42.]

Compare *Hancock v. State* at 908, where the court, although not considering the exact same issues as those weighed in *Ward*, did not hesitate to characterize stolen programs as "property possess(ing) an ascertainable value." See also *United States v. Sampson*, 6 C.L.S.R. 879 (N.D. Cal. 1978), in which the use of computer time was found to be property capable of being stolen under applicable federal statute.

The difficulties of defining how software and programs may be classified as property additionally burdens prosecutors and the courts. As previously mentioned, the dearth of criminal legislation addressing the problems unique to computer crime results in prosecutors bringing indictments under unwieldy criminal statutes never intended for use in criminal prosecution of computer violations.

In the Fourth Circuit, two major cases have been decided that illustrate the difficulties of attempting to prosecute computer crimes under traditional statutes. The first case, *United States v. Jones* [441 F.Supp. 964 (D.Md. 1976), rev'd, F.2d 351 (4th Cir.), *cert. denied*, 431 U.S. 968 (1977)] involved a prosecution under a federal statute. The District Court of Maryland dismissed the indictment. Only when the Circuit Court of Appeals characterized the case as one of theft and fraud by ''computer abuse'' rather than forgery was the US attorney allowed to continue prosecution (533 F.2d at 353, 356).

The second major case, *United States v. Seidlitz* [589 F.2d 152 (4th Cir. 1978), *cert. denied*, 441 U.S. 922 (1979)] presents identical problems. The defendant had violated the computer system of a former employer by using his knowledge of certain data codes to gain remote access by telephone hookup. The original indictment included two counts of wire fraud and a third count of interstate transportation of stolen property. The District Court granted a motion for acquittal on the latter count on the grounds that the transmittal of impulses by computer telephone hookup did not constitute transportation of property. The decision was similar in rationale to that in the *Ward* case. The defendant's conviction on two counts of wire fraud, 18 U.S.C. Section 1343 (enacted in 1934), was upheld because the Court of Appeals specifically acknowledged that the evidence at trial was sufficient for the jury to have found the stolen program to be property (by implication overruling the District Court's dismissal of the third count of the original indictment).

## LEGISLATION ON COMPUTER-RELATED CRIMES

In the past several years, numerous private and government studies analyzing the existing and projected problem of computer-related crime have concluded that legislation is needed to define certain customary crimes in terms of computer technology and to address the specific issues of criminal acts peculiar to computer operations. To date, state and federal legislatures have exhibited rather lax postures on computer crimes, but certain indications suggest the situation will improve. Fifteen states have enacted specific legislation on computer-related crime: AZ, CO, FL, MI, NM, RI, CA, IL, NC, and UT. A number of others, including MA, have passed legislation making criminal various acts involving computer technology in the field of telecommunications. (M.G.L.Ch. 166, Sec. 42A).

The Florida Computer Crime Act (Fla. Stat. Ann. No. 815.10 et. seq.) appears to be the most comprehensive of all the state legislation. It includes sanctions for theft of or damage to hardware (computer equipment and suppliers) and software (computer programs and data). The Florida act makes willful, unauthorized access to computer systems criminal. It also applies to theft or damage to data or programs, whether they are stored in a computer or not, and whether they are off-line or on-line. This legislation represents a major step toward saving the courts the task of defining the contents of a system. Electronic impulses, for example, which were deemed not to be property or tangible in *Seidlitz* and *Ward*, would fall within the protection of the Florida act without any ambiguity.

A Federal Computer Systems Protection Act was introduced to the US Senate in 1977 by Senator Abraham Ribicoff (D-CT), then chairman of the Governmental Affairs Committee. A revised version was submitted by Ribicoff in 1979, but did not pass. (**Editor's note:** *H.R. 3970, currently in the House Judiciary Committee, is titled the Federal Computer Systems Protection Act of 1981. No action has been taken, nor is any planned, and no Senate version has been introduced as of June 1982.*)

If this bill is enacted, it would be the first federal law aimed at curbing computer crime. The debate and comment on the proposed legislation [*Congressional Record*, S.240, 96th Cong., 1st Sess., 125 Cong. Rec. 710 (1979)] offers an excellent overview of the multiple issues involved in the application of law to computer crimes.

S.240 identified four main types of computer crime:

- the introduction of fraudulent records or data into a computer system;
- the unauthorized use of computer-related facilities;
- the alteration or destruction of information and files; and
- the theft, whether by electronic means or otherwise, of money, financial instruments, property, services, or valuable data.

Three facets of the proposed bill merit special attention. First, it provides specific sanctions for violations relating to EFT systems, thereby increasing the protection afforded financial institutions. Second, by being broadly written, the proposed act ensures it will be possible to institute criminal proceedings by overlapping the criminal sanctions of other federal statutes. For example, with respect to intellectual property, the proposed act and the Copyright Act [17 U.S.C. Section 506 (1976)] both make criminal the reproduction of a copyrighted piece of software. Fraudulently obtaining information from a federal agency may violate both the proposed act and the Privacy Act [5 U.S.C. Section 552(a) (1976)].

The third element of the bill, and perhaps the most troublesome, is its failure to define precisely a proscribed unauthorized usage of a computer system. The absence of such a definition would seem to leave overly broad discretion in the hands of federal prosecutors. The character of the computer industry and the nature of the technological services employed are not labelled easily. Attempting to ascertain when the use of a computer, program, computer time, or the like is adverse to the interests of the proper user would be more useful than seeking to further define what constitutes unauthorized use.

For a complete discussion of the proposed legislation and the ramifications it would have on the prosecution of computer crime, see Roddy, ''The Federal Computer Systems Protection Act,'' [7 *Rutgers J. Comp. Tech. & L* 343 (1980).]

Even should legislation addressing computer crime pass, the responsibility for prevention, detection, and reporting of computer crimes rests with business and industry. Such legislation would, however, give US attorneys, at the federal level, and local prosecutors at the state level, a better weapon with which to prosecute identified and reported offenses.

# CHAPTER 8

## Put Information Assets on the Balance Sheet

Dr. Alan G. Merten
University of Michigan

Partrice Delaney
Hewlett Packard/DISC Security Division

Beth Pomerantz
Great Lakes Steel

Paula Kelly
Arthur Anderson & Co.

"Our database and software packages are two of the most valuable resources this company has," claimed an EDP manager to his fellow executives in the executive lunchroom. Everyone at the table nodded their heads in agreement. "And furthermore," he continued, "these resources should be valued, depreciated, and accounted for in the same manner as all other balance sheet assets." The reaction at the table this time ranged from a few bemused "those strange people in EDP" smiles, to a number of "hmm, I'll have to think about that" replies.

In light of the Foreign Corrupt Practices Act and moves in Europe to value data for tax purposes, many managers are seriously thinking about broadening the definition of assets to include data and software. This approach would have far reaching effects on most US corporations, ranging from tax implications, to the need to redesign the balance sheet. Such an approach would also influence the whole field of data processing controls.

If software and data are viewed as assets, then it follows that they should be valued and depreciated in the same manner as other assets. This valuation process would also help to make managers more sensitive to and aware of the need for controls. We believe that if managers were forced to stop and think about the value of a specific

Reprinted from the January 1982 issue of *Risk Management*, a monthly publication of the Risk and Insurance Management Society. Used with permission.

data resource in terms of efficiencies gained, impact of loss, and costs, they would begin to recognize the importance of security and controls.

Most managers realize that software, hardware, and data are resources to be protected, but there has been a large gap between recognition and actual installation of adequate controls. Awareness of the economic and/or monetary value of software and data would certainly be one step toward closing this gap.

How, exactly, would a firm benefit from valuating its information assets? When current data applications are implemented, in most cases they are studied extensively before they are introduced to determine their cost effectiveness and what accompanying control procedures they require. Once operational, however, applications seem to assume a momentum of their own. Changes and new features are added without formal recognition that new risks may result and that new controls are needed. If an asset valuation procedure were applied, management would be forced to continually re-appraise the value of an application, making them increasingly aware of the need to expand and change controls accordingly.

Adequate controls may also be lacking because of upper management's naive assumption that competent EDP personnel automatically install adequate controls. If management required valuation procedures, it would have more information on which to base the value of its EDP resources. It would be better able not only to understand what controls were in place, but also to ascertain where controls were needed. And a cost/benefit analysis for ranking the implementation of controls in order of priority could then be developed.

Having become aware that data and software are assets and are exposed to risks (natural disaster, human error, hardware/software failure, and abuse), managers would realize that data and software should also be insured. Insurance is currently provided only to a certain extent by disaster recovery plans and a good system of internal/administrative controls. The need for a secondary line of defense, such as fidelity bonding and disaster insurance, would become clearer to managers. Furthermore, because of the valuation process, they would be "allowed" to purchase such insurance. Resources can be insured only if a monetary value has been placed on them.

## ASSESSING THE INTANGIBLE

To understand how information assets might be valued, think of them as intangible assets, such as goodwill or patents. First, establish the initial cost of this data and software. The cost should include the purchase price, if any, plus costs incurred in enhancing its use. Examples of purchased data include mailing lists, market research data, independent laboratory analyses, economic forecasts, and policy studies. Internally developed software programs should reflect any development costs that can be traced. The value of internally obtained data should be defined as the cost of collecting or generating that data.

With the cost of information assets established, the next step is to determine the useful life of data. As with other assets, information assets change over time and their value deteriorates. For example, while the need for generic software and data—such as accounting or payroll systems—is likely to exist as long as the firm does, individual, specific programs will probably not remain static. Changing business conditions and changes in regulations or internal policies could force program changes. Data may also have to be revised. Installing new hardware or software could make current programs suddenly obsolete or incompatible. Shifting to a new data-processing policy, such as centralized data administration, would require revising data files and programs. Newly discovered program bugs often result in untested emergency program patches. And computerized data, like any other form of information, eventually becomes outdated.

The cumulative effect of these kinds of modifications and patches is that the original program no longer exists. It may no longer do what it was originally intended to do, or it may perform less effectively and efficiently and be less productive for the firm. A depreciation schedule based on the useful life of the programs and data should be formulated to reflect this fact of economic life. The above factors should be considered in determining such a depreciation schedule. However the extent to which any of these factors affects the system will vary from firm to firm.

Until this method of calculating depreciation of information assets becomes more widely practiced, a company's experience is probably the only way to define the depreciable life of its information assets. Past lives of similar programs may be the most direct measure. A program's activity level—the frequency of its use and the volatile nature of its ''subject matter''—should also be included in this useful life estimation. A more frequently used program, or one that operates in a more volatile environment, will be subject to more changes and will, therefore, have a shorter useful life. Program complexity is another factor that affects life expectancy; as programs become more complex, they become more vulnerable to program bugs.

Depreciating information assets serves several specific control purposes. Most obviously, the current monetary value of information assets can be specified. Also, a replacement and maintenance schedule can be outlined. Such a schedule contributes to effective control by keeping programs healthy—that is, correct, properly documented, and efficient. Estimating the durability of information assets focuses attention on the nature and life cycle of particular software programs and data. By depreciating such assets, the current phase of their life cycle can be pinpointed and the appropriate controls taken.

For example, programs in the latter phases of their life cycles, which are likely to be more vulnerable to illicit changes and manipulation, could be identified, controlled more stringently, and audited more frequently. Through this method of depreciation, a corporation might also discover the most effective control mechanisms for its information assets based on their nature and age. Overall, understanding the life cycle of information assets gives companies the information they need to deploy their control resources more effectively.

While this concept of value is helpful, particularly for internal management use, it does not capture the full essence of the value of information assets for the corporation. Full economic value goes beyond the notion of book value to incorporate contributions made by these information assets to the company's successful operation. By attempting to construct and value this intangible benefit, the overlooked importance of information assets to the firm's existence will become readily apparent to management and will prompt implementation of appropriate controls. This expanded measure of value should include the dollar loss that would result if the software and data were unavailable or compromised. Added to this loss should be the cost of restoring the programs and data. These amounts can indicate the ultimate value of information assets.

A "what-if" approach can be used to speculate about the probable ramifications and expected dollar losses should the information assets be unavailable suddenly. What is the role of a particular program or class of programs and data? Are they crucial to continued operations? How will the company recover the functions provided by a class of programs and data?

To measure the value of this capability, look at the time and costs required to reconstruct and implement programs and data. This estimation should then be further broken down to include the time needed to establish minimal functioning, and the time required to establish full operations. The ability to recover capabilities quickly would reduce the total loss.

Defining the overall importance of information assets could be very useful in developing a control strategy. Each of the two approaches discussed—characterizing information assets by noting which ones hold the largest potential losses, and defining an appropriate set of controls for the age and nature of the information—provide the beginnings of a more reasoned approach to allocating control resources than the methods used currently.

## WHAT ASSET VALUATION CAN'T DO

We would be remiss if we left the impression that implementing an asset valuation process is a panacea for discovering and controlling all risks associated with EDP and information assets. While it is a crucial step, especially for increasing control awareness, it is important to understand and examine what the procedure will *not* do.

To determine a little more precisely what an asset valuation procedure will and will not do, first try to understand what lies behind management's failure to successfully control risks, and then determine what procedures asset valuation might fail to address. For this analysis, resistances to control awareness, development, and implementation fall into three categories: psychological, organizational, and educational.

Psychological blocks to developing control procedures include a lack of information about the future or protection of turf, and the human tendency to take the easy way out whenever possible.

Imagining the future is difficult, and as long as EDP fraud, problems, and risks are seen as unlikely possibilities, it's hard to take a long range view of events. An asset valuation model is not likely to prevent individuals from thinking, "It can't happen to us."

Furthermore, even though people at all levels in the organization may be more aware of the value of the data and software that affect their work, they still may resist using control procedures if they seem to criticize standard operations, or if the procedures interfere with departmental "turf."

Finally, we'd have to admit that once countermeasures or controls are in place, the process of asset valuation will not really help maintain their use. For example, if control totals are added to a computer-based application, the data entry clerk might just stop computing the totals because it is easier not to do so.

Also, a particular department could dominate EDP functions, causing costly resources to be devoted to relatively unimportant systems while other potential users are denied access to available resources. With an asset valuation procedure, the organization would have a more comprehensive picture of the relative worth of each department's information and could prevent misuse or misallocation of control resources. However, it still could not force cooperation among users, nor guarantee the controls would be implemented through appropriate segregation of duties and responsibilities. In addition, if EDP processing has become fragmented because users have obtained DP facilities outside the organization, even an asset valuation procedure will not make it easy to integrate various DP installations with corporate-wide control policies, a necessary step in controlling risks.

One last point should be mentioned in terms of organizational structure. The dynamic nature of organizations—turnover of personnel, restructuring, applications designed or modified—continually presents new risks and control needs. As we have tried to demonstrate, an asset valuation model could be useful in this instance since, as systems change, their values change and the model should theoretically reflect such changes.

A final hindrance to the development and installation of controls is that managers and users often receive inadequate training and information about computers or the risks they present. However, because they would become more aware of controls through an asset valuation model, management is less likely to be ignorant of EDP risks. Knowing the value of information assets, they would be less willing to simply assume "those people in EDP" must be taking care of everything. Using our proposed model, management would be more likely to take an active interest in information assets protection.

On the other hand, unless special efforts are made to educate users, their role in controlling risks through the implementation and subsequent maintenance of the systems design may not be effective. Lacking knowledge and/or imagination about the best way to process an application, they may continue to suggest familiar, but still risky, procedures. Education, not asset valuation, is needed to determine controls required by specific transaction flows.

Despite its shortcomings, an asset valuation model would force management to take a good, close look at its EDP assets instead of leaving their valuation to intuitive judgement. While putting a monetary value on such assets might be difficult, attempting such an exercise would at least focus attention on their importance and the costly consequences of their loss.

Admittedly, human resource accounting, a similiar concept which deals with hard-to-quantify data, has long been controversial and is not widely used. However, formalized valution of EDP assets seems to be a topic that will receive more attention at all corporate levels—from the EDP auditor who says "that which is measured is controlled," to the company president who calls for a definition of assets which goes beyond the CPA's dictionary to include the value of all information.

# CHAPTER 9

## The Basics of EDP Risk Assessment

James R. Wade
The Scott and Fetzer Company

Just what is all the fuss about risk assessments? Are risk assessments some dream child from the ivory tower or the imaginings of a professor in some think tank in California? Are they some government programs we must try to comply with no matter what?

The answer is no. Rather, risk assessments, or risk analyses, are nothing new. Insurance practitioners have made use of risk analysis for years. What is new is the application of many of the principles and concepts of risk assessment and management to data processing systems.

Electronic data processing (EDP) managers and data processors both may hope the whole issue of risk assessment will blow over. However, today, when money is so tight, it is becoming increasingly necessary for all of us to justify the cost of what we do, including the protective program used for computer facilities.

As a corporate director of security, I find that I need to do more than identify where we have problems and where we need to apply controls in the manufacturing process. I also have to do some cost-benefit analysis to prove to company management that our risk management program is cost-efficient. I may ultimately suggest that we self-insure in some situations, insure other risks through an insurance carrier, or do something ourselves to alleviate a risk. But I can't know which route to suggest until we have really studied the situation.

Whether your company has an unsophisticated computer room or a very complex command and control system, the security director must determine the probability of survival of the computer or data processing (DP) system in the face of particular risks and threats. Critical operations must be designated in the event that damage to the system allows only partial operations. The possible maximum loss in case of catastrophe should also be determined.

This article was originally presented by the author at the June 1980 ASIS Computer Security Workshop in Boston, MA. Reprinted with the permission of the American Society for Industrial Security, from *Security Management*, March 1982, p 56.

Traditionally, planning for computer security programs has concerned only the actual equipment (hardware) and the programs that make it operate (software). However, to protect a data processing center effectively, it must be looked at as a system. The elements included in this broader definition of the data processing center are the hardware and software, communications, personnel, documents and media, procedures, and environment.

*Communications.* This category includes not only communications within the computer system, but also communications with the outside.

*Personnel.* A computer system cannot operate without people, and they must be included in a systems approach to computer security.

*Documents and media.* This element is an often ignored but significant one. For example, how long can you survive without your paper stock, especially pre-printed forms? A supplier may promise to get these for you within six hours, but when a catastrophe occurs, you may find they're not available for six months. The paper storage area, then, must be considered in a computer system risk assessment.

*Procedures.* The procedures for operating the hardware and for the programs are of critical importance. You can put identical computer systems in similar environments, but how the people involved implement the procedures makes each system unique. (This is why you cannot transfer a risk analysis of one location to other systems and have the risk evaluation for the first site be applicable to the other sites.)

*Environment.* The environment of a data processing center must be considered from the outside to the inside, proceeding from the system's geographic location to the actual room(s) it is in.

To be effective, a risk assessment program must consider all these elements as a system. Concentrating security efforts on individual pieces of hardware or software, no matter how critical they may be, is unreasonable. Equipment is of little use without the rest of the data processing system.

Risk assessment is a method of estimating the anticipated or expected loss from some adverse event. The ultimate goal of such an assessment is a ranked order of specific threats that shows which parts of the EDP center need security most. The ranking should run from the least to the most vulnerable.

Risk assessment is a methodology, which means it must be practiced by people and it must be implemented to have an effect. Simply buying a risk management manual or appointing a risk manager doesn't mean you've done the job.

Risk assessment is a method of estimating; it is not a science. If it were, we could provide you with a formula that would give each user the same results in each different situation. But because risk assessment is an art, it can be approached in a lot of different ways.

The approach to risk assessment I will give here is one that has evolved over the last five or six years. I'm using it now in my job to assess what loss controls I need to implement, and it works.

Estimating the threats to a data processing system is difficult because we are dealing with unknowns. We must find a way of anticipating some of what may happen in case of an adverse event.

First, we must realize that the words threat and vulnerability cannot be used interchangeably. A threat is anything that could conceivably affect a data processing system adversely. A vulnerability is any weakness, hole, or flaw in the system that could be exploited by a threat. As a simplistic analogy, diseases such as cancer, heart disease, influenza, and the common cold are threats present in our daily environment. For any number of reasons, some of us are vulnerable to one or several of these threats. Not everyone will get all or any of these diseases because not everyone is vulnerable to them. If you can distinguish between these two terms, you will find it helps as you go through the risk assessment process.

A risk assessment methodology must be hierarchial and modular to be good. The assessment of a complete data processing system is comprised of a number of risk analyses performed in a certain order. Thus, each step brings more information to the next step in the process. This particular methodology can be applied with some adaptation to almost any kind of system in just about any kind of environment.

The assessment process is one that should be cyclical, rather than a one-time linear event. If you operate under Office of Management and Budget (OMB) regulations, you know that OMB Circular A-71 Transmittal Memorandum 1 tells you to perform a risk assessment every five years as well as any time there is a major change in the computer system. If the frequency of these assessments is not specified for a facility, the security manager should see that they are carried out on a regular basis.

The risk assessment process results in recommendations based on the information found in individual analyses. Often, some of the recommendations are implemented and that is the end of the process. Ideally, the assessment should be reviewed after the changes have been made because the exposure to risks is altered by the changes. Another complete risk assessment may not be necessary, but you will want to know if the recommendations have, in fact, improved the security as proposed.

The risk assessment methodology (see Exhibit 9–1) begins with preparation for the initiation of the process. The decision to start the risk assessment process is not one that can be made Friday afternoon and put into action Monday morning. The purpose and starting point of the process must be defined first, and the rest of the process planned from there. If not planned properly, the assessment process will fall apart. Early in the process research should be conducted into company policies and any statutes and regulations that apply to your particular company. This information will prove invaluable at several stages in the risk assessment process (see Exhibit 9–1). For those who work for government agencies, this step is quite simple because most agencies must comply with certain regulations written specifically for them. If you are a government contractor, you must implement certain government policies, as well.

On the other hand, private companies may be responsible for adhering to state or federal laws that may not specifically mention the work they do. Some of these statutes, such as the Freedom of Information Act and the Privacy Act, exact penalties from companies that do not comply with their provisions (see Exhibit 9–2). Private companies must be aware of all such laws that affect what they do; however, regulations like the FOIA do not always specify that they apply to data processing systems. Have

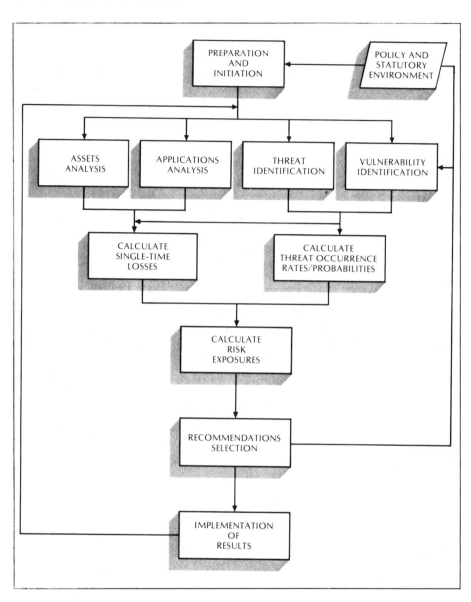

**Exhibit 9–1.** Risk assessment methodology.

someone review all applicable laws and summarize their impact on your company's EDP operations. Knowing this information can help you keep your system from being vulnerable to legal recourse if these obligations are not met.

In addition to checking for laws that apply to your business, you also need to look for company policies that affect your risk assessment. Does the company have any policy about conducting any kind of a risk assessment? If your company is typical, it probably does not. If this is the case, you may want to ask the CEO or whoever has cognizance over security matters to establish a policy that risk assessments will be performed for the firm's data processing operations. Written support will help you avoid conflicts with the data processing department.

Once you are familiar with the policies and statutory or regulatory requirements pertinent to your facility, tackle these further preparations for a risk assessment:

## RISK ASSESSMENT PROCEDURES

### Establish the Scope

You and your boss may have different ideas of what a risk assessment of a data processing center is. Others affected are also likely to have conflicting views.

Sit down with the data processing manager, the director of the corporate management information system (if your company has such a position), the person who chartered the whole process, and other appropriate personnel, and decide with them exactly what is to be included and what is not. It is typical in setting up an EDP risk assessment to exclude certain operations, but what these will be must be settled in advance. Are you going to consider the security of all computer terminals? Every remote job location? All parts of the data processing center?

Decisions such as these must be agreed upon before you begin, but review them during the course of the assessment to ensure that the decisions made were correct.

### Appoint a Project Manager

A risk assessment must have a boss. If the directors of corporate security, internal audit, and management information systems all participate, who will be in charge?

One person should be specified to manage the project. This should be someone with a line of communication to the highest levels of management. Often the individual chosen is the person we can most easily spare, but this is not an acceptable choice. You must take a person who has visibility and communication with the CEO or another high level of management.

The person chosen for project manager should also have some credentials. He or she doesn't need to be a pro in data processing, but some knowledge of the subject is important. The person should know something about security, as well. You will undoubtedly have a tough time finding this person; it will take some work. But pick the best person and proceed with your plans.

| Citation | Title | Issuing Authority | Activities Covered | Summary |
|---|---|---|---|---|
| 5 USC 552 | Freedom of Information Act | Congress | All company records and documents | Establishes policy for public access to information, documents, and records maintained by the federal government |
| 5 USC 552a | Privacy Act of 1974 | Congress | All company systems of records and related activities | Establishes policy for collecting, maintaining, disclosing, and safeguarding personal information in federal systems of records |
| 18 USC 641 | Public money, property, or records | Congress | All company activities | Establishes criminal penalties for embezzling, stealing, or knowingly converting any company records or property to personal use or use of another |
| 18 USC 1361 | Government property or contracts | Congress | All company activities | Establishes criminal penalties for anyone committing malicious mischief against US property, including company DP system |

| 18 USC 1905 | Disclosure of confidential information generally | Congress | All company personnel | Establishes criminal penalties for disclosing trade secret information |
|---|---|---|---|---|
| 18 USC 2071 | Concealment, removal, or mutilation generally | Congress | All company records and reports | Establishes criminal penalties for misappropriating, mutilating, or destroying any record, report, or document including those associated with company DP system |
| 18 USC 2511 | Interception and disclosure of wire or oral communications prohibited | Congress | All company communications | Establishes criminal penalties for intercepting or attempting to intercept any wire communication including data communications of company DP system |
| 44 USC 3508 | Unlawful disclosure of information; penalties; release of information to other agencies | Congress | All company activities | Establishes criteria for releasing information obtained in confidence between federal agencies |

**Exhibit 9–2.** Inventory of policies and regulations.

63

### Plan the Project

Planning the risk assessment process is one of the most difficult tasks involved in conducting such an assessment. On the basis of the scope you established, you know what is included, and from a flow chart like that in Exhibit 9–1, you know the various steps you'll go through to accomplish the task.

But how do you approach the project? Do you start at the beginning and let your team run in all directions at once? Or do you concentrate on one area at a time? Do you do the assets analysis and the applications analysis simultaneously? What level of effort are you planning, i.e., how many hours do you intend to spend and over how long a period? Your answers to these questions will determine how many people will be needed to accomplish the risk assessment.

Do your job right in the planning stage. If you don't, you won't be able to achieve what you set out to do. Take the flow chart and decide exactly what you're doing and when you're going to do it.

As I said before, risk assessment is not a science. Your plan is just that—a plan. As you go through the process you'll probably find that here and there you didn't accurately project what needed to be done or the level of effort required. If this happens, amend the plan; it is not set in concrete.

You need to let management know that although you plan to start the risk assessment process on the first of July and hope to finish by the first of September, it may take longer. Executives need to know that risk assessment is, at best, an art requiring lots of experience combined with trial and error to be accomplished properly. Don't let them think that clear answers to all your problems will come out at the end of the process.

### Select Your Assessment Team

Often people who don't do their jobs too well or whose jobs are being phased out or cut back are chosen for this type of job. This way of choosing team members does not suit the process or the purpose of a risk assessment.

You should pick team members because of their professional qualifications. Just because someone is a director, vice president, or manager does not mean he or she is the best qualified person for the team. Often the people with the greatest knowledge, who can contribute most to the process, are those who perform a nonmanagement job in your organization. At higher levels you frequently find people who know a lot about many different things, but who are not experts in any one of them. People tend to lose that expertise as they go up the ladder. Those contributing to the risk analyses need to know what's going on right now, to have the most up-to-date information.

Finding the right person to serve on the risk assessment team will be a tough job. With the project manager and those who helped establish the scope of the project, select two, three, or four people. They must be people from whom you can obtain a commitment to do the work, but don't expect them to be committed to you one hundred percent of the time. If the level of commitment is going to be four hours per day, you need to know that. Participants' supervisors need to know that, and, most importantly, the participants themselves need to know that.

I've had the unfortunate experience of being told that X number of people were working with me on a risk assessment. I was the project manager, and our team met every morning at 8:00. Three or four of these people, committed to my team, would arrive and say, "I've got to do this today; my boss told me I had to get it done." Then the boss's office would call and ask for Joe or Sam or Beth to report to his office right away. Suddenly I was sitting there with one other person. Commitment to the project can be tough to get, but it's a necessity.

### Train the Team

Those who work on the risk assessment need to know what's expected of them. They need to know exactly what they're going to do and when they're going to do it. To some extent the team members will determine how they accomplish the work because they are the experts. However, you must have a general idea of what's going on so you can tell them when, where, and what is expected of them.

### Establish Documentation Requirements

To help team members get started, provide them with background information. Will they need all the corporate policy statements? Probably yes. Will they need all the hardware documentation for the DP system you're studying? Probably not. (Hardware can be examined later in consultation with those who know most about it.) Do they need complete documentation of every application system being run? Probably not.

In gathering this background information, be specific about what you want or you may end up with piles of material to go through, most of which is not pertinent. Decide what you want, assign someone to obtain it, and give it to whoever on the team needs it.

Keep an index of documents distributed in this way. Frequently during the process, especially if it lasts several months, people will ask for certain documents. Knowing immediately whether or not this information has already been provided to some other part of the team is a great help.

### Develop an Outline of the Final Product

Before the team starts working, develop an outline of the final product expected of them. They must know from the start what is expected so they can organize their work to achieve the desired results. This effort will save a lot of time preparing the end product of the study.

The desired result will depend on what those who will use it want. It may be nothing more than a verbal presentation or a brief executive summary—a statement of the problem, recommendations for solving it, and their cost—backed up with documentation. Or it could be a full-fledged report with a section on each step in the process.

Once the preparations I have described are accomplished, you are ready to get the risk assessment project under way.


### Brief Management and Request Needed Support

One of the first things you need to do is brief management. Support from them is needed on two fronts: cooperation and resources. All departments that may be affected, and perhaps even those that are not, need to be briefed. You're going to be knocking on people's doors in all parts of the company and asking questions. If the managers in these departments don't know why you're there and if you haven't established communication with them, they will probably resist cooperating. Without their cooperation, you won't get the information you need to develop an effective assessment.

One of the best ways to overcome staff resistance is to have the CEO say you're doing a program he established. If the person at the top does not endorse your program, it will fall apart. If you come from one part of the organization and violate the territory of another without the charter of the executive at the top, your actions will be resisted.

The second step in achieving staff cooperation is to choose a project manager who is Mr. or Mrs. Wonderful. He or she must explain clearly what is being done and why and convince other staff members that their cooperation is essential to accomplish the process that will give the CEO what he wants. If you choose Mr. or Mrs. Abrasive, you will not get the needed cooperation.

The budget for a risk assessment on the scale I have described must come from the highest level. Since you're drawing people from other departments, the project will fail without executive endorsement and a hardened budget from the executive level. Your security budget won't be able to carry all that is involved in performing a risk assessment.

Brief management, get them on your side. If you haven't done your planning well, you won't be successful because they'll ask questions you can't answer. You must be ready to talk to these executives and to tell it like it is. Request the support you need at the outset. Don't wait until you get further into the process, and then say I can't go any further because I don't have XYZ or PQM or whatever. This honesty shows management that you have not only done your homework, but you have anticipated problems as well. You won't anticipate them all, but at least you've made the effort.


### Become Familiar with the Facility
### and the EDP System

Even if you know something about the system, are you really comfortable with it? You don't want to start the risk assessment dealing with an alien creature.

Following the steps I have reviewed here will get your risk assessment off to a good start. I cannot emphasize enough the importance of project preparation. Combined with carefully carried out analyses, careful preparation means a useful end product.

## Determining the Value of the System

Your first real data collection begins when you try to determine the value of the system and how much you are trying to protect. This information must be determined very early in the risk assessment process. Assets analysis and applications analysis can provide this information.

### Assets Analysis

A list of all the physical materials and equipment in the data processing center should be prepared. One way to accomplish this is by using a checklist such as the following:

1. *Scope of assets under analysis.* Does the risk assessment cover non-general and non-technical data processing center assets such as desks, typewriters, etc.? In some government agencies, this type of equipment can be replaced without cost from items stockpiled in warehouses.

2. *Mode and cost of replacement.* If the existing physical assets of the DP center were destroyed, would they be replaced with identical items? If not, what would they be replaced with? From what source would they be replaced (used market, subsidiaries, or other)? Would the DP center be replaced at the same location? If not, where? Would the DP assets be replaced under the same financial arrangement (lease or purchase)? How many tapes, disks, and related equipment would be required for normal operations? What would it cost to replace these materials? How many tapes and disks are currently owned and what is their worth? What are the requirements for paper and other supplies for normal operations? At what estimated cost?

What are space requirements for a DP center and administrative facility in square feet? What is the estimated cost of reconstruction per square foot in the area where the facility would be constructed? If the new facility would be rented or leased, what is the estimated cost per square foot for preparation of the site and the additional monthly charge for leasing the facility?

How would the replacement costs for the physical assets of the DP center differ from the original purchase price?

3. *Time for repair or replacement.* If the DP facilities and/or equipment were destroyed, what is the maximum time that would be allowed for replacement? Could operations be continued at an alternate site during this time? What would be the cost of alternate operations?

Prepare a chart by exposure zone of both the leased assets and the owned assets in your DP center (see Exhibits 9–3 and 9–4). This should include the replacement

| Exposure Zone | Name of Asset (Quantity) | Vendor & Model # | Replacement Cost | Remarks |
|---|---|---|---|---|
| Computer Room | Printer | IBM 1403 N1 | $ 21,000 | |
| Computer Room | Air Conditioning Units (4) | Edpac (2) Liskey (2) | 100,000 | 4 ten-ton units |
| Computer Room | Keypunch | IBM 029 | 2,683 | |
| Computer Room | Supplies | Various | 2,500 | Paper, forms, etc. |
| | | EXPOSURE ZONE TOTALS: | | |

**Exhibit 9–3.** Owned assets by exposure zone.

| Exposure Zone | Name of Asset (Quantity) | Vendor & Model # | Replacement | | Remarks |
|---|---|---|---|---|---|
| | | | Purchase Price | Rental Cost/Mo. | |
| Computer Room | Disk packs (73) | IBM 3336 | $ 20,805 | $1,117 | @$285 each for purchase |
| Computer Room | Terminals, modems, mini-computers, CRTs | Four Phase | 250,000 | 6,000 | @$15.30 per month for lease |
| | EXPOSURE ZONE TOTALS – | | | | |

**Exhibit 9–4.** Leased assets by exposure zone.

cost for each item. Also prepare a chart of leased facilities by exposure zone (see Exhibit 9–5).

A summary of the tangible assets of the data processing center should be compiled from the information assembled in the assets analysis. This summary list should cover owned assets, leased assets, and facilities, with their replacement costs (see Exhibit 9–6).

Prices for replacing equipment and rebuilding or leasing other facilities should be obtained from the facilities, maintenance, or engineering departments of your company. If you work for a government agency, you may be able to find out replacement costs from GSA. In some instances, estimates from outside contractors may be required to get the most up-to-date information.

### Applications Analysis

Applications programs, the software programs that perform specific functions for your DP center, must be identified. Then, because data processing centers usually have so many applications programs that they cannot all be protected equally, the programs must be ranked according to their sensitivity and criticality.

The risk assessment analyst ranks the applications programs in terms of which require the most security emphasis. This ranking (see Exhibit 9–7) should be based on answers to the following questions:

1. What impact would the loss or modification of these programs have on the company's operations?
2. How often are these programs used?
3. How long would it take to reconstruct each program if it were lost?
4. How expensive would it be to reconstruct each program?
5. What is the value of each program to someone outside the company?

To find the answers to these questions, the analyst must talk to the data processing manager, the programmers, and the primary and secondary users of each program. Because all users will think their programs are the most important, the risk assessment analyst must be the one to rank the programs.

The first step in ranking the applications programs is to determine the criticality and sensitivity of each one. By sensitivity, I mean the program or data's susceptibility to disclosure or modification. Criticality refers to the relative importance of a program in terms of how often it is needed and how much it affects the entire business. The criticality and sensitivity of each program can be summarized conveniently in a chart (see Exhibit 9–8).

A chart of loss totals from the applications analysis should also be prepared, showing the total single-time loss for each type of threat to the programs (see Exhibit 9–9).

| Exposure Zone | Name of Asset (Quantity) | Square Feet | Replacement | | Remarks |
| | | | Purchase Price | Rental Cost/Mo. | |
|---|---|---|---|---|---|
| Computer Room | Facilities | 2,134 | $170,720 | $1,999 | Reconstructed @ $80.00/sq. foot |
| Input/Output Area | Facilities | 735 | 6,652 | 555 | Reconstructed @ $9.05/sq. foot |
| Program Systems Development and Systems Support | Facilities | 2,430 | 21,991 | 1,832 | Reconstructed @ $9.05/sq. foot |
| Managerial and Administrative Area | Facilities | 1,688 | 15,276 | 1,273 | Reconstructed @ $9.05/sq. foot |
| | | TOTAL FOR ALL EXPOSURE ZONES — | | | |

Exhibit 9–5. Leased facilities.

|  |  | Replacement Cost |
|---|---:|---:|
| *Owned Assets* |  |  |
| Computer room | $  176,200 |  |
| Tape library | 24,900 |  |
| I/O room | 19,000 |  |
| Managerial area | 3,700 |  |
| Administrative and systems development | 11,300 |  |
| Program systems development and |  |  |
| systems support | 6,000 |  |
| *Owned Assets Total* |  | $   241,100 |
|  |  |  |
| *Leased Assets* |  |  |
| Computer room | $1,230,800 |  |
| Program systems development and |  |  |
| system support | 18,900 |  |
| Managerial and administrative areas | 1,800 |  |
| *Leased Assets Total* |  | $1,251,500 |
|  |  |  |
| *Facilities* |  |  |
| Computer room | $  170,700 |  |
| Tape library | 25,600 |  |
| I/O room | 6,700 |  |
| Program systems development and |  |  |
| systems support | 22,000 |  |
| Administrative systems development | 10,000 |  |
| Managerial and administrative area | 15,300 |  |
| *Facilities Total* |  | $   250,300 |
|  |  |  |
| Labor costs during reconstruction (company personnel) |  | $   114,800 |
| Cost of leased facilities during reconstruction |  | 111,900 |
|  |  |  |
| **Total Loss Exposure** |  | **$1,969,600** |

**Exhibit 9–6.**   Summary of tangible assets.

| Applica-tion | Mode* | Freq** | Software and Documentation Replacement Costs | Modification and Manipulation Costs | Disclosure Costs | Delay Costs | | | Remarks |
|---|---|---|---|---|---|---|---|---|---|
| | | | | | | 72 Hours | 1 Week | 1 Month | |
| TRI | OL | D | $150,000 | – | – | 1,000 | 3,000 | 14,000 | Reconstruction would require 5 man-years of effort. Delay costs result in approximately 16 man-days overtime per week of delay plus alternate updating. |
| OTC | B | W | 25,000 | – | – | – | 1,300 | 5,200 | Reconstruction would require 1 man-year of effort. Delay costs assume dedicated computer time and labor at $75/hr, plus alternate updating. |
| | | | | | | – | – | | |

*MODE  
OL – On-Line  
B – Batch

**FREQ  
– Frequency  
D – Daily  
W – Weekly  
BW – Biweekly  
M – Monthly  
Q – Quarterly  
Y – Yearly

**Exhibit 9–7.** Applications loss summary.

| Application | Criticality | Sensitivity |
|---|---|---|
| TRI | **Delay:** Backlogs of about 800 transactions per day would build up during any delay. TSO data entry personnel can process about 225 actions per person per day. Delays greater than 3 days begin to impact several other applications and the micrographic system would become less effective. Since data on file would no longer be current, employees would soon lose faith in the data entirely. If delayed more than one week, some batch input at an alternate facility would be attempted.<br><br>**Destruction:** Backup tapes are produced daily for storage both on-site and at X Street. If both backups were destroyed, partial files could be reconstructed. This effort would require about 3 days. The micrographic system would become a manual record system on a temporary basis. | **Disclosure:** Since the output from this application is considered public, there would be no negative effect from the disclosure of this information.<br><br>**Modification:** Intentional manipulation of the data base would not yield any potential gain for the perpetrator. Rather, the manipulation as a result of disgruntlement or a like grievance is the most probable modification for concern. As many as 50 people can enter data. If detected, it would require about 3 man-hours of analyst time, 0-4 hours of data entry time, and 2-3 hours of computer time to eliminate the incorrect data. Examples of effects of modification are: registrants could be considered delinquent in filing a required report when they already had complied; references to filings could be unobtainable; micrographic copies could not be located; etc. |

**Exhibit 9–8.** Criticality and sensitivity summaries.

| | Total Single-Time Loss | |
|---|---|---|
| Replacement of Software and Documentation | $   597,400 | |
| Modification and Manipulation | $     5,000 | (annually) |
| Disclosure of Personal Privacy Act Data | $   750,000 | |
| Disclosure of Commercially Sensitive Data | $6,500,000 | |
| Applications Processing Delays | $     7,100 | (for one week of delay) |
| | $   37,145 | (for one month of delay) |
| Unauthorized Use of Machine Time | $475/hour CPU time | |

**Exhibit 9–9.**   Loss totals from applications analysis.

### Identify the System's Threats and Vulnerabilities

Defining and listing specific threats that apply to your EDP system is important. As your team goes through the analysis process, they can compare the information they find to the threat list, which will help them determine what is relevant to your system and what is not.

In making up the threat list, deciding which threats to include and which to exclude is not always easy. For example, if you are in Boston, do you need to worry about earthquakes? Exhibit 9–10 is a table of basic threat probabilities and sources of information about them. To find if a particular threat applies to your system or location, consult these sources. You can find the gross probability of a particular threat occurring in your locality or facility, or you can look for more specific information, depending on the likelihood of the threat occurring in your facility.

For example, you may find, through information provided by the National Earthquake Center in Boulder, CO, that earthquakes are a more serious threat in your vicinity than you knew. From the earthquake center, you can get a computer printout of every earthquake that has occurred within a particular area. Give them your location and request information within a useful radius, say 150km. I asked for one for a plant I was working with in New Jersey and I was shocked. Earthquakes turned out to be one of the major threats in that location.

Request information like the earthquake histories and other material in Exhibit 9–10 before your analysis starts because it may take some time to arrive.

Threats should be classified as either natural hazards, accidents, or intentional acts. Generic threats in these classifications would be:

*Natural hazards*—flood, hurricane/typhoon, tornado, earthquake, volcano, tidal wave/tsunami, snow, ice storm, and wind storm.

*Accidents*—fire, power anomalies, water leakage, air conditioning failure, telecommunications outage, system error/failure, program/data errors, and human errors.

*Intentional acts*—unauthorized use of the EDP system, unauthorized manipulation, unauthorized disclosure, denial of service, and theft.

System-specific threats can also be listed. For example, fire can be classified as a minor fire, computer room; a major fire, computer room; a minor fire, other exposure zone; a major fire, other exposure zone; or a catastrophic fire.

A list of vulnerabilities must next be prepared for your EDP system. Once again, you may have the problem of deciding which things to include and which to exclude.

The vulnerabilities in the total data processing system—information, hardware, software, communications, personnel, documents, procedures, security management, and physical security—must be systematically identified. Studying each segment of the system separately will help you categorize your problems. Define each segment first. What are its limits? Who do you talk to to find out the problems in each? For equipment, few vendors will admit their systems have problems, but if you talk to enough other users, you'll find out some of them.

Check the hardware to learn what vulnerabilities yours has. You may not be able to do anything about these, since they may be built into the system. But knowing what these are will allow you to compensate for them.

If you bought many systems, like the Department of Defense does, a vendor might build a super system for you for millions of dollars that eliminates these vulnerabilities. You get what you pay for. If you have off-the-shelf hardware, you are likely to have some vulnerabilities. Determine these for both the applications systems software and the operating systems software. Most of us can do very little with the operating systems, but, again, you need to know the problems that exist.

Beyond the hardware, the vulnerabilities of the information stored in or passing through the computer, and of the data needed to process that information must be determined. It's great to protect the hardware, but what about the information that's going to be processed? The information and the data should become the focal point of your vulnerability and threat analyses with the rest of your work radiating from them.

Examine each element in the DP system for strengths and weaknesses. You want to know exactly what these are, so you can see if there is a way for the threats you've identified to reach the information you're trying to protect.

How do you identify your system's vulnerabilities? You begin by interviewing people, from the top down. Interview management, then interview the "doers." Find out what they think they do and then find out what's actually done. Sometimes there is a world of difference between the two.

Observe the work in progress; go in and look. I have been told many times about the third shift, "We have six people; we have a supervisor on site. They never go anywhere." But if you go out during the third shift, you find three people there, and they all leave at about 3 AM to go down to Dunkin' Donuts. That's reality; go look.

Interview, observe, look at the documents, see what the procedures say. Then test these procedures—such tests can be very revealing. I once had a government agency tell me. "Nobody can get into our building. We have TV, guards, gates, alarms." Their greatest vulnerability was the parking lot downstairs. A guard sat across

| Threat | Sources of Information | Basic Probability | Modifying Factors |
|---|---|---|---|
| *Natural Hazards* | | | |
| Flood | Corps of Engineers, FIPS-31, Natl. Oceanic & Atmospheric Administration (NOAA) — Flood Center | .01-.09 | Geography |
| Hurricane or Tornado | FIPS-31, NOAA — Natl. Hurricane Center | .05-.5 | Geography |
| Earthquake | FIPS-31, NOAA — Earthquake Center | .005-.02 | Geography |
| Other natural occurrences | NOAA — Natl. Weather Service, Severe Weather Organization | | |
| *Accidents* | | | |
| Minor fire | Natl. Fire Protection Association, building fire marshal, local fire department | .1-.9 | Local training, fire extinguishing |
| Major fire | Insurance sources, building fire marshal, local fire department | .01-.09 | Distance from firefighting |
| Catastrophic fire | Factory Mutual, building fire marshal, local fire department | .001-.009 | Building construction, local firefighting |
| Power outage | Local utility, FIPS-31, building engineer | .1-1 | Equipment, geography |
| Power transients | Local utility, FIPS-31, building engineer | 2-30 | Power distribution, type of equipment |
| Telephone outage | Telephone company | .05-.5 | Local utility back-up |

| Threat | Source | Probability | Local experience |
| --- | --- | --- | --- |
| Air conditioning failure | Manufacturer, building engineer | .2-1 | Local experience |
| User input errors | Empirical data | Depends upon system | Program edits, local experience |
| Software errors | Empirical data | 1-200 | Software quality, local experience |
| Hardware failures and operator errors | Empirical data, hardware vendors, Federal Supply Service | 10-200 | Maintenance, training, local experience |
| *Intentional Acts* | | | |
| External sabotage | FBI, International Association of Chiefs of Police, building manager | .009-.1 | Facility exposure, company image |
| Employee sabotage | Empirical data | .1-5 | Morale, controls in place |
| Strike/Riot | FBI, local police | .009-1 | Labor unrest, local conditions |
| Fraud/embezzlement | SRI International, FBI | .006-.09 | Attractiveness of assets, controls in place |

**Exhibit 9–10.** Basic threat probabilities and sources.

| Threat | Loss Category | | | | | Total Single-Time Loss | Occurrence Rate | Annual Risk Exposure |
|---|---|---|---|---|---|---|---|---|
| | Destruction | Delay | Disclosure | Modification | Other | | | |
| *Natural Hazards* | | | | | | | | |
| 1) Windstorms | | $ 9,025 | | | | $ 9,025 | .4 | $ 3,610 |
| 2) Severe Storms | | $ 9,025 | | | | $ 9,025 | 1 | $ 9,025 |
| *Accidents* | | | | | | | | |
| 5) Minor Fire— Computer Room | $ 157,770 | $ 5,700 | | | $ 2,500 | $ 165,970 | .2 | $ 33,194 |
| 6) Major Fire— Computer Room | $1,577,700 | $52,225 | | | $ 29,938 | $1,659,863 | .07 | $116,190 |
| *Intentional Acts* | | | | | | | | |
| 18) Unauthorized Use of the System | | | | | $123,500 | $ 123,500 | 1 | $123,500 |

**Exhibit 9–11.** Annual risk exposures and threat effects.

the lot with a TV monitor that showed him the entire lot. People approaching the gate would hold their ID cards out the window and tell him who they were in order to be admitted. I wondered how he could possibly see their cards from that distance.

We decided to test this situation. We sent a man up to the window after hours. The squawk box came on; the guard said, "Who are you?" Our man said, "I'm going to the computer room." The guard: "Identify yourself." "I'm Johnny Jones," said our man, as he held out a bogus ID card. The gate opened and he drove in. Through an open door at the end of the parking lot was the computer room. So, my advice is to test the procedures you're told about, because many times you'll find they don't work as well as people think.

Quantify the risks you have identified. Plot them on charts, broken down into generic threats by location in the system (see Exhibit 9–11). Enter the costs you figured for each threat in the applications analysis and the cost of a total single-time loss on the charts.

Number the threats for easy reference, then rank them in order of amount of exposure calculated (see Exhibit 9–12). In the example, systems errors or failures come out on top, followed by network communications outages and programmer data errors. One error was worth almost a million dollars a year. Just prior to our analysis, this organization went through a conversion from the DOS operating system to OS. We had to go back and play with the figures to identify the risks realistically under the new circumstances. Converting operating systems changed the rank order of threats

| Threat Number | Threat | Annual Risk Exposure |
|---|---|---|
| 14 | System Errors or Failures (Hardware) | $  812,340 |
| 15 | Network/Communications Outage | 448,910 |
| 16 | Program/Data Errors (Software) | 440,695 |
| 20 | Unauthorized Disclosure | 290,000 |
| 18 | Unauthorized Use of the System | 123,500 |
| 6 | Major Fire – Computer Room | 116,190 |
| 17 | Human Errors | 74,461 |
| 19 | Unauthorized Manipulation | 64,250 |
| 10 | Major Fire – Other Exposure Zones | 58,775 |
| 21 | Denial of Service | 52,940 |
| 5 | Minor Fire – Computer Room | 33,194 |
| 11 | Catastrophic Fire | 26,859 |
| 13 | Environmental Problems | 26,600 |
| 8 | Major Fire – Tape Library | 25,458 |
| 3 | Earthquakes | 14,639 |
| 12 | Power Fluctuations and Interruptions | 13,475 |
| 9 | Minor Fire – Other Exposure Zones | 11,057 |
| 7 | Minor Fire – Tape Library | 10,668 |
| 2 | Severe Storms | 9,025 |
| 22 | Theft | 5,000 |
| 1 | Windstorms | 3,610 |
| | TOTAL: | $2,661,646 |

Exhibit 9–12.   Rank order of threats.

| Threat Number | Threat | Annual Risk Exposure |
|---|---|---|
| 20 | Unauthorized Disclosure | $  290,000 |
| 18 | Unauthorized Use of the System | 123,500 |
| 6 | Major Fire – Computer Room | 116,190 |
| 14 | System Errors or Failures (Hardware) | 81,234* |
| 17 | Human Errors | 74,461 |
| 19 | Unauthorized Manipulation | 64,250 |
| 10 | Major Fire – Other Exposure Zones | 58,775 |
| 21 | Denial of Service | 52,940 |
| 15 | Network/Communications Outage | 44,891* |
| 16 | Program/Data Errors | 44,070* |
| 5 | Minor Fire – Computer Room | 33,194 |
| 11 | Catastrophic Fire | 26,859 |
| 13 | Environmental Problems | 26,600 |
| 8 | Major Fire – Tape Library | 25,458 |
| 3 | Earthquakes | 14,639 |
| 12 | Power Fluctuations and Interruptions | 13,475 |
| 9 | Minor Fire – Other Exposure Zones | 11,057 |
| 7 | Minor Fire – Tape Library | 10,668 |
| 2 | Severe Storms | 9,025 |
| 22 | Theft | 5,000 |
| 1 | Windstorms | 3,610 |
| | TOTAL: | $1,129,896 |

*Discounted 90% due to conversion problems

**Exhibit 9–13.**   Revised rank order of threats.

by annual risk exposure in a very substantive way (see Exhibit 9–13). We projected what the major problems would be with the new system by looking at the previous year's analysis.

Once your risk assessment team has completed all the research you need, it is time to make some recommendations keyed to the vulnerabilities and threats. Exhibit 9–14 is an example of one recommendation sheet I have used. The category is security management. I have ranked the item as a severity of one because of its implications. The sample company has no one to monitor and control the development of its data base system, which makes it likely that control of the information is irregular. We recommend a permanent staff position be designated for data base administration.

Look at the vulnerabilities you've determined and what each one's possible impact could be, then come up with a recommendation for each. Try to give a cost for implementing the change, or you'll have less chance of getting what you ask for. You want to provide management an idea of what the risks are so they can make the decisions as to which threats need to be treated, which can be self-insured, which they should insure through an outside firm, and what can be done if your company decides to accept the risk itself.

CATEGORY: PROCEDURAL CONTROLS

SEVERITY: 1

VULNERABILITY: **Printouts Disposed of in Normal Trash**
There is no established written policy requirement to shred all sensitive DP output and console listings.

*Impact:* In the absence of an established written policy requirement to shred all sensitive DP output and console listings, sensitive data, including privacy and confidential business information as well as program information, is being thrown out in the normal trash. This could lead to unauthorized disclosure of this important data. The potential for this unauthorized disclosure is greatly increased by the fact that the company employs a contractor to sort through all trash, separate all discarded output, and remove it for recycling.

RECOMMENDATION: Shred all discarded paper products containing sensitive and privacy data.
Input and output documents that contain sensitive or privacy data must be effectively rendered useless prior to disposal. Since the company has a shredder, all paper products containing previously identified sensitive data (e.g., console printouts, personal-in-nature, confidential business, etc.) should be shredded prior to disposal.

Lockable, secure trash containers should be positioned throughout company facilities. All personnel should be instructed to dispose of sensitive or privacy data documents in these containers. A standard procedure should be established for emptying and shredding the contents of these containers.

*Relative Cost:* Low

**Exhibit 9–14.**    A sample recommendation.

The recommendations that are implemented are usually low cost, quick-fix actions. When they are implemented, look at the adjusted operation again. You don't need to keep a full risk assessment team operating forever, but you or someone should continue to update the risk assessment information so you can have an up-to-date and accurate idea of what the risks are in your company's electronic data processing system.

# CHAPTER 10

## Computing Security Risk Analysis: Is it Worth it?

James A. Schweitzer, CDP
Systems Security Technology Manager
Xerox Corp.

Responding to numerous articles and stories in the press, business managers are concerned about computer security. Many are uncertain about the level of protection of their business information.

Computer operations, in an organization of any significant size, can be complex and technical. Managers trying to determine what to do to ensure some acceptable level of information security are faced with a bewildering problem. The potential sources and types of attack on computing systems appear endless. Total protection is prohibitively expensive, and established security organizations are usually poorly equipped to deal with the matter.

Risk analysis is the popular way to deal with the problem of information security. Many different forms of risk analysis have been developed by government and business. The Bureau of Standards has published one of these methods and a commercial software package supporting risk analysis has been offered. Unfortunately, all of these methods have inherent flaws, and all are extremely expensive.

All risk analysis methods studied by the author involve similar procedures. While some variation occurs, traditional risk analysis systems share the following characteristics:

- Since a wide range of business systems, activities, and vulnerabilities must be considered, a risk analysis committee must be set up. Members of the committee generally include the functional users of the computer systems, the computer operations group, the systems design group, and the security department. The committee applies its combined knowledge of the business operation and computer functions to develop decision base information.

Reprinted with the permission of the American Society for Industrial Security, from *Security Management*, Aug. 1982, p 104.

- The committee lists all computer functions and describes the various vulnerabilities of each one.
- The committee assigns risk values, usually in dollars, to each potential *event* or breach in security.
- The committee estimates the probability of each event occurring.
- The last step of the procedure involves a simple mathematical equation: the risk value of the event is multiplied by the probability of the event, thus producing a *decision value*. The decision value is then used as a guidepost for deciding where and how to invest in security.

## THE COST

In a large corporation, with multiple divisions spread over wide geographic areas, the size of the risk analysis committee must be large. In most cases, the committee would be broken down into division or area sub-committees. The task of the committees—identifying all vulnerable business activities—is mind-boggling.

Consider one function, for example, that of customer billing. A cursory look at billing operations shows that vulnerablities occur:

- whenever information changes form, as from paper to digital, or is transmitted via communications circuits.
- whenever information is moved within the organization or function, e.g., when an order is processed from accounts receivable and routed through the organization to the file clerk.

The potential areas of vulnerability in the typical billing system of a large business could number in the hundreds. Vulnerable areas in the operations of a large corporation could be in the tens of thousands.

The committee's task, then, is a huge one. Even with knowledgeable, capable people assigned to the task of identifying potential vulnerabilities, the process takes a tremendous amount of time. The time factor alone—in terms of cost per man hour—makes traditional risk analysis methods extremely costly. The potential flaws in the procedure make it difficult to justify its cost.

## THE FLAWS

Since the potential number of vulnerable points in a company is so high, there is a reasonable probability that the risk analysis committee will overlook a serious vulnerability. Locking all doors except one does not provide protection at home. The same holds true for a computing system. When the potential for omission is so great, a security program based on a committee's identification of required protection points cannot be considered reliable.

Another inherent flaw in traditional risk analysis methods involves the assessment of probability. When the insurance industry figures premiums for covering a risk, a mortality table or other records of actual experience are used to develop estimates of risk. No such historical data is available to the risk analysis committee. The probability assigned to each vulnerability point, e.g., the likelihood of a security breached occurring at that point, is determined by a consensus of the committee members. Using this method, a vulnerability estimated as a one-in-a-million shot may occur three times in the next year, while a one-in-ten estimated probability may never occur.

The committee must also figure the risk value for each potential vulnerability. For example, if the payroll file is compromised, what will it cost the company? The usual recommendation is to apply order-of-magnitude values, in other words, the risk is either one thousand, ten thousand, a hundred thousand, a million dollars, etc. Generally, proponents of traditional risk analysis methods recognize the fallibility of such an estimation. The major flaw of such value assignments is that the values assigned may be in error by one order of magnitude.

## COMPUTING THE DECISION BASE

The data generated by the committee is used to compute *decision base results.* These results, in the form of dollar figures, represent the risk involved in each vulnerability point. Based on this information, management will make decisions on computer security investments. The decision base value is computed as follows: (value of event) times (probability of event) equals (decision base value); or $Ve \times Pe = DBV$.

By now, the committee will have compiled a huge listing of events and decision base values. Unfortunately, the flaws inherent in its methods cast doubt on the thoroughness and value of the results. Consider the decision base equation in terms of the potential for error: Value of event (which may be in error by an order of magnitude) times the probability of event (at best a dubious assumption, at worst pure guess) equals: the list of decision base values (which has a high probability of being incomplete, and may overlook high risk).

A Honeywell-sponsored survey of users of risk analysis methods, discussed at the Privacy and Security Conference held in Phoenix, AZ in April 1979, showed that a majority of those who tried traditional methods were dissatisfied with the results. No wonder.

## AN ALTERNATIVE

An effective, less expensive computer security system can be developed based on a program of business information security. The system consists of the following activities, in sequence:

1.   Establish a value rating system for the company's business information. Assuming three levels are selected, classify them high value, limited, and confidential.
2.   Divide all business information into the value rating categories chosen. Most

information will not have a high value rating, because it will not require special protection. Only about one percent of business information should be assigned a high value rating.

3.    Assign value ratings at the element level to information in the computing system. This simplifies transfer of information within the system.

4.    Establish rules for the handling, processing, and communicating of oral, paper, and digital forms of information at the three value levels.

5.    Ensure that computing systems development and audit processes include security requirements, starting with information evaluation. Systems must also include measures to ensure data integrity and credibility. While these are not security issues in themselves, integrity and credibility may require security measures. Usually, processes that ensure data integrity and credibility are a part of the business control system, and represent good business practice. Without them, a security program is pointless.

Using information security management techniques as a basis for a program of computer security has an important secondary effect missing from most other risk analysis methods. That is, this method protects information in *all* forms, whether in computer, on paper, or passed by word of mouth. To be effective, an information security program must provide protection for all forms.

A study of actual cases of computer crime reveals that most instances are the result of administrative carelessness—exposure of information on paper. Locking up computing systems without safeguarding paper-borne information defeats the purpose of computer security. The computer security effort must be part of an overall, comprehensive information security program.

Use of a traditional risk analysis method may be justified in a narrow context, such as for one application system, when the following exist:

- a well-defined problem in which the security vulnerabilities are obvious—for example, a case where only physical risk is involved, such as data center contingency planning;
- a history of attempted penetrations of this or a similar system, and the methodology used is understood, or where records of risks, such as tornados, earthquakes, etc., are available;
- the potential for damages that could be extremely serious.

Outside of these narrow boundaries, a computer security program based on the five steps suggested will be dependable, effective, and cheaper to implement than traditional risk analysis methods.

# CHAPTER 11

## The Hidden Risk in Risk Analysis

### Howard R. Keough, CPP
### The MITRE Corporation

Since the publication of the Willis H. Ware report[1] in 1970, a new field of security —automatic data processing (ADP) security—has emerged.

In 1978 the Office of Management and Budget issued a circular[2] that required executive branch agencies with computing facilities to develop computer security programs, conduct risk analyses of their facilities, and develop contingency plans to safeguard their ADP operations from disruption. Many agency heads have complied with the directive, but many others have not. Some plead they do not have the in-house expertise to carry out the tasks required. Others claim that even though they have the expertise, their employees do not have the time to devote to such tasks.

Contractor firms have benefited greatly by being able to assemble the expertise to perform the required security tasks within an acceptable time. These contractor firms were, however, the first to discover they had underestimated the time needed to complete one of the first steps of the risk analysis process—data collection. Almost none of the articles and books written on computer risk analysis warns of the time, money, and effort involved in determining what resources require protection and what their replacement would cost.

However, authors do present formulas that describe how to estimate annual loss exposures. Cost-of-living figures, actual labor costs, and information about changes in costs due to advances in technology are available, making it possible to calculate the difference between initial costs and replacement costs of data processing and related equipment. Because this information is available, the data collection problem does not lie here.

The problem emerges when the risk analysis team goes on to, say, the purchasing department and has the following conversation:

"Do you have a copy of the current inventory of all the ADP equipment?"
"Yes."

---

Reprinted with the permission of the American Society for Industrial Security, from *Security Management*, April 1985, p 77.

"I see you have a long list of items, but not the cost of each item."

"That's another department."

"Oh, what department?"

"Try Budget."

Budget says, "Try Finance." And that's only for the data processing equipment.

Another consideration is that many devices in the ADP facility were purchased four or five years ago, and all cost data have since been sent to the archives for storage. This fact causes a lengthy delay because forms have to be filled out and submitted, and the boxes containing the data have to be found, opened, checked, and forwarded to the team.

The risk analysis team also has many other figures to compile, for instance, the costs of:

1.  construction of the computer facility;
2.  laboratory grade power;
3.  the building housing the computer facility (either lease costs per square foot or, if owned, construction costs per square foot);
4.  construction of the raised floor;
5.  air conditioning;
6.  the operating system, including the costs to modify it for operational needs;
7.  software packages and any required modifications;
8.  backup, redundancy, and maintenance;
9.  disk and tape storage space, on-site and off-site;
10. consoles and remote user terminals;
11. access control systems:
    a.  guard force
    b.  closed circuit television
    c.  alarm systems (intrusion and fire);
12. ADP personnel:
    a.  operators
    b.  supervisors
    c.  programmers
    d.  support staff.

The list goes on; the problem in gathering reliable cost information lies here.

To gather the data essential to form a true picture of costs, the team must locate the costs of items such as those listed above. Should the team's client be part of the federal government, the data will usually be found in the General Services Administration, scattered among its various departments.

Many government and private organizations record inventory items by serial number only, rather than by their description or location. Some organizations assign serial numbers in which the item's general identity is coded in the first two digits. For instance, the first two digits may be 94, which to the logistics office means the item is a typewriter. But nobody else can identify the item without a master list of the codes. And master codes can be difficult to come by.

Should the team obtain a master copy of the codes, the next challenge is to determine if the item is located in the area of interest or somewhere else. Is it in the computing area, in a support area, or in the company garage?

Few organizations, government or private, have all the essential information in one place. Unquestionably, they need the information to calculate annual loss exposure ratings and to prepare the cost-benefit recommendations made to senior management. These costs must be obtained to establish the baselines for later risk reduction calculations.

The problem is no one has ever asked anyone in the organization for this kind of information. Consequently, the organization's staff is not in a position to supply it. That is why assembling the information needed may take three months instead of the allotted two to three weeks. This difference is expensive for both parties if a contract extension becomes necessary. And since the contract could not be completed within the time originally specified, the contractor's reputation could easily be tarnished.

Security contractors and the government agencies hiring them should be alert to the hidden hazards in compiling costs and developing an assets inventory. The solution is to make sure, the moment a contract has been awarded, that the contracting office's technical representative initiates the requests for this information within his or her own organization. To ensure the costs of the relevant equipment are compiled easily and quickly, the contractor should prepare a detailed checklist of items needed.

The best way for a government agency to start the analysis is to have the contractor hold an initial briefing of all personnel involved. At this briefing, the contracting company's staff can be introduced and the object of the analysis explained. The contractor will also be able to brief those of the client's staff directly involved about their roles in the analysis and explain why the checklist should be completed promptly.

## REFERENCES

1. *Security Controls for Computer Systems: Report to the Defense Science Board Task Force on Computer Security* (February 1970).
2. Office of Management and Budget, *Security of Federal Automated Information Systems*, Circular A-71 (July 27, 1978).

# PART III

---

# Focusing Protection Efforts

Security resources are inevitably limited and must be applied selectively where they will have greatest effect. This selective protection approach often evolves from the findings of an EDP and information risk assessment and seeks to concentrate resources on protecting the most valuable assets and those that would have the greatest impact if stolen, damaged, or misused.

Because data processing functions frequently spread through an organization in seemingly haphazard fashion, computer security efforts may become equally disorganized. One company's approach to unifying computer security efforts is examined in this section.

Business communications and the common practice of transporting business information outside the office both bear consideration when establishing information security programs. These topics are discussed in this section, as is the advisability of debriefing employees who are leaving the organization as an additional protective measure for sensitive information.

The final article in this section takes a look at some lessons the retailing industry, which uses computers extensively, has learned about the importance of integrating security controls into computer-based information systems.

# CHAPTER 12

## Selective Protection

Frank T. Roedell
Manager, Security-Field Engineering Division
IBM

Even to the uninitiated, it is apparent that conventional security methods have not been completely successful in preventing the loss of critical proprietary business information. Hardly a day passes without some mention in the news media of industrial espionage, computer theft, or the outright disappearance of valuable goods from warehouses, loading docks, or offices. Few can doubt that these reported thefts are but the tip of the proverbial iceberg.

One way to prevent the loss of proprietary information and physical assets is to selectively protect a company or corporation's most valuable and creative work. Selective protection offers a more sophisticated approach to improve security, making use of both traditional security measures, such as badges, locks, document classification, and security officers, and the newer technical security devices such as CCTV and intrusion detectors. This approach, however, requires much more in the way of critical analysis. Security managers and top management must outplan and outsmart those wearing the black hats.

A protection plan must be created for a company's products, trade secrets, or programs at the earliest moment. This plan must be prepared in conjunction with top management, or the responsible product manager if the asset is a new product under development. The product manager's early involvement helps to motivate lower managers and employees and underscores the importance of the plan. If upper management offers only lip service to security needs, the most aggressive asset protection plan is just so much wasted effort and time. A key ingredient to success is giving the top manager responsibility for deciding what to protect and how. Toward that end, while the plan's actual writing should be the responsibility of the product security manager or coordinator, the plan must be completed under the close supervision of the product manager or other top management.

Reprinted with the permission of the American Society for Industrial Security, from *Security Management*, March 1982, p 17.

## THE DEVELOPMENT STAGE

When a protection plan is in the development stage, the owner or developer of a product must realistically assess the cost of his or her product. He or she must ask what would happen if a particular asset was lost to competition, or just plain stolen for monetary gain. The corporate protection plan should incorporate a specific list of critical assets requiring protection. The key word here is *critical*—inclusion of too many assets tends to weaken any protection plan. Indeed, a security plan perceived as having an excessive number of assets, each requiring top security, weakens the credibility of the plan among employees. Far better to have a tight, respected security plan for a relatively small number of assets.

A good protection plan takes the development and production cycles of a product into account. Remember that during the initial development phase the plan should concentrate on methods for identifying and protecting proprietary documents, technologies, and expected technical advances.

As the product moves from the preproduction cycle into the production cycle, the plan should include additional physical security precautions for production areas and parts. Obviously, one of the most critical security periods is from just before the announcement of a new product through actual shipment of the product to customers. That period may even be two years or more after a product is first conceived.

A protection plan should also include measures to safeguard personnel records and all documents deemed critical to business needs, such as blueprints, equipment guides and specifications. Policy guidelines and a basic plan for protecting a product during every stage of development should be delineated.

Ideally, the final form of a protection plan should have five sections:

*Section I.* Include the basic security strategy. Outline what assets and information are important and why. The total development schedule of products, from concept to assembly, should be included.

*Section II.* Discuss what items and information are considered classified. Any information relating to classified items, it should be pointed out, is also considered classified. This would include any records pertaining to product documentation, marketing objectives, specifications, classification, and patent status.

*Section III.* Physical security requirements should be outlined here. Perimeter security areas requiring restricted access, such as computing centers, terminal rooms, vital record areas, and laboratories, should be listed. Rules for controlling access to product parts or drawings should be explained, and procedural rules and audit routines for vendors and consultants outlined. Explain that strict controls must be placed on the hiring of temporary employees and consultants.

*Section IV.* Outline the educational aspects of the security plan, that is, what information top management or product managers must relay to other employees. Audit and review procedures should be identified.

*Section V.* This final section should have a schedule of all product manufacturing cycle updates. Without fail, the production plan should be updated as product cycles, or the product itself, is altered. This section should stress that the development cycle of a product, from concept to marketing to production, necessitates an ever changing cycle of security.

Once an initial draft of a plan has been formulated, the plan must be distributed to other business groups or divisions within the company that will be associated with the product or individual assets. No plan is ever formulated in a vacuum. Manufacturing, service and support groups, and, of course, the business planning areas should be encouraged to submit their views—and suggestions for revision—to the security department.

## PROMOTING A PRODUCT PROTECTION PLAN

When a plan is presented in draft form to management, the security manager should describe why each asset included in the plan is worthy of so many precautions. Bluntly speaking, this task calls for a sophisticated selling job. To prevent security from taking a back seat to other management concerns, the product manager must go to bat for asset protection as often as necessary just as he or she would for any other important business goal.

The presentation should include mention of:

- the dollar value of each product and/or asset being protected (dollar values should be predicted by taking into account the cost of design and technology). Mentioning a product's monetary value to the company adds emphasis to your argument.
- the direct methods to be used to protect each asset. The security classification levels of each asset should be explained at this point, and it should be made clear that every department within the company will have responsibility for asset protection, including engineering, planning, forecasting, legal, support, and manufacturing departments.
- the planned schedule of product audits. This schedule should follow through each development stage of each protected asset, so that a system of checks and balances is established for the protection of each product.

If you follow each step described here with care, you should end up with a solid security plan for your products and assets. This plan is not, however, meant to remain the same for all time: updating your corporation's goals and priorities should be an integral part of each plan.

# CHAPTER 13

## Information Security Strategy

Donald J. Coppotelli
Manager Information Systems,
Planning & Financial Administration
G. E. Corporate Information Systems
Planning Operation

General Electric (GE) is a large, decentralized corporation that spans several continents. While GE's many businesses are autonomous, the corporation's information processing system is, by comparison, highly centralized. Over ninety percent of our processing expenditures represent work being done at one of our twelve regional centers (the remaining ten percent is primarily processed externally or by small, decentralized computers). We also have computer centers in other countries. This diversity of processing environments presents a real challenge in terms of security and information control.

Our policy of central information processing began in 1972. Faced with the existence of more than one hundred small and medium-sized computers, our corporate policy committee authorized a program to exhaust the potential of the older, smaller computers while consolidating workloads into our modern, large-scale centers.

Our strategy of centralization has been highly successful over the years. While the workload has increased at an annual rate of twenty-eight percent, operating costs have increased only twelve percent. The cost to produce a unit of computing work has decreased seventeen percent a year on the average. Overall, approximately $40 million in processing costs have been avoided.

As GE increases on-line capabilities, more people have access to the central information base of the company. Appropriate security measures are required for each category of system user (including vendors, independent distributors, and government personnel) to control access. During this time, management saw a need for more corporate security standards and guidelines that are consistent with the new information processing environment. A standard risk assessment methodology for use by the various

Reprinted with the permission of the American Society for Industrial Security, from *Security Management*, May 1982, p 86.

businesses within the company is also needed to evaluate cost effective security and control measures.

To address these needs, GE is developing a corporate information security program. One part of this program involves a shift to dual vendors for our computer equipment. This step was recommended by a corporate study conducted in 1978.

The obvious benefit of this dual vendor approach is an improved ability to exploit new technologies, use an increased number of packaged applications, and generally provide added flexibility in meeting information processing requirements. Our goal is to engineer a well-integrated dual vendor system so that system incompatibilities are not visible to the user. Undoubtedly, however, the dual vendor system increases the complexity of information security operations.

Another step toward improved security involved the formation of a task force, which I head, to study a variety of security-related issues. The task force represents those responsible for information security and control throughout GE. A review board, made up of senior management, was also appointed, to review the progress of the task force and to evaluate any task force recommendations.

The thirteen-member task force is responsible for researching a comprehensive set of tasks and then presenting suggested recommendations. The objectives of the task force are to:

- assess the status of security and control currently implemented for the company's information systems and to define the primary issues.
- develop a corporate information security program to provide direction and consultation to company businesses on cost-effective security and control measures within their businesses.
- establish security awareness and specific responsibilities for security and control at both the corporate and operating component levels.
- recommend specific areas where further corporate security and control standards and/or guidelines may be required (i.e., physical security, logical access, application security and control, personnel controls, contingency planning, compliance with federal/state legislation, etc.).
- recommend a standard risk assessment methodology that can be used by each GE business to evaluate risk exposure and investment required for additional security and control measures.
- recommend a corporate-sponsored plan for disaster preparedness and recovery, including guidelines for standard procedures to be developed by each computer center and its assigned users.
- recommend a standard data classification system that specifies the security measures required for identifying, handling, storing, using, and destroying data for each classification level.
- recommend a corporate-wide security education program to improve awareness, communicate corporate direction, and provide an understanding of the alternatives available for reducing risk exposure.

The task force has been aided in its activities by a comprehensive information security survey conducted this year. All facets of security and information control, in their broadest senses, were studied. Our dual vendors and several other consulting firms helped write and administer the survey, which was sent to all GE businesses in the US and Canada.

We are now in the process of digesting, organizing, and evaluating survey returns. While the survey was not intended to be an audit, it has provided a reference data base for the task force.

Our initial responses seem to indicate that:

- Security and control programs for computer centers, data bases, and the application development process vary considerably throughout the company.
- Plans for alternative computer resources and detailed recovery plans in case of disaster or extended outage are generally inadequate or incomplete.
- The businesses require a practical risk assessment methodology to develop a security and control program and a means of evaluating cost-effective security measures.
- Security focus and responsibilities within a business are often unclear, left to the discretion of several functions, or delegated to relatively low levels.
- Investment in security programs tends to be a low priority since security measures are generally costly, defensive in nature, and provide no measurable benefits. The sense of urgency is often lacking since GE has not experienced any computer center catastrophes or significant frauds. Most managers prefer to devote resources to programs that will improve profits or productivity or increase market share, rather than security measures to reduce exposure.
- Corporate Audit Staff has considerably extended the scope of EDP audits over the past years but has encountered some resistance to their recommendations due to lack of corporate security/control standards and guidelines for computerized information systems.

This survey information will help the task force in its assigned tasks, which include studying and recommending changes in these areas: corporate information security policy, physical security of computer centers, computer center administrative controls, access controls, security and controls for software applications, personnel controls, disaster recovery planning, corporate risk assessment methodology, corporate data and/or application classification systems, corporate security education programs, and corporate security organization and responsibilities.

To accomplish this set of comprehensive tasks, each task force member will be assigned to perform the research required to support each task force recommendation. To help members in their work, the task force defined each task as follows:

*Corporate Information Security Policy.* Address organization responsibility, (by corporate and operating component), management accountability, security awareness, data ownership, information classification requirements, and identification of information assets.

*Physical Security of Computer Center.* Review the devices and security measures available to industry today. Establish guidelines to assist business components in evaluating costs of security measures for their specific computer center. Emphasize research of viable power outage controls, physical access controls, and preventive and protective measures.

*Computer Center Administrative Controls.* Recommend the appropriate administrative checks and balances in these areas: separation of duties/responsibilities; control over removable media such as tapes and disks; personal practices (rules about smoking, drinking, etc.); review and control for console logging and retention; use of courier services; console operator activities: physical input/ output controls; access limitations; and destruction of classified materials.

*Access Controls.* Consider and evaluate the security options and provisions of system software provided by computer vendors. Invoke password and encryption controls according to a classification system. Provide guidelines for vendor access to computers during maintenance. Research the impact of security measures on processing overhead costs.

*Security for Software Applications.* Consider what security and control measures can be taken as software is developed, whether developed in-house or by vendors. Define role of auditor and user clearly. Establish straightforward lines of responsibility and roles of authority for all persons involved in all computer operations (designing, programing, testing, maintaining, and operating.)

*Personnel Controls.* Review current practices and recommend standards and guidelines to achieve or maintain a high level of integrity (including non-disclosure agreements, annual personnel review policies, and firing procedures, for example).

*Disaster Recovery Plan.* Establish a corporate disaster contingency plan, including evaluating off-site processing, storage, and transportation alternatives.

*Risk Assessment.* Evaluate current risk management methodologies and develop a standard corporate procedure, including identifying risks and estimating vulnerability, probability of problems occurring, and recovery countermeasures. Test proposed risk management methodology, document the proposed standards, and adjust methodology.

We are pleased with the progress of our task force up to this point, and look forward to developing a cost-effective information protection and preservation strategy that fits the needs of GE.

# CHAPTER 14

## Effectively Securing Business Communications

James A. Schweitzer, CDP
Systems Security Technology Manager
Xerox

All business communications activities, each of which has implications for information security, fall within one of several well-defined processes. By recognizing the processes, we can establish proper information protection for each. This analysis of the processes and assignment of security elements ensures a consistency of protection and avoids the confusion that may surround novel or unusual communication methods. The processes include preparing, storing, processing, delivering, transmitting, and receiving messages. Appropriate security elements can be identified for each process.

### PROCESS 1: MESSAGE PREPARATION

Keep in mind that "message" (as used here) refers to all kinds of communications, including letters, memos, charts, telegrams, voice telephone calls, data transmissions in digital form, image transmissions in digital or analog form, and combinations of these.

Message preparation consists of retrieving information from files (paper or electronic); processing and assembling information (by human thought, perhaps supplemented by manual or electronic processes); and packaging information, including printing, enveloping, and other related tasks if the message is in paper form.

A most critical information security activity occurs during this process: namely, the decision about the value of the information involved. Does the message require classification? Important information can be left without protection unless a decision is made at this step. Improper decisions can result in an exposure, or in less protection than is needed.

Reprinted with the permission of the American Society for Industrial Security, from *Security Management*, Sept. 1982, p 157.

Decisions about classification or information value rely on the motivation and knowledge of the person preparing messages. The decision to classify, for example, may be based on:

- *the source of information used* in message preparation (i.e., if information from classified files was used to prepare the message, the message should be classified);
- *the inherent value of the information* contained in the message, as evaluated by the message preparer or his/her supervisor, and;
- *the type of information used*. Often companies will decide that certain categories of information will automatically be classified at a certain level of secrecy. By such a process it might be decided, for example, that all financial summaries are to be kept top secret.

No matter what system is used to prepare messages, the decision whether to classify (as well as what level of classification is required) should be made in advance. The effectiveness of any classification system depends on management support of the security manager and good training and publicity programs that stress employee awareness of security concerns.

## PROCESS 2: MESSAGE STORAGE

If information is deemed classified, how the message will be stored should be indicated from the start. A good security program will have the necessary storage containers for each information value or classification. If messages are stored on magnetic tape or disk, employees must be made aware that these media must also be protected.

Improper storage of valuable information represents a real threat to businesses of all types. When people without proper authority browse through papers or computer files, they may stumble across valuable or embarrassing information. Messages that should be restricted to circulation among only a few participants can become public knowledge when the medium containing the original message is not safeguarded. Even original handwritten notes serving as the prelude to a telephone call should be protected.

## PROCESS 3: MESSAGE TRANSMITTAL

Sending or transmitting a message includes all those activities involved in the process of entering the message into the originator's delivery system. This includes:

- company mail, where special marking, wrapping, or courier delivery may be appropriate;
- public mail, where an additional wrapper or special designation (such as registered or insured) may be needed;
- facsimile systems, where digital or analog signals convey an image to a distant machine and where special arrangements at the receiving end must be set up to protect the information from unauthorized observation;

- electronic computer-driven systems, where digital messages may require encryption; and
- telephone voice messages, which may require voice encryption, masking, or the use of code words.

To protect messages effectively as they are being transmitted, the sending person must not only be aware of the established requirements for protecting the particular classification or value of the information involved, but he/she must also have the means to provide that protection. The security manager must ensure that security elements are made available by coordinating with computer, telecommunications, mail, and other services. Otherwise, the effort at training and awareness will not pay off in added protection.

## PROCESS 4: MESSAGE PROCESSING AND DELIVERY

While businessmen and women have never had to worry about how the postal system or a telegraphic network handles their messages, the security manager cannot afford such a blasé attitude. Although out of sight, information in the delivery process should not be unguarded. Many messages pass through environments outside the business premises, and the security manager must be concerned with and aware of the resulting exposure. Company computer and telecommunications managers must be consulted to provide adequate protection.

Each form of processing or delivery dictates different security issues to be considered:

First class mail is probably the most secure message system available, even in the computer age. Once a *correctly addressed* letter is in the post, one can be fairly certain it will not be opened by anyone other than the addressee.

Internal company mail may be another matter. Security managers should review internal mail handling procedures to make sure obvious security exposures are eliminated. In one company, for example, business mail was being carried on belts through a public parking garage. The security manager recommended a change in procedure so people could no longer reach onto the belt to pick off internal mail envelopes.

Electronic message systems involve many more concerns. Telegraphic messages are extremely suspect, since they are routinely available in switching centers and in message centers for perusal by various people, some of whom will not be your own employees.

Telephone and computer message traffic also passes through switching centers operated by service carriers and vendors. In these cases, messages are routinely scanned or copied for purposes of traffic analysis and quality control.

Electronic messages cannot be considered totally secure unless they are encrypted between the sending and receiving units. Link encryption is not satisfactory, as the need for intermediate regeneration implies availability in clear text at midway points. By considering all possible weak points in a message delivery system, the security manager can plan effective countermeasures.

## PROCESS 5: RECEIVING MESSAGES

Receiving messages includes the actual reception of the message (which may be a memo, letter, telephone call, telex, or computer data stream) *and* the disposition of the message. The latter action involves deciding who is to see the information and how it will be stored.

The employees who receive messages, including the business' mail room or mail processing vendor, must understand the security system. The various classification markings or value indicators required by established policy must indicate to the receiver how the message is to be handled.

In establishing a company-wide policy on information security, remember that information value indications established in one division may be meaningless in another. Unless the employees receiving messages are capable, trained, and motivated, the security elements applied by the sender may be disregarded, resulting in an exposure. Such exposure can be caused by intentional distribution, as when a manager doesn't know enough to restrict an item of news. Carelessness can also cause problems. Misfiling or leaving sensitive messages in the open frequently results in impaired information security.

How sensitive messages coming into an office should be stored should be regulated by established policy and the proper valuation markings on each message. The process of retransmitting messages should also be governed by information security policy. Certainly the top level or most sensitive information classification should not be further distributed without the approval of the originator.

## THE OVERALL PICTURE

We have seen that message processes are replete with risks and the possibility of security exposures. Vulnerabilities occur:

- at the site where messages are prepared, sent, and stored;
- en route, especially in electronic systems; and
- at the receiving site, where people may not have a clear understanding of the value of information classification or value indicators.

Effective information security measures must address the employees, the systems used to transport messages in any form, and external carriers and systems. The security manager must understand his business' communications methods and systems thoroughly, and must work closely with systems designers, computing managers, office managers, and telecommunication people to achieve information security. By recognizing the processes inherent in all business communications, the security manager can develop standards for all circumstances.

# CHAPTER 15

## Protecting Information Outside the Office

M. L. Proctor
Manager, Corporate Security Programs
R. J. Reynolds Industries

Almost everyone takes work home from time to time. Sometimes there aren't enough hours in the workday to complete an important project; sometimes creative thinking can thrive only with a change in environment; and sometimes documents are needed for traveling and meetings taking place the next day. When work assignments involve a company's proprietary information, which could be of value to competitors or affect the privacy of employees, the whereabouts of that information becomes a security concern.

An assignment to handle sensitive information for the company is an indication of an employee's reliability, trustworthiness, and maturity, and provides a good test of his or her readiness for promotion and additional responsibility. Such confidence on the company's part must be matched by an awareness of responsibility by the employee. Special care should be taken to protect work taken out of the workplace from unauthorized disclosure.

Classified company materials should not ordinarily be removed from work premises. These materials have information that could hurt the company's growth, competitive stance, or employees if disclosed at the wrong time or to the wrong person. If an employee authorized to use classified material finds it necessary to take a portion off the premises, a record should be maintained in the office file listing the material taken, the date, and the person taking it. If anyone else needed the material while it was off the premises, they would then know where to find it.

Work removed from the premises should be carried in a briefcase, folder, or envelope; not as loose papers. If any of the material is sensitive, the briefcase should be locked and the envelope sealed. It is better to take a moment to lock the material in a car trunk than to risk a theft while performing an errand on the way home. Placing

Reprinted with the permission of the American Society for Industrial Security, from *Security Management*, April 1983, p 92.

material on the floor behind the driver is also a good idea. Intruders have been known to seize materials from a front car seat when a driver stops for a light.

Family members may be very proud of the position an employee holds in a company and the important work he or she does. However, family interest should not prod the employee to reveal any information the company would want protected. Family and friends not privy to the proprietary information training employees receive are not likely to understand fully the importance of protecting the company's information. As a result, family pride and neighborhood gossip frequently cause substantial proprietary information leaks, especially those involving inventions, salaries, promotions and terminations, and new products.

The relaxed atmosphere at home can make guarding against imprudent conversation difficult, and casual interruptions may allow relatives or friends to see something they shouldn't. Conscientious employees will find ways to satisfy their families' curiosity and to be responsive to them without compromising the company's trust.

Travel imposes special problems in the protection of sensitive information. When an employee is on the road, outsiders can easily overhear conversations or casually observe classified papers or activities. Unknown individuals can approach employees without screening and without opportunity to verify identity and purpose. Locks and keys become less reassuring, as hotel proprietors or business associates may not employ adequate security measures. While traveling, an employee must always be alert and discreet.

When it is necessary to remove classified materials from the office for travel, the original documents should remain in their proper location and copies taken on the trip. Authorization must be obtained before the travel copies are made, and the copies' existence should be logged on the master file.

The traveler should place the copies in a sealed, unmarked manila envelope in a locked case that can be carried with him. Sealed material that has been tampered with will show intrusion, while the unmarked envelope protects the material from view if the traveler needs to open the case for customs clearance, airport security, or removing unclassified materials.

Sensitive material should only be carried in luggage that can be carried with the traveler to avoid loss or delay en route. A briefcase holding such materials should be treated like a wallet or purse. It should not be left unattended on a plane while stretching, checked with a coat at restaurants or conventions, or left vulnerable in hotel rooms. No one other than the traveling employee should use the case or fetch materials from it on the employee's behalf. The case should be kept locked at all times, and keys should not be shared with fellow travelers or subordinates.

Some luggage brands issue keys that unlock all cases in that luggage line. A combination briefcase coded by the employee or by the company or a case in which the entire lock system has been replaced is more secure.

If the proprietary item being transported is film or tape, special precautions may have to be taken at airport checkpoints to avoid damaging the material. If the item is a scale model or oversized artwork that should not be seen, similar care should be planned. If the case or material must be opened, it should be done in a private room with airport security personnel present, never in the passenger line or in a public corridor.

If multiple copies of classified material are needed for a meeting and cannot be mailed in advance, duplicates should be made at the meeting and only one copy transported by the traveler. The fewer copies made, the easier it is to look after them.

At the highest levels of a company and in the case of sensitive subjects, the identity of the employer and the nature of a traveling employee's position with the company may reveal more to a travel companion than is prudent. Luggage, particularly carry-on luggage, should not bear company identification. If putting a home address on the luggage tags is not desirable, use a post office box or the address of a friend or relative (with their knowledge and permission).

Employees who travel on company business have more opportunities to reveal information than those who do not travel. Refrain from discussing business on public transportation or doing company work on crowded public carriers. At conventions or meetings, speak generally and sparingly about known projects and products and suppress urges to brag about company advances and foresight.

Recently, the use of minicomputers and home CRT terminals has grown rapidly. This may be part of a program to take advantage of the services and skills of handicapped personnel, or it may be to accommodate special schedules of key employees. Or it may simply be an attempt to cut down on necessary office space and travel at the headquarters building. To the extent that such off-site computer data bases access company proprietary information, special security considerations are necessary. The equipment itself should be used only for company business, not for teaching family and friends about computers. Just as in the office location, classified materials should not be accessed from off-site computer terminals in the presence of unauthorized persons. Printouts and data to be transmitted should be protected as in the office setting, which may necessitate buying locking cabinetry or oversized files.

Work removed from the premises should be returned as soon as possible, generally by the next workday. A company provides many controls and protections for its information, such as locking cabinets, handling procedures, and careful selection of employees, but these techniques will not guard information taken off the premises. Each employee should be aware of the sensitivity of company information and protect it wherever they may be.

# CHAPTER 16

## Don't Forget to Debrief

M. L. Proctor
Manager, Corporate Security Programs
R.J. Reynolds Industries

Not every employee is qualified to handle classified and sensitive company information. While many companies have developed preemployment screening tests and continuing education programs to underscore the importance of information security, too little thought has been given to information drains caused by departing employees. When an employee who has worked with sensitive documents walks out the door, so can a lot of vital information.

Whether an employee is leaving voluntarily or is being fired, and whether he or she is full-time or seasonal help, a debriefing procedure should be undertaken. Few companies realize that exit interviews, especially those conducted by personnel departments, are insufficient for departing employees who have had access to confidential information. Personnel departments have no knowledge of the specific information entrusted to the employee, and thus cannot effectively question the employee about it.

The suggestions for debriefing employees outlined here work equally well for all types of employees. A debriefing need not be burdensome or lengthy; if used routinely for all departments, the debriefing process will not focus undue attention on any individual.

Upon receiving notice of an employee's impending departure, a department manager or supervisor should set a time and date for a debriefing session and outline for the employee exactly what the session will entail. In all cases, the debriefing should be handled by someone at the managerial or supervisory level.

Prior to the debriefing, the manager should retrieve from the employee all company identification, keys, equipment, and sensitive materials. During the debriefing, the status of sensitive projects the employee has been working on should be reviewed. This should be done regardless of where the employee is going, even if he or she is simply moving from one department within the company to another. Job responsibilities

Reprinted with the permission of the American Society for Industrial Security, from *Security Management*, May 1982 p 28.

and information gained while working in one department should not be the subject of discussion in the employee's new department.

Most companies require employees who will be handling sensitive projects to sign an agreement when they are hired not to disclose the nature of their assignment. A departing employee should be reminded of his or her promise to protect the information of the employer. The manager should review with the employee the confidentiality agreement that was signed, and discuss with the employee any perceived conflicts of interest that may be faced as the employee moves into a new position.

An employee should also be reminded that he or she has no right to take or copy written company materials. If the material is classified, the employee should not even be allowed to take copies of work products that he or she authored or compiled, even if the new job requires work samples. Employees who are leaving the company to return to school should be warned not to submit any information in term papers or reports that might violate the confidentiality agreement.

Talk with the departing employee about technical or privileged knowledge gained on the job. Legally, an employee is entitled to use scientific skills and knowledge in his or her new job, as long as trade secrets and proprietary information of the former employee are not revealed in so doing. This fact should be considered in planning who will be allowed access to research logs and files. While research logs provide an accounting of daily activities, they also provide evidence of the development of ideas and trade secrets that could be patented or otherwise protected. The employee should be told that although the logs are maintained by individuals and reflect the work accomplished by those employees, the logs themselves remain the property of the company. The logs should never be removed from the premises or left unprotected.

Prior to an employee's departure, it is important to discuss where duplicates or copies of classified documents may be found. Secretaries who report to the departing employee may have copies in their master files, or copies may have been distributed to colleagues, contractors, libraries, or record centers. If the departing employee is the author or compiler of these documents, he or she should be able to account for any copies still in circulation. If the company has a policy of logging recipients of classified materials, this duty should not be onerous. In jobs where an employee works at home or other sites, particular attention should be paid to retrieving materials from those locations.

The files of a departing employee should also be reviewed for clarity and completeness. If file notes and documents are not in order and self-explanatory, the productivity and effectiveness of the person inheriting the assignment will be proportionately diminished. Communication about classified matters to a former employee, even in the interest of a smooth transition, is inappropriate, so be sure all such matters are settled well before the employee's departure date. Even completed projects done by the departing employee should be fully reviewed; a file no one else can understand is useless to the company and could become a liability. For each file in his or her office, the departing employee should indicate an information retention and declassification schedule and note the location of existing duplicates of files.

A manager should be prepared for the possibility that the employee will refuse or fail to appear for debriefing, or appear but fail to provide sufficient information on the classified data in his or her assignment. In such cases, the manager should consider withholding the final paycheck (make sure you verify that the employee does not receive automatic deposits to the bank account), withholding a recommendation, recording noncompliance on the employee's permanent record, or, for serious instances, alerting the company security department or legal officer.

Consider using a debriefing procedure at the close of contracts with consultants, suppliers, and vendors whose services are retained for sensitive projects. Of particular importance is the retrieval of documents, product samples, advertising scripts, etc. that may have been shared with the contractor during the course of the project. Copies of all work products the contractor produced during the term of the agreement should be retrieved as well. When the company and a vendor or supplier enter into a contract for services or goods, the contract should include nondisclosure provisions specifying that all trade secrets and unpublished know-how are properties of the company. The contract should require the contractor to agree to preserve the confidence of the trade secrets and know-how, and to use them only in the performance of the contract. The nondisclosure agreement should require the contractor to return all confidential materials (including copies) at the end of the contract period in order to minimize any chance of losing trade secret rights because of negligent disclosure to others.

The final step in the debriefing procedure requires the manager to notify others of the employee's departure. Receptionists should be alerted not to allow the former employee free access to department premises, and coworkers assigned classified projects should no longer share project information. Passwords should be changed in electronic equipment such as word processors and computers, and automatic ID card readers should be programmed to reject the former employee's card. In short, privileges of the workplace accorded to the employee because of his or her job assignment should be effectively closed.

Even if you have no reason to question an employee's actions or loyalty, take an opportunity to clean house when he or she decides to change jobs. Debriefing is an effective way to clarify what an employee has done during his or her tenure and to underscore the importance of safeguarding proprietary information. These days, this simple precaution can make the difference between secrets kept and secrets—and money—lost.

# CHAPTER 17

## Data Security—Key to Protecting Your Store's Assets

Charles Jackson
EDP Systems Manager
Frederick Atkins, Inc.

Retailing is one of the most vulnerable industries in America today. The nature of the business itself accounts for this openness to attack.

- We have million-dollar days.
- We have as many as 100 different departments.
- Vendors ship merchandise in to us.
- We ship merchandise out to our customers.
- We exchange merchandise.
- We handle returns from customers.
- We return merchandise to our vendors.

To handle large volumes of merchandise and the corresponding paperwork properly, controls must be built into the various stages of the retail cycle. Development of controls must be an integral part of the design of a computer-based system, insuring its reliability and accuracy. Adequate controls should be developed to prevent or identify and isolate errors at the earliest point in the processing flow. In addition, controls must prevent the unauthorized or fraudulent use of the system and related data files. Controls should also provide an audit trail of transactions from their original source through the manual and mechanical processing to the final reports.

Controls should be developed so they can be efficiently and effectively performed and monitored. Such controls should be as simple, logical, comprehensive, and as standardized as possible. In deciding what controls to use, the cost of implementing each control should be considered in relation to the risks involved if that control is not implemented.

Two distinct aspects of operations in a retail environment should be controlled: the movement of goods in and out of stores (Physical security), and the flow of data through the store (Data security).

Reprinted with the permission of the American Society for Industrial Security, from *Security Management*, September, 1978, p. 68.

113

This article will discuss the problems relating to data security. These problems are of a compounding nature, so users, controllers, data processors, auditors, managers and security experts must become involved in the solutions. Security of retail data must limit three adverse effects: modification, destruction, and disclosure, either accidental or intentional. Some of the inherent problems in data security are illustrated in the following case studies.

## CASE STUDY 1

Merchandise worth $200,000 was stolen over an eighteen-month period by manipulation of the inventory data on a company's computer system. Covering this loss would require an increase of two million dollars in net sales.

The employees involved worked in the warehouse or loading docks, and had access to books showing the location of each piece of furniture in the warehouse. They managed to get different locations for the furniture keyed into the host computer through the CRT terminals.

When a stolen item was requested on the terminal during the eighteen-month period, it was reported as "misplaced." The piece would then be "found" when another piece of furniture was substituted which, in turn, was reported as "misplaced." Consequently, although no one piece of furniture showed up as permanently missing, many pieces were listed as "misplaced." Stores commonly misplaced furniture but not as consistently as this store unless theft is involved.

The accused employees, including the warehouse foreman, dock workers and truck drivers, allegedly sold the furniture from the warehouse where it was loaded either on the store's trucks, or on trucks subcontracted by the store. The operation was uncovered when the wife of an employee, while waiting outside the store near the loading docks, thought furniture was being loaded in a suspicious manner. She notified the store manager who called the police.

The number of people arrested in this case was expected to reach twenty. This total includes people who are accused of having received the stolen goods.

## CASE STUDY 2

This retail store had good data controls, or at least its management thought they did. Yet, $50,000 per year was being embezzled in the accounts payable department.

The company employed a key-rec system, which handled the following functions:

- Bulk receiving
- Detail receiving
- Ticket making
- Relief of open orders
- Stock ledger input
- Class inventory

- Unit inventory
- Key-rec number control
- Accounts payable input

After the merchandise was received, counted, marked, and sent to the stores, the original copy of the key-rec with the invoice attached was sent to the accounts payable department for processing. Key-recs with no invoices attached were classified in a "do not pay" category, and were batched separately and sent to the accounts payable department for processing. The accounts payable department entered the information into the computer system. Both categories were maintained in the accounts payable computer master file. At the time an invoice was received for one of these key recs, a document was created to transfer the item from the "do not pay" to "ready for payment" category.

Each month two aged trial balance reports were created: the regular trial balance, and the do not pay trial balance.

At year's end, management reviewed the "do not pay" trial balance, and removed any items that were a year old.

An accounts payable clerk realized that this computer category could easily be tapped and proceeded to develop a plan. He knew that as a result of the recession, management had eliminated a half-time position, one that matched the paperwork (key-rec, invoices, etc.) to the duplicate copy of the remittance check.

The employee first created a dummy company, a simple operation because, like many stores, the vendor name and address forms were not controlled. Once the master was created, the next step was to change the vendor number on an invoice to the dummy number thru the use of the "change detail form." He then decoded the item from a "do not pay" to a "ready for payment" category.

Now all this person had to do was to wait for the computer to create the next set of checks. The check to the dummy company was mailed and cashed.

After the fraud was discovered, management reinstated the half-time position for verifying the paperwork with the remittance check, and established controls on all input forms.

## LESSONS LEARNED

When planning EDP security methods, many aspects of the process must be controlled. Procedures used to protect the total system generally fall into four categories:

- Personnel controls
- Systems controls
- User controls
- Processing controls

Personnel controls are both important and powerful. Their primary rationale should be to protect the employee from unnecessary failure, temptation or suspicion.

If properly designed, they will also have the effect of deterring, limiting and detecting malicious acts.

A control objective in hiring procedures should be to hire individuals who are sufficiently competent for the task to be performed. This policy can result in the lowest cost over time by reducing errors and training. It will also help to avoid frustration because of an employee's inability to perform assigned tasks.

1. *Reference checks.* All persons under consideration for employment in the data processing department should undergo an extensive employment history check by the security department. The latest employer should always be contacted and questioned about the work habits of the prospective employee. Special investigation should be considered for potential data processing employees who are reluctant to have their latest employer contacted.

    The initial review should include a special screening of all applicants who might handle management information. Possible conflicts of interest for personnel working in data processing, such as relatives working in other parts of the organization or secondary employment responsibilities, should be investigated.

2. *Bonding of Employees.* The bonding of employees in sensitive positions should be considered. Bonding companies usually perform thorough and efficient investigations of an applicant.

3. *Mandatory vacations.* Vacations serve to reduce errors by improving morale and reducing fatigue. Also, a policy of mandatory vacations can conceivably deter some fraud, as the probability of discovery increases when the perpetrator's job is taken over by someone else. More embezzlements are detected by this control than any other method. Many more attempts are probably thwarted by the potential embezzler's perception that he will automatically be detected at vacation time.

4. *Changing of Assignments.* Assignment changes sometimes meet with resistance from managers who are aware of the merits of specialization. But admirable as specialization may be from the perspective of efficiency, it can be an invitation to trouble when maintaining tight internal controls. Periodic switching of assignments mitigates this threat to security, without completely abandoning the idea of specialization. In addition, the practice fosters staff development.

5. *Immediate separations.* If an individual is terminated, the following steps should be considered.
    a. Collect all identification including badges, ID and business cards (new business cards and ID cards indicating retired status may be considered for retiring employees).
    b. Revoke all powers of attorney including bank signature cards. Change or revoke all codes or passwords to which the employee had access. (Note that the ability to change these codes must be considered when selecting systems using passwords.)
    c. Collect all keys (including magnetic stripe cards), signature plates, and other evidences of authority.
    d. Settle all accounts including expense accounts and courtesy accounts.

e.  Reconcile accounts of any resource over which the employee had control, such as petty cash, parts inventory or tape library. Where indicated for the protection of the employee who will assume accountability, an audit should be considered.

f.  Reclaim all proprietary information in the custody of the employee.

g.  Remind the employee of any ongoing contractual obligations to the company, including restrictions on use of data to which the employee had access in the course of employment.

The system controls that are not purely physical fall under the following headings: separation of duties, machine time, library and programming.

Separation of duties means that certain tasks will not be performed by individuals with incompatible responsibilities. The following separations should be made:

- Separate custodianship of assets from keeping of related records.
- Separate responsibility for initiating transactions or master file changes from data processing.
- Separate systems analysis and programming from computer operations (particularly during production runs).
- Separate operation of the computer from program documentation.

The next group of controls in the systems category deals with machine time. Machines should be metered to assure that all time is accounted for. Logs should be kept consisting of computer printouts accompanied by explanations covering every period of inactivity. The explanation should be subject to supervisory review.

Since the printout has internal control significance, it should be secured. Several methods are possible. Numerical control over the pages can be maintained (preferably through the use of numbers entered by the business forms company) or the log output can be run to a special tape or disk, removable only by an authorized person.

A new information environment is now available in the users department. The user has the ability to enter, alter, and delete data from the computer system without the required documents passing between departments. The addition of on-line terminals requires a careful investigation into the procedures which will be established for the use of these terminals.

Of prime importance in maintaining the integrity of information entered through a terminal is the identification of the person who is entering the information. The problem of erroneous or fraudulent information being entered into the system is greatly reduced if the person entering the information is always identified. Currently, research programs are being developed which evaluate terminal operator identification through voice, fingerprint or signature recognition. However, these recognition methods do not promise to be economically feasible in the near future.

Password identification is used in most systems today. However, the shortcoming of this method is that a password can be easily exchanged among individuals. For this reason, the following procedures should be established in conjunction with password identification in an on-line network.

- The terminal device should require some type of locking mechanism which must be deactivated before the terminal can be entered.
- Password identification by the department manager should be required to sign the terminal onto the system. This procedure would insure that someone on the management level has acknowledged that the system is being used.
- Each operator must then identify himself by signing onto the terminal with password identification.

When information that creates or deletes critical records is entered into the system or when new critical informational fields are entered into the system, further password identification should be required.

A transaction log of all computer transactions is essential. This log should identify the operator who entered the transaction, identify the manager who authorized the systems availability, and record the time the transaction was entered.

Manual control should insure the proper departmental approval of all transactions prior to their entry into the computer system. The use of on-line terminals does not negate the responsibility for proper procedural controls for information handling.

Many companies have excellent controls on the prime shift, but few or no controls on the second or third shifts. For example, one retailer discovered that the data processing manager operated the company's computer as a service bureau after hours and pocketed the proceeds.

The third group of system controls concerns the library function. A librarian is a necessity—not only as an internal control, but also to insure that materials are returned in a timely fashion. The library should be off limits to unauthorized persons, and the records in the library should be identified by external labels.

Last in the systems control category are programming controls. Initially, the program itself must be logical and acceptable to the user. This means, above all, that it must be easy to understand.

The retention of test data is also important. It supplies evidence that the required testing has been completed, and provides information that may be usable by internal auditors. Also of prime importance are the final approvals of programs and changes to existing programs by programming supervisors. These changes should be recorded numerically. Numerical control means more than just numbering, it also means accounting for the numbers in use.

Finally, periodic comparisons should be made between the program in use and the master control copy. This check (which ideally should be carried out on a surprise basis) is an effective way to make sure that the version of the program being run for production is authorized and up-to-date. The internal auditing department can assume the responsibility for the master control program testing, at least where significant accounting applications are involved.

The third aspect of security controls involves the users and operators of the computer system. The first important user control consists of a document count or totals used for the ultimate reconciliation of output with input.

Another user control is the review and resubmission of rejections by the user department. In one company where this control was lacking, the "float" of rejected accounts receivable rose to an alarming figure, much of which turned out to be unrecoverable.

A third control in this category is the reconciliation of a listing of master file changes with original input. When changes in retail prices or personnel have been processed, these changes should be recorded in a "change register," which should be sent back to the user department for reconciliation. Failure to reconcile means that mistakes may pass unnoticed. Some of these errors may be costly, like the retention of a separated employee on the payroll.

The last category of EDP security processing controls, begins with pre-data processing validation, a routine designed to assure that approval has been obtained for data about to be converted. Key verification, accuracy and the completeness of transmission are essential to the maintenance of a secure system. Internal labels should be used and updated insuring that the proper files are on hand. Dollar or cash totals should be carried from one run to the next to make certain that there has been no unauthorized addition to, or loss of data.

This last control is by far the most critical to data security. When a new on-line terminal is added to the computer system data security methods should be reexamined.

Involving the internal auditor in the design of the data security system is imperative. The institution and maintenance of internal controls is a responsibility of management. But the auditors must verify the existence and proper functioning of the controls. Thus, the internal audit is in itself a control, the broadest and most important of all because it evaluates the others. In the final analysis, great opportunities exist for exercising creativity in the quest for security.

# PART IV

## Identifying the Threat

Just as assessing risks is a basic part of developing any security strategy, so too is identifying who or what is likely to be a threat to the assets to be protected. The two articles in this section analyze the evidence of actual cases of computer crime and abuse for patterns among individuals or groups who have threatened computerized information systems thus far. Their findings can help sharpen the focus of threat analyses.

# CHAPTER 18

## Who Are the Computer Criminals?

Jay Becker
Director, National Center
for Computer Crime Data

The fashion for journalists and criminologists is to see all computer criminals as geniuses. Donn Parker, in his book *Crime by Computer*, reflects this when he writes: "Perpetrators are usually bright, eager, highly motivated, courageous, adventuresome, and qualified people willing to accept a technical challenge. They have exactly the characteristics that make them highly desirable employees in data processing." F. W. Dennis, writing in *Security World* in September 1979, paints the same picture: "The common denominator in nearly all cases of computer fraud has been that the individual is very much like the mountain climber—he or she must beat the system because it is there."

But is the picture accurate? Does it help us to prevent computer crime? Based on my analysis of many of the cases in the files of the National Center for Computer Crime Data, I must answer both questions with a resounding "No."

Many computer criminals just aren't that clever. Their crimes are not that technically sophisticated. And even if it were true, this view of computer crime wouldn't be very helpful. No test has been devised to separate computer geniuses who are prone to crime from law-abiding computer geniuses. Lacking this type of test, it wouldn't make much sense to ask a personnel director to screen out all geniuses lest they commit computer crime.

### AS THE CRIMINAL SEES IT

Environment, not personality, seems the most useful factor in predicting and preventing computer crime. The data suggest that certain "criminogenic environments" are pres-

This article first appeared in the 13 March 1980 issue of *New Scientist*, the weekly review of science and technology, published in London, England.

ent in most computer crimes. By criminogenic environments I mean the computer system, *as the criminal perceives it*, immediately before he or she decides to commit a computer crime. For example, one type of computer criminal will see the computer environment as a cookie jar—the source of enough money to meet sudden needs. Another may see it as a playpen—simply a place to play computer games as long as he or she likes. These different perceptions, and the attitudes they reflect, will generally lead to very different types of computer crime and require different types of security to prevent them.

In this article, I suggest seven views of the computer system that seem to summarize most of the cases I have seen.

### The Playpen

The American educational television network recently broadcast a one-hour show about computers as tools in the education of nine and ten year olds. About the only discordant note in this paean was one teacher's observation that her students kept erasing each other's names from computer sign-up lists, or destroying the sign-up lists altogether. The teacher tolerated this aberrant behavior, apparently delighted that her students enjoyed playing at the computer.

Older students have the same morality. Professor John Carroll found that 34 percent of the students in two courses on advanced information systems at the University of Western Ontario had tried to obtain computer time without paying for it. The same percentage had tried to penetrate the computer's security system.

These examples demonstrate the fact, obvious to anyone who has watched people play computer games, that simply using a computer can be intrinsically satisfying.

**Exhibit 18–1.**   Playpen perception of the
computer environment.

They also suggest that the drive for this satisfaction can violate others' rights. When computer crime results from the attempt to gain satisfaction from working with the computer, I categorize it as an example of the playpen perception getting out of hand. Unfortunately, there is no standard within the computer industry to define precisely *when* the playing has got out of hand. Thus, if a student uses an hour of computer time without permission, one university computer department considers it criminal theft of services and another views it as commendable ingenuity.

In addition to the unauthorized use of time (and often as a necessary prerequisite to it), attempts to compromise computer security systems are common to those with a playpen point of view. An English group calling itself Crank boasts of expertise in "computer piracy and security cracking." Members of Crank claim to have obtained files from universities and companies in England, including one whose security "has never been broken," all with the ostensible purpose of making sure computer security is improved. But it would take only a small change in the motivation of Crank members to wind up with someone who seeks to outsmart the computer for his or her own benefit.

This may have been the dominant motivation behind Stanley Rifkin's infamous computer crime. When Rifkin pleaded guilty to charges arising from his theft of $10.2 million from an American bank, he described his reaction to what he had done. "I was aghast," he said, explaining that his arrest was the first indication he had had that his scheme really worked. He further explained his failure to hide the diamonds he had bought with the stolen funds, saying he hadn't made any plans for this contingency. Implausible as this story may seem, it is consistent with Rifkin's general ineptitude as a thief and his rapid arrest once he returned to America. Further support for the idea that Rifkin had a playpen perspective comes from an associate who once taught with Rifkin. "The guy is not a bank robber, he's a problem-solver," was Professor Gerald Smith's opinion.

In view of what I have already said about the playpen attitude towards computer environments, certain security implications immediately become evident. Norms that clearly define allowable and excessive computer use will develop, and if the industry does not develop them, it's quite likely that the law will. In the meantime, each computer user must evaluate its rules and practices. Unless these clearly communicate the limits on unauthorized computer use, and the rationale for these limits, the user will continue to be vulnerable to the computer "game player" who goes too far.

### The Land of Opportunity

Not too far removed from the playpen perspective is the attitude that there's nothing much wrong with exploiting an obvious vulnerability in a computer system.

Unlike the game players in their playpen, those who see the computer environment as a "land of opportunity" seem to be motivated not so much by challenge as by lack of challenge. Where the game player might try hundreds of codes to find one that gives entry to the computer's operating system, the employee in the "land of opportunity" just finds and exploits a vulnerability in the system—often in the course of learning his or her job. For example, the operator of a device for printing checks pressed the repeat button again and again when his own check was being produced. Hardly the computer genius the media would have us think all computer criminals are, he took a dozen checks and attempted to cash them all at the same time.

More sophisticated, but similarly opportunist, Jack Polak exploited his position as a purchasing agent in the county of San Diego, CA. Knowing the troubles the county was having installing a new computerized system to control its payments for goods bought, Polak set out to compromise the system. He created fictitious vendors, charged the county for non-existent supplies that had ostensibly been delivered, and collected approximately $50,000 in payments. He knew the county's system too well. Only his impatient questioning about a $70,000 check he awaited led to his detection.

One needn't be a profound criminologist to realize that motivation is directly proportional to opportunity, and opportunity is inversely proportional to the security of a system. If the opportunities are obvious enough, even the least sophisticated employees (or outsiders, for that matter) may be expected to try to exploit them. Consequently, the need for systematic and extensive security cannot be underestimated. Simple measures such as taking particular care of employees' accounts that are under the computer's control, rotating personnel from job to job, and looking for any trends of irregular work habits that might either give rise to or explain computer crime, are just some of the measures a company might take to reduce its vulnerability to those who see the computer as a land of opportunity.

### The Cookie Jar

A gambling debt, a drug habit, sudden losses on the stock market, may all lead an employee to see the funds in a computer as the best solution to his problem of the

**Exhibit 18–2.**   Cookie jar perception of the computer environment.

moment. As though the computer were a cookie jar, the "hungry" criminal dips into it to take what he needs. In such circumstances, the criminal's motivation is much more pressing than his observation of a loophole in the system's security. Criminologists have identified such "situational pressures" as frequent accompaniments to white collar crime in general; since computer crime is a subclass of white collar crime, I am not surprised that these pressures operate here as well. Case histories of computer crimes bear me out.

One head teller at a bank in New York City was found to have stolen $1.5 million when his bookie was raided and it turned out that he was betting up to $30,000 a day. And in Denver, CO, Raymond Ressin financed numerous gambling trips to Las Vegas by falsifying the input to the computer of the stockbrokers for whom he worked.

To counteract people whose need drives them to cookie jar crimes, companies must investigate employees before they are hired. But situations change, and security must be responsive to these changes. Ideally, the relationship between employees and their supervisors and management in general will be such that the employee will seek out help when a problem arises.

### The War Zone

Some people see the computer not as a solution to life's problems, but as a symbol of their cause. Disgruntled employees, who feel that management is out to get them or that they have already been hurt unfairly, may express their resentment in attacks on the company computer. This type of employee sees the computer as a "war zone," the battlefield in the struggle between employer and employee.

In Sacramento, CA, three employees of the state Department of Justice, apparently annoyed by the paltry amount of their pay increase, deleted certain arrest records from the state's criminal records. There are numerous other tales of computer library tapes erased, misfiled, or mislabeled, or of instructions to erase all company records two years after a certain programmer is fired. Employees have even literally attacked the computer with sharp instruments, screwdrivers, and guns.

In one of the most extreme cases I know of, an employee of a large produce company, feeling cheated out of a substantial pay raise, created a "shadow corporation" for revenge. The shadow was almost exactly like the real corporation, except that it was about .75 percent less efficient—more vulnerable to theft, spoilage, and so forth. All of the financial differential between the shadow corporation and the real corporation went into the pockets of the disenchanted employee.

As in the case of the "cookie jar," good management is the best prevention. Where no acceptable avenues exist to express resentment toward the employer, management should not be surprised when unacceptable avenues are used instead. There is also the possibility that the employee's resentments are well-founded. Corrective action will not only reduce the threat of the resentful employee, but also demonstrate to all employees the folly of perceiving the computer as a war zone.

### The Soapbox

In the war zone, the criminal gets at the employer through the employer's computer. The soapbox computer criminals find computers themselves anathema, and see computer crime as a way to strike out *against the computer*. Thus, they see a war going on, not between the employer and themselves, but between themselves and any one of a number of different forces.

In some cases, the slogan of the 1960s—I am a human being; do not fold, staple, or mutilate me—has been converted into an unreasonable dislike for the computer itself. In one case, a programmer sabotaged a computer by short-circuiting the computer's memory. He told the police he had an "over-powering urge" to shut the computer down, and that he had no grievance against the owners of the machine.

Terrorist bombings reflect a much more extensively developed symbolism. In Italy, the Red Brigades produced a telling document, *Resolutions of the Strategic Directorate*, that depicts increasing computerization in Western countries as part of a sinister plot to "maximize social controls." The *Resolutions* explain that because computers are instruments for the "repression of the class struggle . . . it is important to attack, unravel, and dismember these networks of control."

Where the computer symbolizes personal frustrations, the security measures to deal with the problem are not much different from those called for in the war zone. But soapbox crimes are as likely to be committed by nonemployees as by dissidents within. These sorts of attacks on the computer emphasize the need for attention to physical security. The common practice of making the computer center the highlight of a public relations tour is thus a questionable risk, and companies should ensure that they stay aware of the activities of terrorists.

### The Fairyland

If any category of computer criminal completely belies the major myth, it is this one. Some of the participants in computer crime appear to act as though the computer environment were totally divorced from reality. A telex operator may routinely transfer millions of dollars from bank to bank without recognizing how important each transaction is. The computer simply isn't real.

In *Computer Capers*, Thomas Whiteside tells of a fraudulent transfer of $2 million. The culprit convinced his girlfriend to transfer this amount to his bank in New York, telling her he wanted to play a joke on a computer-operator friend who worked at that bank. The friend and the money disappeared before the girlfriend realized she had been conned as well as jilted.

Although it is perhaps dangerous to take assertions of ignorance at face value, the message behind cases such as this is quite clear. Where people associated with computer systems are unaware of their own power, and act as though there were no dangers of computer crime, the company who employs them is exposed to an enormous risk. Just as management cannot afford to ignore the new vulnerabilities a computer creates in any business, so it cannot afford to have employees who are ignorant of these vulnerabilities. Clear communication of the responsibilities of the job, as well as clear standards for its performance, are the most obvious management tools to combat this problem; the company should make it clear that each employee has a stake in computer security.

The other side of the fairyland mentality is that even if the employee's ignorance of computing does not facilitate a crime, it may stand in the way of that employee detecting the early warning signals which, if acted on promptly, might reduce crime. It is clear to me that one of the important security devices in a manual system is that lots of people see each piece of paper, and they can tell unusual entries just because they run counter to common sense. To some extent we lose this security advantage when systems are computerized—and no longer easily understood by many people. If we could only get the game fanatics to teach the residents of fairyland about computing, both might develop more realistic perceptions of the computer environment.

### The Toolbox

To some computer criminals, a computer is simply a computer. Thus, we have cases of so-called computer crime where the computer is not the target, but the implement in a crime that in no other way involves computing. The phone freaks, who use microprocessors to test phone circuits and develop strategies that enable them to use phones for free, exemplify this attitude towards computers. The Equity Funding personnel, who used computers to create false insurance policies by the thousands, seemed similarly clear-headed about what a computer can do. Perhaps the most ludicrous example is the Los Angeles brothel owner who used a minicomputer to keep track of his customers.

**Exhibit 18–3.** Toolbox perception of the computer environment.

These examples suggest a type of computer criminal we can call the technological crook, who sees the computer as another tool in his kit. This type of person is more likely to already be a criminal than any of the individuals whose attitudes I described above. As the key to this sort of crime is computer *use*, all those strategies that limit access to the computer are important security. But none of these "limited access" security procedures will be at all effective against the owner of a micro- or mini-computer who has worked out a way to use the computer to commit crime.

## WHAT TO DO NEXT

The categories listed here are not mutually exclusive, exhaustive, or chiseled in stone, and I encourage feedback—particularly about attitudes I appear to have missed. Furthermore, the categories may not be much use when we want to predict whether a specific individual is likely to become a criminal (unless we can develop tests to discover if a "suspect" is abnormally likely to perceive the computer environment along the lines the categories suggest). Still, if the company sees the environment as a playpen, a cookie jar, or any of the other models I've discussed, it may be inferred that some would-be computer criminals will see it that way as well. I hope the security measures I have outlined here will offer some strategies to change or prevent these potentially dangerous perceptions.

# CHAPTER 19

## Computer Abuse
## Research Update

Donn B. Parker
SRI International

Coverage of computer abuse research in the mass media, magazines and trade publications, the law enforcement community, and legislature continues to expand. Interest in such research reflects the proliferation of computers in all segments of business, government, and society at large, as well as increasing reports of computer crime. The US Chamber of Commerce estimates that losses from business, economic, and white collar crime may cost more than forty billion dollars per year.

SRI International has conducted a Computer Abuse Research Project for the past nine years with funding from a series of grants from the National Science Foundation. A central objective of the continuing project was to lay a foundation on which the relationship between the *proliferation* of computers and the *increasing reports* of computer crime could be studied. Methodologically, it was important to determine both the nature and the extent of their coincidence. Other objectives included achieving an awareness and understanding of the means of deterrence, detection, and prevention of computer crime.

The Computer Abuse Research Project is *not* a rigorous sociological, statistically-based crime study. An abiding aim of the project is to develop a body of knowledge that will attract the interest of qualified sociologists, statisticians, computer scientists, criminologists, and criminal justice experts. The work pioneers in a new field of inquiry in a science (computers) that itself is not much more than thirty-five years old.

The project is organized to explore and assess the new and changing problem of computer abuse on the basis of a limited, somewhat biased collection of reported cases. The project has shown a problem exists, and some of its ramifications for computer technology, computer management, and the law have been illustrated.

Few researchers have attempted serious work on computer abuse because valid

*This paper was prepared for SRI International. Points of view, opinions, and conclusions stated herein are those of the author and do not necessarily represent the official position or policies of SRI International.* Reprinted with the permission of the American Society for Industrial Security, from *Security Management*, Sept. 1980, p 89.

material is difficult and expensive to obtain. The principal source of information is the cases that have been discovered *and*, in many instances, publicly reported. Such cases reveal little, however, about those abuses that have not been discovered because of the perpetrator's success and those that have not been reported for various reasons. Because of this slanted data base, the amount of white collar crime that actually occurs is unknown. Unlike other areas of research, criminological research is usually performed empirically, using individual case studies to study limited, narrow aspects of the subject.

Computer abuse as defined in this project is necessarily broad and diverse enough to cover any kind of crime, civil suit, or dispute between two or more parties that involved a computer. The possibility is remote that an exhaustive search across this spectrum could provide a statistically valid population for the determination of statistics such as mean, standard deviation, etc. Therefore, the project has been self-limited to recording all reported cases that can reasonably be found, and to verifying as many of them as possible. In this way, at least a lower bound of the number of reported cases can be established. From these, we may report on the nature of the perceived problem by case example. The results of this procedure have been most valuable, both in improving computer security and in finding shortcomings in the law. The study continues, and the results change as more loss experience becomes known and computer technology and its applications change.

## THE PROFESSION AND SOCIETY

Data processors are in positions of high trust. If they were not an honest community, use of and reliance on computers would already have been slowed by an onslaught of abusive acts. Data processing people are well paid and in great demand. They invest much effort to achieve their technical capabilities and find their work interesting and challenging. All of these factors contribute to a low incidence of abusive acts in the data processing profession.

Nevertheless, as in any occupation of large size and high mobility, certain people are dishonest or become so under certain circumstances. Others have ethical standards, but have learned to ignore them in a technical environment that treats individuals equally regardless of their ethical standards and in which abusive acts can be easily concealed. Documented experiences in this project have shown that such people do exist and that their potential for doing harm is growing as the percentage of assets and asset records processed by computers increases.

Contact with the media is a part of computer abuse research. Information varies considerably in accuracy, precision, and thoroughness. Cases reported in computer trade publications, such as *Computerworld*, tend to have relatively greater validity. They are based on direct inquiries and information from technically knowledgeable persons. In the general press, more than one article by more than one reporter generally increases the accuracy and quantity of information. Problems from conflicting information are resolved by choosing the information point by point and rating it according to plausibility, reliability of source, and in-parallel coverage by the latest available dated report.

Contact with the media is a two-way street. The SRI project staff and management have been continually concerned about distorted reporting of research results by journalists worldwide. At one time, all cooperation and all interviews with the media were brought to a halt. This action, however, resulted in even less accurate, more distorted reporting of the project's findings. It was then agreed we would maintain a policy of not seeking publicity, with the exception of press releases to announce the completion of studies. Full cooperation, including reporting positive as well as negative findings, is now given at the media's request. Unfortunately, misquotes and distortions still occur, but with less frequency as journalists become more familiar with the technical problems and more appreciative of the positive aspects of computers.

## COMPUTER ABUSE DEFINITIONS

A working definition of computer abuse was necessary from the outset of the SRI project. This definition, then, became a working hypothesis. It also served as the basis for the discovery of unanticipated types of cases that could be categorized and studied. The omission of a type of case could have severely restricted the exploratory nature of the project.

The definition of computer abuse used is necessarily broad: *any intentional act associated in any way with computers where a victim suffered, or could have suffered, a loss, and a perpetrator made, or could have made, a gain.*

This definition relates to computers in the most general way possible. If a stronger relationship between computers and abuse were used (for example, ''an incident in which a computer is directly and significantly instrumental in an abusive act''), the problem of specificity remains. The definition is made more general by extending it to include any case that directly aids in revealing vulnerabilities or legal shortcomings in computer use and that supports the use of computer security safeguards or new computer legislation. Another refinement is the identification of the four roles that computers are found to play in computer abuse:

1.   *Object.* Cases include destruction of computers, data or programs, and supportive facilities and resources, such as air-conditioning and electrical power, that allow computers to function.
2.   *Subject.* A computer can be the site or environment of a crime, or the source of, or reason for, unique forms and kinds of assets, which can be manipulated in unique unauthorized ways.
3.   *Instrument.* Some types and methods of crime are complex enough to require the use of a computer as a tool or instrument. A computer can be used actively, as in automatically scanning telephone codes for working combinations that can be used to make unauthorized use of a telephone system. Or it can be used passively, simulating a general ledger in the planning and control of continuing financial embezzlement or fraud.

4.    *Symbol.* A computer can be used as a symbol for intimidation or deception. This could involve the false advertising of nonexistent services, as has been done by several computer dating bureaus.

The broad definition is focused somewhat by eliminating cases where the substitution of another device for the computer or computer-related device would not materially change the nature of the incident or the nature of the skills and knowledge needed by the perpetrator. Stealing a terminal and fencing it for resale would not be a computer abuse case when, if a typewriter were substituted for the computer, there would be no difference in the methods, motivations, skills, knowledge, or resources involved.

The application of this broad definition of computer abuse to specific cases is difficult. For example, most credit card fraud is excluded from the file because the perpetrator did not have direct contact with a computer and was not in collusion with someone who did, or did not use a characteristic of the computer system to make the fraud workable. The difficulty of specific application requires considerable judgment and experience for consistent classification. Because sufficient information is difficult to obtain, cases are classified on a best effort basis initially, then reclassified when more information is obtained.

Theoretically, all types of crimes—fraud, theft, larceny, extortion, conspiracy, espionage, sabotage, burglary, embezzlement, and murder—could involve the computer. However, separate consideration of computer-related incidents is warranted by the following factors, which can differ markedly when computers are involved:

- the occupations of the perpetrators,
- the methods of the crime,
- the environment of the crime,
- the form of assets involved,
- the timing (milliseconds and less), and
- the geography (long distance computer communication).

## THE FILE OF REPORTED CASES AND ITS USE

Central to the Computer Abuse Research Project, both in method and purpose, is the working case file of reported computer abuse. Our method of collection includes data relevant not only to verified cases, but also to other reported but unverified cases that are plausible, indicate possible forms of computer abuse, or suggest types of computer vulnerability. The file is indexed to reflect the status of each case. Periodically, we publish the number of cases in the working file by type of source and remind readers of the difficulties of case collection and the variable quality of the file's information sources.

Testimony before the US Senate Subcommittee on Criminal Law and Procedures in June, 1979 stated that "about 75% of the cases have been verified. The remainder have not been investigated and include reports for which sufficient data . . . have not been reported. Sources of case information include newspapers. . . ." In an SRI report, "Computer Abuse Assessment," published in the *Encyclopedia of Computer Science and Technology* in 1975, it was stated that:

"The value of the research results is limited by the extent to which the database of reported cases represents all cases. Conclusions must be based on the universe of the [cases] rather than the total universe of experience. Applying the conclusions to [all] cases beyond those represented by the [data base] is subject to statistical uncertainty. . . . Two instances have occurred where verified cases were subsequently found to be fictional, or at least not to contain sufficient basis in fact. Several unverified reported cases in the file are suspected of being without basis in fact, but remain in the file as real cases until proven otherwise. A number of cases were removed from the data base after discovery that they either did not occur, or occurred in ways that did not meet the requirements of the database definition."

The most basic difficulty in collecting and reporting case information is that the results can be based only on discovered and reported cases. Even though the number of reported cases per year appears to be growing at an exponential rate, the real or total number may be growing more slowly or even reducing in number. However, we believe there is greater value in taking action to make computer use safer based on known reported cases and good judgment than in ignoring cases for lack of complete knowledge. We must accept that this may preclude protection from repetition of unknown loss experiences. In addition, we believe that reporting as much as is known of reported cases has a beneficial effect in motivating management to take prudent action and in aiding the criminal justice community.

## RESEARCH VALUE

The greatest value of the case file is in the application of example cases to computer security and criminal law research. Regardless of its stage of verification (including even fictitious cases), each case is useful for determining the feasibility of recurrence, the effectivess of computer security controls, and the adequacy of the law to deal with it. For example, the project shows that most cases involving the use of magnets to erase magnetically recorded data are fictitious. This discovery generated enough interest for SRI and the National Bureau of Standards (NBS) to test the feasibility of this practice in the laboratory. The low potential threat from the intentional use of magnets was found to be small.

In another instance, a series of incidents were reported, some real and others possibly fictitious, in which offenders replaced the blank deposit slips banks place on customer convenience tables with their own MICR codes preprinted by the bank. This resulted in deposits being credited to the offender's account. Many financial institutions changed their deposit procedures after learning of this.

The working file contains cases that have occurred since 1958. Case materials include news clippings, excerpts from magazines and books, court proceedings, reports of law enforcement agencies, interviews with individuals involved, questionnaires from computer users, and documentation from everyone willing to report a case.

The collection of cases from news clippings is compiled by project staff members who scan local news media and review clips sent to the project by interested parties. The project engages a newsclipping service to collect all US clips reporting nonviolent crime, suspected fraud, and civil suits. About fifty clips per week result, and these are scanned for involvement, or likely involvement, of computers. During the nine years of monitoring news reporting and verifying reported information, the quality and accuracy of the reports have improved as reporters have become more knowledgeable about computer technology. Off-beat and human-interest news is often unreliable. However, general news about an abusive act is usually accurate enough to conclude that an act occurred if the names of participants and their quotes are used, and if the report is from a reliable publication (i.e., one that other research organizations use as a source). Parallel articles on the same case by different reporters are cross-checked. Even when technical facts are inaccurate, the text of the report will usually reveal whether or not computer technology played a role. The project currently has hundreds of news articles in a separate file pending examination to determine if they qualify for unverified status in the working file.

The reported case file is not a statistical sample and is not intended to be statistically based because the total population of actual cases cannot be known. The file is biased in some known and probably some unknown ways, but this has been carefully stated in most of the project research papers published recently. This point is usually omitted in news and magazine articles written by others who reference the project's work. We have loosely called the computer abuse file of reported cases a computer crime file when taking the time to explain and define our precise meanings for a general audience would be secondary to another theme.

## SPECIFIC RESEARCH RESULTS

The specific results of the research are not based on the entire reported case file except for gross characterizations to show how the reported cases have grown and how trends have developed in the types of cases reported. Rather, the specific research results are based on subsets of applicable cases. For example, computer abuse perpetrators were characterized on the basis of information in twenty-six interviews, and the average reported gross loss per case in a subset of forty-two cases of banking-related abuse was found to be $430,000. The number and type of cases used have been stated in definitive project findings and are usually limited to those investigated by the project. As resources allow, from five to ten cases per year are investigated in the field.

In mid-1979, 669 cases were reported (this number was subsequently reduced to 668 when field investigation revealed that the Penn Central boxcar theft case did not involve computers). Approximately sixty new cases have been collected since then, but have not yet been categorized and entered in the working file. In addition, news clippings collected in the last eight months have not yet been examined for computer abuse incidents. The degree of case verification is established by using the eight rating code levels described below. The first character is alphabetic and is used as follows:

Y = The case has been verified.
N = The case has not been verified.
D = It is not certain that a computer was involved.

The second character of the rating code is numeric and orders the level of verification from high (for example, 1) to low (for example, 4). The full set of codes used and numbers of cases by level are shown in Exhibit 19–1. The level N3 cases are documented in letters; one was documented orally. These include five cases personally investigated and described in a memorandum by Stanley Rifkin, who is now serving a federal prison term.

The application of the definition of what constitutes an unverified or verified computer abuse case has been under periodic study and change. The goal is to include all types of cases, anticipating changes in computer technology and use that make ultimate research purposes unpredictable. Published gross tabulations are derived from the entire reported-case file including unverified, partially verified, and possibly a few fictitious cases. Recent cases too late for inclusion are always omitted.

Collecting and studying reported cases that may be fictitious could lead to dis-

| No. of Cases | Code | Verification |
|---|---|---|
| 147 | Y1 | Legal or law enforcement agency documentation sufficient to identify an act and the role of a computer. |
| 141 | Y2 | Description of the act obtained directly from at least one reliable source or case participant or other reliable person if names of case participants have been supplied. |
| 246 | Y3 | Reliable public media reports identifying the victim and quoting descriptions of an accomplished act or statements of the official disposition of the case by named investigating officials. |
| 20 | Y4 | Description of the act obtained directly from at least one reliable case participant or other reliable person in which names of case participants have not been revealed. |
| 554 | | *Total verified cases* |
| 45 | N1 | Reliable public media reports identifying a victim, but quoting no investigating officals or agencies. |
| 59 | N2 | Reliable public media reports with no identification of participants. |
| 7 | N3 | Other. |
| 3 | D1 | Not certain that a computer was involved. |
| 114 | | *Total unverified and uncertain cases* |
| 668 | | *[Total case (80% verified)]* |

**Exhibit 19–1.**    Computer Abuse Cases by Type

covery of new abuse methods being discussed publicly and anticipation of possible abuses in the future. This anticipatory awareness is necessary in the development of computer security because long lead times are needed to install system controls.

Data are tabulated by levels of confidence in case validity and by types of cases. As more cases are collected and experience in cataloguing increases, studies have more meaning. In turn, this improvement motivates increased sophistication in data tabulation. The project has never achieved complete agreement among all staff members in categorizing all cases. This problem was partly overcome in the most recent vulnerability analysis (not yet published), which was performed by two people working independently with a single set of rules and tabulating for case validity at several confidence levels.

It is expensive to validate and research cases. An increasing number of cases reduces the proportion that can be adequately treated under fixed levels of project funding. Fortunately increased funding is now anticipated, and a greater part of the project resources will be used to improve the quality of the case file.

Presentation of data has been limited to selected tabulations. Cross-tabulations and other statistical analysis have not yet been attempted because of the limited quality, quantity, and accuracy of the case data. The working file of reported cases has never been published for reasons of privacy and copyright protection and because it is a working, changing file. The file is available for others to examine at SRI's facilities in Menlo Park, CA. Copies of the file have been made available to several serious researchers.

## AVAILABILITY OF THE DATA

Data from the case file are now in a computer-stored data base accessible from SRI terminals. A computer program is in production use that provides twelve reports with data tabulated as follows:

1. Incidence and loss by year and type of abuse (1958–1978 and four types).
2. Identification and tabulation of cases by size of loss (twenty-one ranges).
3. Identification and tabulation of cases by type of abuse (forty-seven types).
4. One-line case descriptions by source of information received.
5. Identification and tabulation of cases by geographic location (state and country) and type (four types).
6. Case identification by victim name (private).
7. Identification of cases by perpetrator or defendant name and occupation.
8. Identification of cases by employee status, class of victim, number of perpetrators, and collusion (yes or no).
9. Identification of cases by perpetrator or defendant occupation.
10. One-line case description by key words.
11. One-line case description by case number.

A manual describing the data base and access systems has been prepared for project use.

## COMPUTER-RELATED CRIME

A questionnaire was developed by SRI International in 1979 under a grant* from the National Criminal Justice and Information Statistics Service of the Law Enforcement Assistance Administration (LEAA), US Department of Justice, and sent to seventy-two district attorneys who participate in the Economic Crime Project of the National District Attorneys Association. The purpose of the questionnaire was to determine the degree and nature of computer-related crime among offices focusing on economic crime programs. Responses came from forty-six people. (See Exhibit 9–1.)

Within the past five years, forty district attorney's offices had a total of 244 cases of respondent-defined computer-related crime brought to their attention. Of these cases, 191 were prosecuted and 157 convictions were obtained by plea and 10 by trial. Many more cases of fraud were handled that involved data in computer-readable form: 311 reported, 215 prosecuted, and 158 convictions obtained by plea and 20 by trial. Averages of both types of cases are in the range of 5 to 8 per office. Foremost in the number of cases reported are the offices in Nassau, NY with more than 100; Cook County, IL with 30; and Baltimore, MD with 20. Other offices reported 10 or less. This concentration of computer-related crime in only a few offices probably occurred because of the localization of computers and of prosecutors who have knowledge of and interest in this type of case.

A significant number of prosecutors are acquiring the ability to deal effectively with computer-related crime. Of the individual prosecutors responding, sixty percent had read a book or manual on computers and attended one or more courses or seminars on computers.

To determine the respondents' level of technical knowledge, the questionnaire asked whether they could explain various technical computer concepts to juries. Over one half said they could explain the components of a computer, how a computer program functions, and what a programmer does. Slightly fewer could explain the source and object code forms of a program and on-line computer terminal protocol. However, few could explain a program branch function, distributed processing, multi-programming, computer crime methods (such as "Trojan horse" and "salami"), and the meaning of DBMS (data base management system). Only one knew the meaning of ROM (read-only memory). We concluded that many prosecutors have more computer-related knowledge than would be expected, but this knowledge is relatively

---

*This report was prepared for the National Criminal Justice and Information Statistics Service of the LEAA, US Department of Justice, under Grant Number 78-SS-AX-0031, awarded to SRI International. Points of view or opinions stated herein are those of the authors and do not necessarily represent the official position or policies of the US Department of Justice or of SRI International.

shallow and limited. Only one individual answered that he could speak to all these subjects, while ten were knowledgeable on at least half the subjects.

Little agreement exists on what constitutes computer-related crime. Ten examples of computer-related crime as defined in the SRI study were described on the questionnaire. Only one prosecutor agreed that all cases qualified as computer-related crime. All agreed that welfare payment fraud using a computer terminal and a computer to create falsified inventory data qualified as fraud. All but five and eight respondents respectively agreed that theft of a computer program from a computer and falsification of computer input forms for payroll processing are computer-related crimes. Six voted for falsely claiming the use of a computer in an advertised service, about twelve for theft of a computer or computer terminal, and one half agreed that theft of a program from an office and use of a computer to plan and manage a fraud were computer-related crimes. This lack of concurrence on what is considered a computer-related crime could partly explain the disparities in the number of cases reported.

The district attorneys' offices reported dealing with alleged crimes in which a computer or program played a number of roles in illegal acts. Following are the roles with the number of offices reporting them in parentheses; they are marked from the most to the least frequently encountered: contained evidence (28), used as an instrument (24), produced output material (19), was the site (14), was the object of theft (11), was the object of sabotage (5), and claimed use falsely to deceive or intimidate a victim (5). Several offices reported ten to thirty instances involving the more frequent roles. The reason for so few cases of sabotage and theft may be that the questionnaire respondents deal more with fraud and may be unaware of the more common cases of damage and theft.

The number of offices that reported using various computer-related items for evidence varies from a few to half the sample. Computer output listings have been used by twenty-eight of the forty-six offices, including twenty-one that requested specialized output reports. Computer programs were used in output listing form by fifteen, eleven on printed paper, seven in punch cards, and six on handwritten forms. Only six used programs or data on magnetic tape as evidence, and two used them on disk packs. Computer media used in the order of most to least include output listings, punch cards, magnetic tape, punch paper tape, and disk packs. The use of disk packs will probably increase, and of punch cards and paper tape decrease, as technology changes.

About half the offices indicated they had experience in interrogating computer employees and computer terminal users. Several offices reported ten to thirty such interrogations.

To a question asked about best evidence forms of data, twenty-seven respondents chose handwritten pages. Only four chose magnetic tape, and seven would not favor one over the other. Factors considered included "understandability, mistrust, and precedence." One respondent indicated that the issue of fraud may lie in the difference between handwritten material and data on tape.

Respondents to the SRI questionnaire were asked to rank the quality of four different draftings of a search warrant for the contents of a computer and adjacent rooms to look for evidence of an alleged computer program theft. The search warrant draft selected as best by a large margin was:

> Search for personal property consisting of remote plotting programs, specifications, and user documents in the form of: key punch computer cards, reels of magnetic tape, magnetic disks or packs, computer printout sheets, and computer printout sheets produced by execution of computer output programs from the computer's storage.

Ranked second and of moderate quality was the text used in an actual search warrant in the *Ward v. California* case.

> Search for personal property in the form of keypunch computer cards punched with the remote plotting programs, computer printout sheets with printouts of remote plotting programs, and computer memory bank or other data storage devices magnetically imprinted with remote plotting computer programs, related documentation.

Ranked next, as of poor quality, was:

> Search for personal property consisting of remote plotting programs and documented specifications and user documents in printed, punch card, magnetic media, or computer stored forms.

The draft ranked last appeared to be generally unacceptable:

> Search for personal property consisting of remote plotting programs and related documentation.

Respondents suggested the following variation as alternatives for the search warrant drafts. Search for:

1.    user source documents;
2.    user source deck (cards or other formats);
3.    object decks (cards or other formats);
4.    printouts of questioned program in action;
5.    copies of computer logs, journals, etc. for the time period in question.

Drafting this variation requires a person familiar with "source deck," "object deck," and "source documents." Another respondent pointed out that wording must not only be understandable by laymen, judges, and executing officers, but must also be technically precise and inclusive. Item (5) above, requiring copies of computer logs and journals for the time in question, is an important inclusion.

Another variation suggested is as follows:

> To search for evidence or fruits of a crime in the form of data or information contained in or recorded upon computer-related devices and mechanisms included but not limited

to computer cards, computer cards punched with the remote plotting programs, computer printout sheets, computer tape, magnetic disks or packs, or other computer printed or encoded devices or mechanisms, and data and information contained within the magnetic or electronic data storage capacity of the computer or computers at said location; you are commanded to use the facilities of the computer or computers of said location to produce said aforementioned data or information in printed and legible form.

This variation is the most comprehensive, except it lacks Item (5) of the previous variation. However, it may be too comprehensive, because it provides for seizing any materials or information whether or not related to remote plotting computer programs.

These examples display some of the problems associated with legal definitions of computer-related crime.

*Research Limitations of the Survey.*   This survey of district attorney's offices was conducted as part of a larger project, to develop a manual on investigation and prosecution of computer crime, and not to characterize the computer crime activities of the thousands of prosecutor's offices. The questionnaire was not pretested, and follow-up sampling has not yet been done. Additional support will be sought for a statistical analysis of the survey data based on cross-tabulation and further sampling to answer the following questions:

- What characterizes the offices that did not return the questionnaire?
- What characterizes the offices at the extremes of the data range?
- What factors explain the disparate number of cases reported and prosecutors' concepts of computer crime?
- What are the differences in response by office based on the number of crimes reported by each?
- What methods were used by the offices to produce the data they reported?

*Conclusions of Survey.*   The most surprising result from this SRI questionnaire is the large number of prosecutors gaining or having technical knowledge about computers. Numerous books and seminars make this information available. On the basis of the frequent inquiries that SRI receives from an increasing number of law students, the students are not only learning about, but also are specializing in computer technology.

The next step is more advanced computer training for investigators and prosecutors who have some familiarity with computer technology. Such programs should make them fully capable of dealing effectively with computer-related crime.

## CONCLUSION

Other research efforts are starting to expand the work of the computer abuse project. The National Computer Centre in Manchester, England is developing a similar case file. The Caulfield Institute of Technology has a computer abuse project in Australia; its data on cases collected bear a marked similarity to the characteristics of SRI project data, although there are also some significant differences. The US General Accounting

Office (GAO) performed a study with SRI assistance of sixty-nine computer crime cases in the federal government in 1976. The original manager of the project, John R. Schultz, indicated that thousands of cases of fraud were reported in large payment systems such as Welfare and Social Security where evidence resided in computer media. In the GAO study, an appropriate narrowing of the definition of computer abuse resulted in a more pertinent and manageable number of cases for their purpose. Jay Becker has started a collection of cases in Los Angeles in the National Center for Computer Crime Data. As computer abuse studies expand, the researchers will choose definitions and apply them in ways relevant to their end purposes with methods suited to their fields of endeavor.

The SRI project does not claim that the results of its research are representative of all abusive computer acts. As in all empirical research, partially supported hypotheses abound, which must be further supported or not, as experience and knowledge dictate. In the meantime, this project remains the only serious, comprehensive, ongoing study of computer abuse. We hope efforts to support or improve the results will be based on new, more valid, and more accurate information.

## 1975–1979 PUBLICATIONS RESULTING FROM THE SRI COMPUTER ABUSE PROJECT

### 1975

Parker, Donn B. "Computer Abuse Assessment." SRI Report and *Encyclopedia of Computer Science and Technology* (Marcel Dekker, New York).

Parker, Donn B. "Computer Abuse Perpetrators and Vulnerabilities of Computer Systems." SRI Report and *AFIPS Conference Proceedings, 1976 National Computer Conference.*

### 1976

Nycum, Susan H. "The Criminal Law Aspects of Computer Abuse: Federal Criminal Code." SRI International, Menlo Park, CA.

Nycum, Susan H. "The Criminal Law Aspects of Computer Abuse: State Penal Laws." SRI International, Menlo Park, CA.

"Criminal Sanctions Under the Privacy Act of 1974." SRI International, Menlo Park, CA.

"Testimony of Donn B. Parker for the U.S. National Commission on Electronic Fund Transfers." SRI International, Menlo Park, CA.

Nycum, Susan H. "Legal Protection of Proprietary Rights in Software." SRI International, Menlo Park, CA.

### 1978

Parker, Donn B. and Russell Dewey. "EFTS, A Guide to EDP and EFT Security Based on Occupations." Report for Federal Deposit Insurance Corporation, SRI International, Menlo Park, CA.

Parker, Donn B. and Susan H. Nycum. "Programmer Criminality." SRI International, Menlo Park, CA.

Parker, Donn B. and Susan H. Nycum. "Computer Crimes: Case Histories and Proposed Legislation." *Proceedings of the DHEW Secretary's Conference on Fraud, Error, and Abuse.*

Nycum, Susan H. "Trade Secret Protection for Proprietary Interests in Software." *AFIPS Personal Computing Digest, 1978 National Computer Conference Proceedings.*

Parker, Donn B. "Computer Security Differences for Accidental and Intentionally Caused Losses." *AFIPS Conference Proceedings, 1978 National Computer Conference.*

"Testimony of Donn B. Parker and Susan H. Nycum for the US Senate Subcommittee on Criminal Law." Federal Computer Systems Protection Act Hearings before the Subcommittee on Criminal Law and Procedures of the Committee of the Judiciary, US Senate, June 21, 22, 1978.

Parker, Donn B. "New Approaches to EDP Security." *American Bankers Association Automation Conference Proceedings* (May 1978).

Parker, Donn B. and J. Don Madden. "ADP Occupational Vulnerabilities." SRI International, Menlo Park, CA.

Parker, Donn B. "Computer Misuse." *Information Privacy* (IPC Science and Technology Press, London, November 1978).

Parker, Donn B. "Ethics and Computers." *Information Privacy* (IPC Science and Technology Press, London, September 1978).

Parker, Donn B. "Computer Crime Can Spell Doomsday." *Los Angeles Times*, January 10, 1978.

## 1979

Parker, Donn B. "Computer-Related Management Misdeeds." in Robert K. Elliott and John J. Wellingham, *Management Fraud: Detection and Deterrence* (Petrocelli Books, Inc.).

Parker, Donn B. *Ethical Conflicts in Computer Science and Technology.* (AFIPS Press, New Jersey, 1979).

Parker, Donn B. "Vulnerabilities of EFTS to Intentionally Caused Losses." *ACM Communications* (December 1979), pp. 654-660. [Association for Computing Machinery.]

Parker, Donn B., "The Race To Prevent Major Computer Attack." *Reader's Digest* (to be published).

Parker, Donn B. "Computer Abuse in White Collar Crime." *Sage Criminal Justice Systems Annuals*, Vol. 13, Gilbert Geis, Ezra Stotland, editors.

Nycum, Susan H. "Security in EFTS." *University of San Francisco Law Review* (to be published).

Nycum, Susan H. "Liability for Malfunctioning Computer Programs." *Rutgers Journal of Computers and Law* (to be published).

Nycum, Susan H. "Product Liability Exposure for Computer Programs." (to be prepared for *Trial*, Monthly Journal of the American Academy of Trial Lawyers).

"Computer Abuse Assessment and Control Study." SRI Final Report under NSF Grant MCS7601242. SRI International, Menlo Park, CA (March, 1979).

"Computer Crime." Criminal Justice Brochure for Executives, US Department of Justice LEAA, 1979.

"Criminal Justice Resource Manual on Computer Crime." US Department of Justice LEAA, 1979.

# PART V

## Managing EDP and Information Security

The articles presented in Part V of this book address specific procedural safeguards for computers and their contents. Selection guidelines for off-site storage facilities, contingency planning, and policies regarding time-sharing, remote processing, and distributed computing environments are among the topics discussed. Security practices in data processing service bureaus are also examined, and the use of computational cryptography is considered.

# CHAPTER 20

## Some Basic Bytes on Keeping Computer Security Thieves Out of Your System

Arion N. Pattakos, CPP
Consultant

National losses from computer theft are estimated at $3 billion to $5 billion, depending on who you read or talk to and how willing they are to make a guesstimate. Much computer theft goes unreported, and it's believed much more goes undetected. The loss statistics are huge, and such big numbers often make it difficult to relate them to our individual situations. But we've been warned time and again that without appropriate safeguards, computers can be a source of serious security problems.

It doesn't take much to notice that computers with considerable power have become smaller and much cheaper and, thus, the computer's presence throughout the public and private sectors has become widespread. Computers are also becoming easier to use. Systems have multiple users, and some of these users may be many thousands of miles away.

The proliferation of users and equipment clearly has made business more dependent on the efficiency and productivity a computer brings to the workplace. In turn, businesses' dependence on computers makes them more vulnerable if something happened to a system or someone tampered with it.

Among the more significant computer crimes are the theft of assets, including the computer and its software; embezzlement of funds; fraud; and the destruction or alteration of data and software. An American Bar Association committee survey of 283 large corporations reported in June 1984 that 48 percent of the responding companies had experienced some form of computer crime in the last year. Among these companies, total annual losses were estimated to range from $145 million to $730 million, which is considered a conservative estimate, since respondents were to report only "known and verifiable" incidents.

Reprinted with the permission of the American Society for Industrial Security, from *Security Management*, Feb. 1985, p 31.

Crime, however, is not the only challenge confronting the security or computer professional concerned with protecting a computer system. The potential for fire, electrical outages, flood and water damage, and other natural, accidental, or deliberate disasters, must also be considered in computer security planning and implementation. Loss of access to such basic information as accounts receivable, customer lists, shipping data, or formulas can put you literally out of business. According to a survey conducted last year (1984) by the Chubb Group of Insurance Companies, more than 90 percent of all companies that manufacture and/or depend on data processing systems and experience a serious interruption or loss to their data processing operations, go out of business after the occurrence.

To avoid such devastating losses and curb the damage from computer crime or accident, a security plan should be developed, implemented, and tested for all computer facilities or systems. The term "minimax" can serve as a shorthand reminder of the security goals that should be established for a computer system: to **minimize** loss, both accidental and intentional, and to **maximize** the availability of data, equipment, and processing capability. These goals are achieved by establishing in-depth security safeguards that follow an overall security posture appropriate to the operational uses and value of a particular computer system.

## COMPUTER SECURITY SURVEYS

The best way to start assessing your computer security requirements is to conduct a survey. The survey should tell you where security efforts stand at present, what security goals should be, and how to achieve these goals. Most security professionals are familiar with and have used security survey techniques, and similar methodology can be used for computer security surveys.

Many approaches to performing a security survey are qualitative, some are quantitative, and some are both. A few have been computerized to make data manipulation easier and more effective.

Whatever the approach used, the survey must consider four types of security: administrative, personnel, physical, and technical. Administrative or procedural security covers the "how" of security management operations; personnel security, the people part of the equation; physical security, such concerns as physical access, environmental controls, and hazard protection; and technical security, technical access to the system, including system applications, hardware, and operating systems and telecommunications.

Much literature has been written on the specifics of conducting risk assessments or security evaluations, and the federal government is a good source for some of this information. The National Bureau of Standards issues government guidelines in its federal information processing standards (FIPS) publications. While some of the terms used in federal and commercially available publications may differ somewhat, the various approaches to analyzing the security environment of a computer system have many points in common.

Basic to most survey or assessment techniques is a threat and vulnerability analysis. The sources of potential threats, the methods employed by the threat agent, and the consequences of an occurrence of the threat must be identified. As the analysis is conducted, take care to document all assumptions. Significant threats such as natural hazards, accidents, and intentional acts should be related to targets as well as to the threat's effect on various targets. Various outside factors that affect threats should also be considered; some of these are listed in Exhibit 20–1.

After evaluating a computer system's security controls, you should be able to identify specific vulnerable points in the four areas noted—administrative, physical, technical, and personnel security. The potential effects from an occurrence of each identified threat should be assessed. Among other benefits, a vulnerability analysis should clarify existing security strengths.

A comparison of threats to vulnerabilities will provide a security profile of the computer system, which can serve as a sound basis for recommending prudent and practical security controls. However, some security managers may want to crank more structure into their analyses by quantifying the costs and benefits of their recommendations and significant alternatives. Specifically, these individuals can run a loss-exposure analysis to determine the single-time losses that would occur if a threat were realized, the annual risk posed by each threat, and the rank of threat effects. Of course, to conduct a loss exposure analysis, one must determine the value of all assets associated with the computer system. Such analyses provide the basis for calculating annual loss

Geographic location
Proximity to population centers
Detection features
Weather patterns
Proficiency levels of employees
Emergency training
Local economic conditions
Employee crime
Security policy implementation
Compliance with procedures
Redundancies in equipment and key
   services
Facility environment
Protection features
Visibility
Flood areas
Security awareness
Morale
Local crime
Security policy
Written procedures
Data sensitivity

**Exhibit 20–1.**   Factors that can affect threats.

exposure, which essentially combines the results of the asset value analysis and the threat and vulnerability analysis. Annual loss exposure (ALE) = single time loss × the occurrence rate of the threat.

This numbers game has come under attack from many quarters. Many people doubt you can do more than guess when doing a value analysis. You can get "good" numbers when determining equipment costs and replacement costs. But it gets more difficult to assign good numbers when dealing with software, and the approach breaks down when you try to estimate the data's value.

This concern with the subjectivity of the values used has led some people to develop analytical techniques that take a qualitative approach to risk assessment. Some examples are fuzzy metrics, RIM, risk ranking, and threat scenario methodology. Others have suggested the highly structured numbers approach not be used because it is too elaborate and based on questionable data.

Donn Parker of SRI International is not too keen on using structured survey methodologies as a kick-off for determining what is needed to secure a computer system. He and his colleagues suggest using what they call a "baseline approach." Baseline security controls are "a set of generally used controls meeting commonly desired control objectives that should be present in every well-run computer center. The justification for having them is derived from common usage and prudent management, rather than from explicit identification of vulnerabilities and the reduction of risk." Eighty-two data security practices and controls are suggested as part of this approach.*

The baseline approach is *not* seen by Parker et al. as an alternative to quantitative and qualitative risk assessment methods now in use. However, they do believe these baseline concepts should be implemented before such assessments are used.


## RISK ASSESSMENT

To choose which approach to threat analysis is best for you and your company, first assess the management style of the people in the organization who make the decisions. Are they number crunchers? If yes, the obvious choice in making your study of computer security requirements is to use the ALE approach to risk assessment. You may argue about a few of the numbers (values) you assign, but these can be adjusted in your final report.

On the other hand, if your managers are prepared to accept "expert opinion," you can probably get them to accept the baseline controls suggested by Parker before

---

*Baseline controls were determined by surveying what were considered well-run computer centers. It is interesting that none of the centers studied used a formal cost-benefit or risk analysis approach to arrive at security controls. These methods were thought to be too elaborate and not cost-effective. Quantification was not considered appropriate because of the lack of valid data. Subjective techniques were used, with such words as "prudent" and "common sense" describing their approach.

For more information about this approach to threat analysis, read the US Department of Justice Bureau of Justice Statistics publication, *Computer Crime: Computer Security Techniques*. The publication is undated but appeared in circulation in late 1983.

you launch into something more ambitious. If the decision-makers lie somewhere in between, the threat and vulnerability analysis approach as a basis for security recommendations is probably the best one to take.

Before choosing a method of assessment, however, it can be helpful to consider the benefits and limitations of conducting formal assessments. These factors are listed in Exhibit 20–2.

The survey/audit/assessment/analysis technique you use must be credible and must meet the security needs of your computer system and the needs of your management to achieve effective decision-making. To reach this balance, get management involved in the process early.

To start the analysis approach, determine your present security situation, your future security posture, and your road map to that future security posture. Develop short- and long-term programs that will lead to the implementation of effective security controls. Test these new controls to determine if they work as anticipated. Establish and monitor a lively feedback system to ensure problems can be identified and solved early.

The use of an appropriate security survey technique provides solid insights into what needs to be done if the unthinkable happens. Disasters *do* happen. Outrages *do* happen. Sabotage *does* happen. Environmental problems, hardware failures, floods,

---

**Benefits:**
Pinpoints security needs.
Relates security program to the
    organization's operations.
Gets management involved to provide
    guidance, understand alternatives,
    assigns priorities, make decisions.
Alerts management to near-term risks.
Provides guidance for action plans and
    associated expenditures.
Increases security awareness.
Provides the basis for recovery planning.
Provides the basis for developing security
    test, evaluation, and monitoring plans.

**Limitations:**
Values and other estimates are often
    based on imperfect data.
Assumptions may not be valid.
Varying levels of detail are available and
    must be integrated.
Large number of potential variables exist.
Costs in terms of resources needed to
    conduct the analysis are high.

**Exhibit 20–2.**    Benefits and limitations of formalized analyses.

The base or **introduction** should include the purpose of the plan, the responsibilities involved, the contingencies considered, job/system priorities, and the succession of personnel.

A section on the **protection of records and documentation** should list records and documentation to be protected; its storage locations, both on and off site; and an outline of the safeguards for all locations.

A section covering **contingency operations at alternate sites** should include designation of the sites to be protected; a description of the system configuration and the security, communications, and personnel at each site; the points of contact with outsiders at each site; and the coordination requirements and emergency movement capabilities for each.

Detailed **emergency procedures** should be described for each threat: fire, water, flood, storm, bomb, electrical, etc.

Last should come a list of key **telephone numbers** and a comprehensive **index.**

**Exhibit 20–3.**   An outline for a recovery plan.

earthquakes, lightning strikes, and other equally disabling occurrences can put a system, and the organization it supports, out of business. Such dismal scenarios can be avoided with proper recovery planning and effective execution of emergency plans.

Obviously, an important goal of any emergency plan will be early restoration of services. But "early" must be defined in terms of user needs, so critical systems can be operational again within a specified time. This time is fixed by assessing criticality—the importance of the continued availability of computer records to the survival of the organization.

The recovery procedures you plan for emergencies in a computer system should be designed to achieve goals very similar to those of any security controls. Returning to the concept of minimax, your goals should be to maximize the availability of the resources in the computer system and to minimize the effect of the emergency on the system. Particularly, the impact each type of crisis would have on resource availability must be determined. Crises to plan for include equipment failure; damage to software, files, and documentation; absence of key personnel; inaccessibility or loss of major company assets; severe damage or destruction of the facility; and denial of services to users.

To protect against these threats, the following considerations should be part of your planning process: protecting data files, computer programs, and computer documentation through in-house backup and alternate files storage; contact with organizations or departments supported by the computer system; and coordination with mutual aid organizations. The resulting plan must be written clearly and concisely and be well indexed. A brief outline of points to be covered is given in Exhibit 20–3.

Simply writing the plan, of course, is not sufficient to protect a computer system. Key elements must be implemented, such as assigning responsibilities to individuals and establishing the chain of succession. People must then be trained to execute their responsibilities, and the plan must be tested. The actual operation or simulation of every element of the plan should be exercised and the results should be recorded. This information can then be used to modify the plan if problems are disclosed.

Providing security for a computer system is only good sense. We depend on computers, and without prudent and common-sense security controls, we are vulnerable. Although the computer environment is complex, it is also manageable. A thoughtful approach to computer security can determine the what and why, the where and when, and the who and how of needed safeguards.

# CHAPTER 21

## Insurance Against a Data Disaster

Bernard Balter
Dataguard

Where would the future of any company be if it lost the vast repository of vital information stored in the data banks of its computer system? Such records as historical data, customer or payroll files, tactical management data, mailing lists, and inventory, billing, or tax records are frequently entrusted to a computer. These often irreplaceable corporate assets are the lifeblood not only of many daily operations, but also of long range corporate decision-making.

While businesses regularly insure themselves against various forms of damage and loss, insuring against the loss of data is not given the same priority. Top management frequently overlooks the sensitivity of their computerized functions and seems unaware of the extent to which daily operations depend on it. As a result, the responsibility for the security of a company's data bank, including recovery in case of loss, is usually left to the data processing department, which often has other priorities.

Data processing personnel are professionals who understand the critical nature of the information stored in their systems. But as a former data processing manager, I'll admit that when the time came to submit my annual budget, I'd be more likely to request a new piece of equipment than funds for what I considered an intangible security service, like off-site storage of duplicate computer data. It's a Catch-22 situation, and the data gets stuck in the middle.

One data processing manager from a large municipality estimates that if his city's tax records alone were destroyed, the data processing man-hours required to recreate the master file would top 4,000. What if corporate accounts receivable files were destroyed? What havoc would be wrought on a company's cash flow, and how would management explain the loss to its shareholders?

Companies should also consider the likelihood that some day in the near future they may be held liable for failing to take the necessary steps to avoid a data disaster. Insurance, of course, is a key element in reducing financial risks, but its limits must

Reprinted with the permission of the American Society for Industrial Security, from *Security Management*, July 1983, p 69.

be recognized. Insurance can't physically replace data, and even the best coverage can't begin to approximate the true value of data files to a company's operations.

Seen from this perspective, security measures to safeguard data become a corporate responsibility. And the relatively low costs of computer security measures, such as hardware or software controls, physical security of the computer facility itself, and a recovery system including off-site data storage, are well worth the investment.

Off-site storage of data is one of the simplest means of computer security. Companies arrange to have backup copies of their computer tapes containing important data, programs, and operating systems transported to the storage location on whatever schedule they require—monthly, weekly, daily, even twice daily. If something does go wrong with the company computer—be it a bad disc or tape, theft, sabotage, terrorist attack, power outage, or just plain human error—master files are safe. To cover the loss, computer records stored off site need only be updated and put into operation.

Exceptional disasters, such as a fire, flood, earthquake, or other natural disasters, are not the only concern. I was once awakened in the middle of the night by a programmer who had inadvertently wiped out an entire operating system. Without the necessary backup precautions, such an accident could have wiped out the company.

Executives looking into off-site data storage should consider the following criteria for selecting such a facility:

*High security facilities.* An off-site service should itself have excellent physical security to protect corporate data adequately. Access to the facility should be limited to authorized personnel. The facilities should be safeguarded from fire by an automatic Halon system, as opposed to the normal sprinkler system. (Halon is a chemical fire suppressant system that operates by removing oxygen from the air, thus eliminating the possibility of water damage to records. In addition, a facility that has separate vaults rather than one large storage area is preferable so any mishap will be isolated and can be contained.

*Storage Environment.* A dry, dust-free environment is essential to the maintenance of computer data. Look for a company that offers environmentally controlled facilities, including temperature and humidity monitoring. For this reason, storing data in a bank vault is less than ideal (not to mention that access to data is limited to bankers' hours). When considering underground storage, remember it gets awfully damp in basements. Tapes stored in this kind of environment can be destroyed while they sit on the shelf.

*Proximity.* Storage companies should be far enough away from the client's main facility so they don't suffer simultaneous damage due to a local disaster or fire. However, they must be close enough to allow pickup and delivery of computer tapes on a regular and/or emergency basis.

*Service.* Because data is constantly being updated, an off-site storage firm should not only safely store computer media, but also provide regular and reliable transportation. Some storage companies use outside courier services and have little or no control over company data while they are being transported. Look for companies that carefully screen and bond their own personnel and equip vans with emergency apparatus to provide safe delivery service to clients.

*Inventory*. An important measure of an off-site operation is its attention to record-keeping. The storage service should be able to provide each client with a regular report that lists all media being stored, when it arrived, when it's scheduled to return, and what has been returned already. In fact, use of a professional off-site storage operation can improve in-house record-keeping by imposing routine updating of information on the data processing department.

*Personnel*. Look for a firm with a stable track record run by managers with data processing experience. These executives should thoroughly understand the pressures and demands of both data processing and administrative management. Remember, a service organization is only as good as its people.

A simple service like backup storage can make life easier for everyone. Data processing managers no longer have to resort to taking important tapes home over night, and security personnel can sleep soundly knowing they're covered in the event of a disaster. As more and more managers realize how much of their vital information is computerized, companies will make it their business to see that all corporate assets are secure—on or off company property.

# CHAPTER 22

## Quick, Efficient Recovery of the DP Function: A Critical Security Responsibility

Michael Sobol
President
MIS Associates

Imagine that your company's data processing installation has been crippled by a natural disaster. Vital business functions—accounting, invoicing, payroll, research and development—suddenly stop. Business momentum is lost, customer service slows down, and corporate assets begin to dissolve.

If your company is not prepared to make a quick and efficient recovery of the data processing function in an emergency, it is overlooking a critical security responsibility.

Increasingly, businesses rely on the information processing power of the computer. In large firms, all financial information, administrative data, and customer records are computerized. Any loss of data—whether it occurs through natural disaster, vandalism, or theft—is a threat to the viability of the company's operation. Exhibit 22–1 illustrates the decline in business activities experienced by firms during the two-week period following a complete data center failure.

Within a company, two major groups share responsibility for the security of the data processing operation: electronic data processing (EDP) auditors and security professionals. Together, these groups must not only ensure the integrity of financial information processed in the company's automated environment (generally the sole responsibility of the auditors), but also provide protection against fire, environmental stress, unauthorized access, and, most importantly, any disaster that could shut down the computer operation.

Automated accounting systems present new opportunities for the manipulation and diversion of assets (typically, money and inventory). Without the application of

Reprinted with the permission of the American Society for Industrial Security, from *Security Management*, Aug 1981, p 154.

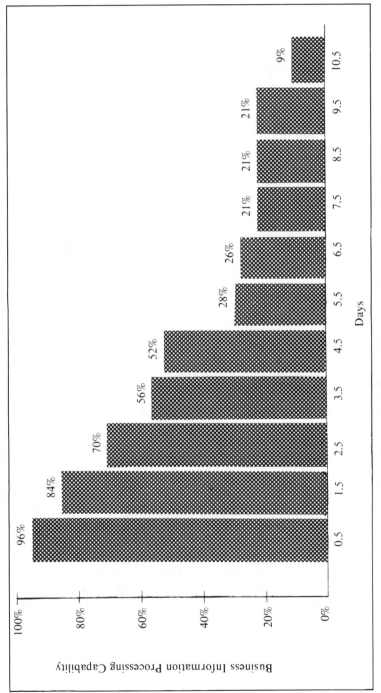

**Exhibit 22–1.** Effect of computer failure on business information processing (for all industries). (Source: *An Evaluation of Data Processing "Machine Room" Loss and Selected Recovery Strategies*. Management Information Systems Research Center. University of Minnesota: Minneapolis.)

proper auditing and security measures, a company cannot satisfy the stringent standards set by the government and by professional accounting associations.

Historically, auditors have approached the issue of examining automated systems by auditing "around" the computer. This kind of audit examines the input and verifies the output. However, because few audit trails can trace transactions through the computer itself, this audit method cannot ensure adequate control or accountability.

The EDP auditor audits "through" the computer system. In addition to looking at system input and output, the EDP auditor traces transactions through the system by examining tape and disk files. Audit retrieval software, marketed by many different software vendors, is one of the tools the EDP auditor uses to verify the integrity of automated system data.

The profession of EDP auditing has been boosted in recent years by federal legislation and guidelines, including the Privacy Act of 1974, the Foreign Corrupt Practices Act, the Office of Management and Budget (OMB) Circular A-71, and auditing standards from the General Accounting Office (GAO). The Privacy Act of 1974 sets stringent limits on the access and control of data and increases the responsibility of security personnel to guard against inappropriate dissemination of data. The Foreign Corrupt Practices Act, in addition to forbidding corrupt payments to foreign governments, contains a number of important accounting provisions. The Act requires companies to keep books, records, and accounts that accurately reflect, in reasonable detail, the transactions and asset dispositions of the company. These "reasonable details" include a secure system of internal accounting controls, restricted access to a company's assets, and frequent audits.

OMB A-71 requires federal data processing installations to provide an EDP security officer who is responsible for performing risk analyses to ensure privacy, and to formulate a contingency plan should the loss of computer resources occur. It continues:

> The objective of these (contingency) plans should be to provide reasonable continuity to data processing support should events occur which prevent normal operations. These plans should be reviewed and tested at periodic intervals of time commensurate with the risk and magnitude of loss or harm which could result from disruption of data processing support.

GAO, in its 1980 standard *Auditing Computer-based Systems*, presented guidelines to facilitate audits of automated systems and data centers. Additionally, it charged auditors and security professionals to "consider the adequacy of contingency plans for continued processing of critical applications in the event of a disruption of normal data processing functions." The GAO standard required companies to make provisions for emergency power and backup hardware, as well as detailed plans for using backup equipment and transporting personnel, programs, forms, and data files to alternate processing locations.

Through its *Statements on Auditing Standards* (SAS), the American Institute of Certified Public Accountants spelled out the guidelines auditors must follow. SAS #3, issued in 1974, defines the auditor's responsibility for verifying internal controls of automated systems. As these guidelines point out, both the EDP auditor and the security professional are crucial to the continuity of a company's data processing operation. Five internal or "built-in" controls can improve the security of a computer system: data communications controls; input controls; processing, storage, and retrieval controls; output controls; and organizational controls.

## DATA COMMUNICATIONS CONTROLS

The proliferation of data communications technology presents new challenges to computer security. No longer is it sufficient to secure a computer room physically; data communications facilities and the possibility of wiretapping necessitate new measures for online and remote job entry (RJE) site security. For example, in 1978, the National Bureau of Standards adopted a Data Encryption Standard (DES) which contains a sophisticated scrambling algorithm. Data is scrambled at input, sent along data communications lines, and unscrambled at the other end.

But encryption doesn't solve the entire data communications security problem. Data security systems must ensure that the remote user is properly identified and authorized to access the computer system. "Authorization tables" must be maintained. These tables show which users can access which programs or data. For example, a payroll clerk at a remote data processing station should not be able to access general ledger records, or execute accounts receivable transactions.

### Input controls

Input controls for both batch (card) and online systems data should verify transactions by means of hash and control totals. Online data validation improves security by enabling users to get good data into the system at an accelerated rate. Bad data can be eliminated by real-time data verification checks. Because online systems tend to eliminate paper, audit trails are lost if transaction summaries or batches are not produced. Auditors need these summaries when reviewing the system. A clear company policy should specify how long data will be retained in the system and how it will be deleted.

Another often overlooked aspect of input controls is the unattended online terminal. Automatic log-off after a period of inactivity at the terminal can ensure that unauthorized personnel do not use online systems. Input irregularities are most often the result of human error or omission, rather than premeditated deceit. But since most crimes result from input manipulations, input controls are the first and most important part of an internal security control system.

### Processing, Storage, and Retrieval Controls

Processing controls depend on internal system files—typically, error suspense files and automated control files—to control processing. Files need to be compared from run to run to verify that no data has been lost and that version and date information is consistent. Integral error suspense files ensure that errors are not lost. Processing should not rely on the application of external controls; automated control systems should handle the bulk of processing controls.

## Output Controls

Although not strictly "built-in," output controls are a necessary part of computer security. Procedures must be designed for the reconciliation of output, for critical review, and for the distribution of reports and negotiable instruments. Any report that falls into the wrong hands can jeopardize the security of the system. The disposal of documents presents another problem. Even if reports reach the right people, there must be a specific retention period for the reports and a clear policy for their disposal.

## Organizational Controls

Many organizational controls can be used by a company to improve data processing security. Some examples follow:

- *Separation of responsibility.* Are vital functions under the control of only one individual? Are staff members aware of functional interrelationships?
- *Program change control.* Who is authorized to change applications programs? Is there a version/date/programmer log?
- *System access.* Are passwords and telephone numbers changed on a regular basis? Has your company investigated the many software security systems available?

## PHYSICAL PROTECTION

Even if a computer system is protected by a comprehensive set of internal controls, the system is still susceptible to a variety of physical security threats. Physical access to the computer center and to remote sites can be strictly controlled by guards or by using badges or entry cards. Although most computer centers are well protected against fire, security personnel must establish emergency procedures, conduct frequent fire drills, and provide training on hand-held extinguishers and breathing apparatus. Companies need to monitor environmental changes, and check for temperature extremes, atmospheric variations, and the proximity of dangerous chemicals. A backup electrical source can assure an uninterrupted power supply that minimizes downtime. Voltage regulators can smooth current to prevent line noise and other transmission problems. All computer installations require the safest in structural materials, including fire walls and fireproof building components.

## RECOVERY PLANNING

A company must have a recovery plan that provides for alternate data processing capabilities in the event of loss of power, sabotage, or natural disaster. The three phases of disaster recovery planning are designing the actual plan, testing it, and then maintaining it.

Designing a disaster recovery plan involves identifying the company's critical systems and resources. What capacity and configuration do we need to support our critical functions? Where can we get qualified personnel if our people are incapacitated? Where can we set up temporary operations? Where can we get equipment and processing power?

One answer to the question of where to set up temporary operations is to maintain an empty shell somewhere on company property. This shell should have a raised floor, air conditioning, an electrical source, and access control—in short, everything necessary for data processing operations except the actual computers. If maintaining an empty shell is not feasible, consortiums and rental arrangements are available.

Computer vendors are usually prompt about getting substitute equipment to users in emergencies. During the period in which staff is bringing up new machines, service bureaus can take up the processing slack. But often the service bureau cannot provide enough capacity. Many companies turn to sources of guaranteed computer power. These sources are expensive, but few companies can afford to be without data processing functions—no matter what the price. Companies must also be sure that vital supplies (such as checks, paper, or special forms) are available if the current supply is destroyed.

The most important requisite for designing a company disaster recovery plan is to make certain that data, programs, master files, procedures, and documentation can be stored offsite. Even if physical recovery is made quickly and new machines are put into operation, no processing can take place if no data is available. The off-site storage location needs a retention/rotation schedule to make sure that current copies are stored at periodic intervals.

Once the recovery plan is formulated, disaster simulations that test it for completeness and applicability should be initiated. Staff members should practice checking the validity of off-site storage data, recovering a critical system on the company computer, and recovering a critical system on another computer.

Finally, the recovery plan has to be maintained. One person who will be responsible for testing and maintaining the plan needs to be identified, and regularly scheduled reviews of the plan must be performed. Maintenance is a critical and never-ending task.

Data processing security is the responsibility of the internal auditor and the security professional alike. In a critical function like EDP, cooperation, understanding, and cross-checking between departments are essential to the security of the operation.

## BIBLIOGRAPHY

*Audit And Evaluation Of Computer Security*. National Bureau of Standards Special Publication 500–19. US Department of Commerce, 1977.

Burch, John Jr., and Joseph Sardinas, Jr. *Computer Control And Audit*. John Wiley & Sons, 1978.

Canadian Institute Of Chartered Accountants. *Computer Audit Guidelines*. 1975.

Canadian Institute Of Chartered Accountants. *Computer Control Guidelines*. 1975.

Davis, Kaegle. *Auditing & EDP*. American Institute Of Certified Public Accountants, 1968.

*EDP Auditing Updating Service*. Auerbach Publishers. [A series of portfolios available through subscription.]

Enger, Norman. *Management Standards For Developing Information Systems*. American Management Associations, 1976.

Fitzgerald, Jerry. *Internal Controls For Computerized Systems*. E. M. Underwood, Publisher, 1978.

Institute Of Internal Auditors. *Systems Auditability & Control*, 3 volumes. 1977.

Jancura, Elise. *Computers: Auditing And Control*, Second ed. Mason/Charter, 1977.

Jancura, Elise, and Arnold Berger. *Computers: Auditing & Control*. Petrocelli, 1973.

Krauss, Leonard. *Computer Fraud And Counter Measures*. Prentice-Hall, 1979.

Mair, William, Donald Wood, and Kaegle Davis. *Computer Control & Audit*. Institute Of Internal Auditors, 1976. [NOTE: A 1978 edition of this book from another publisher contains the same material as this 1976 edition.]

Porter, W. Thomas, and William Perry. *EDP Controls And Auditing*, Second ed. Wadsworth Publishing Company, 1977.

Wooldridge, Susan. *Systems And Programming Standards*. Petrocelli, 1977.

# CHAPTER 23

## How Changes in Computing Practices Affect Security

James A. Schweitzer, CDP
Systems Security Technology Manager
Xerox Corporation

American business has been moving rapidly into the use of terminals for information access via computer time-sharing, remote processing and the developing distributed processing systems. Advancements in computer technology have sharply reduced hardware costs per unit of production while allowing simultaneous processing of multiple jobs. These developments have provided an economy of scale in spreading the use and benefits of huge, high-powered computers over a large, widely dispersed user population. Further, the development of miniaturization of computer components has created the intelligent terminal, which when connected in networks results in distributed computing.

Business users of these systems are typically engineers and scientists who use terminals to access computers as they perform computations and test equipment; managers and accountants, who use terminals to access and process accounting data; market researchers, who operate models of market economies; and programmers, who use terminals to do on-line applications program development. Still other persons within an organization may have terminal equipment at home that can be connected to central computers through telephone couplers.

The advantages from the use of this advancing technology are many. Some benefits are probably critical to continued successful operation of competitive business. But the technology also has a negative side. The new systems are bringing more and more people into direct contact with computers. From a security viewpoint, every contact represents a potential security breach. Where sensitive information may be exposed, the risk is severe and immediate. Where routine business information is accessible, significant risk is entailed because of the volume of information present, the potential for exposing sensitive information from combining or processing several

Reprinted with the permission of the American Society for Industrial Security, from *Security Management*, April 1979, p 42.

files, and the possibility of introducing unknown and unauthorized processes into business information systems.

Technology cannot as yet provide for complete protection of information in computer files, but it is struggling to keep up with identified threats. Most companies, while applying computer technology in the most advanced ways, have not developed or applied computer systems security technology to a degree which provides an acceptable level of protection. Consequently, a level of protection in all parts and at all access points of a system, commensurate with the value of the data being processed or accessed, is not in force.

The existence of many access points, and the development of very large data bases to service multiple applications or functions pose severe vulnerabilities since:

- Current systems security features are often weak, poorly maintained, and in some cases ineffective. Typically, users choose to avoid optional security elements because of the necessary complexity and administrative effort involved.
- Sensitive business information is being transmitted without encryption over public telephone lines, and is being maintained in vendor data centers.
- Effective terminal security practice and terminal site security is virtually non-existent today. Poorly maintained, single-level password protection offers little security against an exploding population of terminal users who have potential for mischief.
- The use of terminals for applications programming represents a severe threat because of the access potential and the technical competence of the terminal user community.
- Data processing installations, with a few exceptions, do not offer encryption of data as a standard service.

These exposures exist because most companies have not had policies which address new time-sharing, remote processing, and distributed computing environments. Further, adequate resources and personnel have not been devoted to the technical security problems. Existing policy and procedure have not been acceptably observed, in practice.

The leading computer manufacturer estimates that ninety-five percent of the risk in data processing stems from a company's own employees. Only a small portion of these cases are actually discovered. Security experts estimate that only ten percent of all violations are reported.

## THE DEVELOPING ENVIRONMENT

In the early days of computer development, hardware was rare and expensive, requiring that all computing work be done at the site of the computer. Typically, the computer occupied a large space because of vacuum tube design. When solid state technology introduced miniaturization, computer hardware costs began to decrease while computer capacity went up spectacularly.

Although the productive unit cost of hardware went down forty percent per year, the increasing size of components kept the price tags high. Managements therefore wanted to make maximum use of this investment.

The arrival of complex operating systems, which permitted multi-programming—that is, the operation of several jobs in the computer concurrently—offered that option. By connecting several terminals to a central computer, each user gains what appears to be a private computer resource. Because of its speed in handling processing requests, each terminal responds as though the user had sole control of the computer. This is called time-sharing.

At the same time, terminals that could input large batches of data and receive volume data transmissions for copying to tape, print or punch cards were developed. These terminals are usually scheduled for connection to a central computer, and a portion of the central computer is dedicated to the terminal's use. Data cards or tapes can be read into the remote terminal along with programs. These data are carried over telecommunications lines to the central sites where processing takes place as though the terminal operator were there. After completion, the output is returned to the terminal site via the telecommunications system. There, reports are printed out or tapes written.

Remote batch processing is an intermediate step to distributed processing, a recent development resulting from the miniaturization of computer components. While the terminals are still connected to a central site, in this case, the terminals now have intelligence—the capability to do computing on their own. In a typical case, programs allow for the processing of input data, editing and certain basic local reporting of activities. After editing, the data is transmitted to the central site for processing against a data base, or general collection of data according to subject matter rather than purpose. Distributed processing, then, distributes computing power to the sites where the output will be used or where input validation may be more effective.

## THE PHYSICAL ENVIRONMENT

The traditional computing environment consisted of a central site containing multiple pieces of computer hardware, medium to large staffs, and a sizeable investment in a facility, including various security systems. As remote processing and time-sharing uses became common, the typical computer environment changed: terminals appeared in remote and unlikely places such as the hallways of office buildings; telecommunications lines became an important and exposed part of the system; small groups of employees, three or fewer, found themselves operating mini data centers using remote batch terminals; and many employees often with interchangeable roles and common access authorizations, were sharing the use of a single time-share terminal.

Central sites have become larger and more sophisticated as cost and load justified uninterruptible power supplies, specialized staffs, and disaster-proof library vaults. At the same time, the number of remote sites with electronic access to the central computer increased geometrically, adding a bewildering variety of locations, physical characteristics, employee access controls, equipment, purposes, and systems. The task of managing one central environment is challenging but possible. Effective management of hundreds of terminal sites becomes impossible, except on an indirect basis through policy.

The proliferation of computer terminals, and the resulting security problems, is compounded by the types of terminals that may be found at locations remote from the source computer. For example, a terminal with a cathode ray tube display, like a TV screen, may display sensitive information without ever making any sort of record of having done so. High speed printers in remote locations have been known to spew out quantities of information by mistake, sometimes to the embarrassment of the owners. Good site planning and effective terminal site security management have become a necessity.

## HOW THE SYSTEM WORKS

Terminals, information networks, data bases, and distributed computing enable users to realize "economy of scale" in profiting from a computing investment. Along with the benefits though, the complexities of these systems must be recognized bringing to light disturbing implications for security management.

In any service arrangement involving computers and telecommunications, three functions are required:

- *Network processors*, controlling the movement of data among the nodes of the networks;
- *Information processors*, performing the manipulation of the data to give desired outputs;
- *Data base processors*, to manage, maintain, and protect access to the information upon which processing is to be done.

Traditionally, the network processor has been in a "front end" or separate computer, which managed the communications effort (see Exhibit 23–1).

Now, however, the movement towards transaction processors and interactive computer uses has made access to the data bases increasingly important and has made accessibility more critical. Possible interference between the data base processor and the information processor is causing a second functional separation to occur. The data base processor now is moved into a separate computer, causing the three basic functions to be located in each of three distinct computers (see Exhibit 23–2).

The three basic functions, then, become bases from which various types of information networks can be constructed. These networks range from time-sharing fully centralized to fully distributed configurations. In between these two types are an almost limitless number of variations. All of the possible variations can be protected by two kinds of security—physical security and logical security. Each of the three basic functions we have described has some shared and some unique requirements from each kind of security (see Exhibit 23–3).

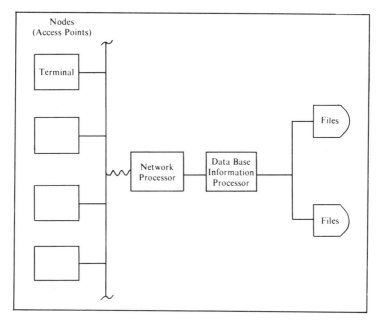

**Exhibit 23–1.**   1970—ERA system.

## PHYSICAL SECURITY

Physical security for the data base processor and information processor functions is the traditional one of limiting access to the site and providing emergency protective systems (fire, storm, flood, etc.). Designating special areas that require clearance levels for entrance, and providing backup storage for files with effective contingency planning contribute to physical security.

Physical security for the network processor is different from physical security necessary in the other processing environments because of the geographic dispersion of the network facilities, such as wires, cables, switching centers, switching computers, telephone switchboards, and so forth. Physical security for the network function is localized and includes locking all telephone service cabinets, placing telephone cables in conduit and securing telecommunications operating centers. Because networks which extend beyond the property of the operator use common carrier facilities, real physical security is virtually impossible. *Therefore, the emphasis must be on logical security.*

## LOGICAL SECURITY

Logical security applies to all three functions in different ways and to varying degrees. Logical security in the information processor and data base processor enhances physical security measures by further stipulating, for those already authorized access to the

172

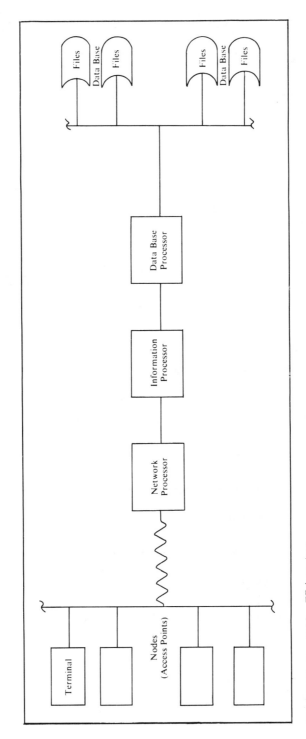

**Exhibit 23–2.** 1980—ERA system.

| Computer \ Security Elements | Physical | Logical |
|---|---|---|
| Network Processor | Facility Security Line Security (Impractical In Most Cases) | Accessor Identification Routing Recordkeeping System Integrity |
| Information Processor | Facility Security and Access Controls | User Identification and Authentication |
| Data Base Processor | Facility Security and Access Controls | User Identification and Authorization Activity Logging |

**Exhibit 23–3.**    1980 ERA system.

computer physically or via terminals, what each person can see, move, or process. Logical security is the primary concern for the years 1977 to 1985.

Several levels of logical security can be provided. The first level can establish that the person contacting the system is in fact authorized to do so. However, at this point, the caller has no access to information. The second logical security level requires that the requestor identify himself as a valid information accessor, and then gives that user the authority to see, change, manipulate, or move one piece, several pieces, or all parts of a file. Controls may also limit access to data bases by applying limitations set up by the data base managers. For example, one stipulation may allow personnel managers at branches to have a code that gives them access to personnel information but not payroll information.

Computer terminals and terminal-like devices are becoming very common, and cheap. By 1985, it is estimated that seven million terminals will be in use in the United States. This proliferation of terminals indicates that security for computer data files must rely on protection at the processor site. Security measures imposed on terminals will be ineffective unless the processing site can somehow screen out those unauthorized terminals seeking access.

Logical security functions within the network processor include supervisory, routing, record keeping, security and integrity, and utilities functions. Each of these functions has a specific role to play in the operation of time-sharing, data base, distributed processing, or other network systems. Some have special security considerations, as briefly described below.

The supervisory function controls the highest levels of software, the ones that provide the executive direction of the system. The highest levels of protection, therefore, must be provided at these points by limiting access to a few key individuals, using effective privilege systems, and giving strict physical surveillance to terminals accessing the supervisor.

The routing function directs the flow of data through the network. Routing system software must be protected by security procedures that prevent unauthorized alteration of routing programs.

The record keeping function journals the network activities, providing a running record of every message, including its source, destination, and delivery data. It also maintains a copy of every message for retrieval and retransmission should such procedures be necessary because of a systems failure. (In practice, most messages are sent several times because of line quality problems.) The journaled information must be kept secure and safe from tampering or access. An effective network must guarantee that information is delivered only to the intended places.

Utility functions are those technical activities necessary to monitor and maintain the network. Security is not usually an issue.

The security and integrity function maintains the accuracy and credibility of the information flow through the system. Parity checks, cyclic redundancy, and other techniques may be applied. This function also detects software or hardware malfunction throughout the network. Restart and recovery systems are provided. These last processes may have security implications if their use threatens established security systems, and they must be so designed that security is maintained.

The integrity and security function also checks the identity of terminals and operators, and can provide complex data base access authorization systems. The software in these elements must be provided with a high level of protection.

## ACCESS MANAGEMENT SYSTEMS

Complete security is possible only when information is processed in a computer that is devoted to a single application, contained in a secure physical environment, and independent of any terminals or other computers or devices. This is not practical in the business operating environment of 1977–1985.

Just the reverse is true. Business computer plans indicate increasing use of terminals, distributed processing, and data bases with large multiprogrammed processors. The security consideration, then, is to achieve some acceptable level of security. Considering the large number of people who will have access to terminals, we obviously must have effective ways of controlling access to the files that will be present on large central processors connected to communications circuits. Terminal users and potential terminal users must be considered as having the basic capabilities to access all business data.

An effective security scenario for a network of computers and terminals requires that an access management mechanism be provided for *all* system/network users. Terminals, or any device capable of contacting and communicating with a computer, will soon be as common as television sets—and probably cheaper. Any effort to control possession of such terminals holds little promise. The next three years will also show an increase in distributed processing. Therefore, the security shield must depend on access controls at the central site. In simple terms, the central computer must be able to determine who a person is and what he/she is allowed to do. An access management system accomplishes three tasks:

- *identification* of potential system users, via a personal claim to be a certain individual (such as by the entry of a password);
- *authentication* of the personal claim to be a specific individual through voice recognition, or a handshake mechanism where the claimant must answer a question randomly selected from a prearranged series (such as "who is your mother-in-law?");
- *authorization* of an authenticated, identified person to do only specified activities (such as display only, read only, display and change, execute program, etc.).

In this context, programs are treated the same as persons when attempting to access information. In a secure environment, program identification, authentication, and authorization are also required, and may use the same access management mechanisms.

Once a system for identification and authentication is successfully used, the caller has been identified to the computer as being a certain person. The question remains, however, "what is this person allowed to do?"

Authorization refers to an administrative process that gives a person authority to perform one of the following functions: read an element of information, a file, or a program, or all of these; write out a data element, a file, a program, or all of these; or execute a program or a set of programs.

Authorizations are typically represented by a matrix with personal identification on one side, information and program elements on the other side and authorized actions in the core. Exhibit 23–4 shows a sample authorization matrix.

| File/Program<br>Employee/ID | AC201 | AC205 | BC609 | BC610 |
|---|---|---|---|---|
| J. Smith<br>ID 72 89 30 | R | | | R |
| R. Jones<br>ID 44 01 12 | | M | E | |
| B. Hall<br>ID 90 27 35 | R | | E | M |

Key
R – Read Only
M – Modify
E – Execute

**Exhibit 23–4.**   Authorization matrix.

## ADMINISTRATION

An administrative procedure is necessary to manage the identification and authorization control mechanism. Essentially, administration keeps track of individual job assignments, hires, discharges and insures that password/code changes are made at appropriate times to preserve security. This check can take considerable effort requiring, in most cases, at least one full-time employee. At a minimum, the following activities are necessary:

- Periodic changes of identification passwords or codes. A password that is never changed becomes ineffective after a time;
- Modification of authorization codes whenever job responsibilities or employee assignments change.
- Adjustment of authorizations and necessary codes whenever operating procedure changes, system changes, or increasing data sensitivity cause the system user to want to restrict or enlarge an individual employee's authorization.

The administrative subsystem for security may be organizationally within the system users' group. Or, in the case of a data base system with many users, it might be in the data base administration group. In any case, the owner system must have positive control over authorization assignments.

## ENCRYPTION

Encryption refers to a process of transforming information, character by character, using a mathematical process. The output from an encryption process is a random substitution of characters, numbers, and symbols from the encoded message. It is theoretically extremely difficult to decipher such an encrypted message unless one has the appropriate key and understands the process used.

Over the past several years, interest in the encryption of computer-processed data has been increasing. This interest has arisen from the requirements for privacy and governmental security. At present two developments are of interest.

The first, and most promising, is the development of an encryption methodology and standard by the US Bureau of Standards and IBM Corporation. This encryption system, called the DES algorithm, has been tested and is generally believed acceptable for commercial use. Several manufacturers, including Motorola and IBM, have announced hardware/software products supporting the DES system. There have been discussions on the potential for breaking the DES algorithm, given large computer resources. From a practical viewpoint, however, an enemy who wished to devote millions of dollars to getting business information could probably do the job more easily and cheaply using traditional industrial espionage methods.

A second methodology for encryption is the "Public Key Cryptosystem," developed by researchers at MIT and Standford Research Institute. This method also uses a mathematical system but revelation of the encryption key does not automatically reveal the decryption key. This means that the keys themselves need not be encrypted, and a message can be signed or authenticated by the sender. Much work remains to be done on this system, but it appears to offer promise for business applications.

To be effective, an electronic information security system must include encryption, which provides a final barrier should the outer defenses be broken. Encryption systems are superimposed on other security systems. For example, passwords or authorization codes may be encrypted while in the computer system or telecommunications network thus preventing eavesdroppers or spies from learning the codes.

Encryption may be accomplished by using a program at the time data processing is accomplished, that is, by software. Encryption may also be done through hardware, where a device encrypts or decrypts as appropriate each time data moves through a "gateway." Most systems will probably use some combination of hardware and software for reasons of economy and efficiency.

The prime cost of encryption will probably be the overhead introduced to computer and telecommunications process budgets. An important secondary cost, however, will be the administrative effort necessary to control the encryption keys. Since having the key is tantamount to having the information, the protection, assignment, change, and control of encryption keys is a weighty matter.

Organizationally, the control of keys has traditionally been the job of the processing organization (data center?), which parcelled keys out to the users. In the future, such functions will probably be within the realm of the data base administrator or equivalent position. Again, insuring that the system owner has positive control over the security subsystems supporting his data is critical.

## SUMMARY

Practical security for time-sharing or other network operations depends on logical security efforts. These include effective identification and authentication for access to the system plus a third level of security which specifies acceptable penetration and limits activity against files. The fall-back security measure in the network is the encryption of all sensitive files so successful penetrators will not get useful intelligence.

A sensitive and critical element in time-sharing computer operations permits users to generate sensitive data outputs, either as printed copy or as displays on a cathode ray tube or gas plasma screen, without the knowledge of others and, in some cases, without accessing a sensitive file. This latter case may occur when the user's program assembles pieces of information from various files and creates data or other processed results that would be considered sensitive.

The central processing site knows only that user X is active and is using certain files. The central site operators do not know what data is being extracted nor do they know what use is being made of that data in the course of the user's terminal-directed processing.

In these cases, the responsibility for the protection of such output must be clearly delegated by the principal user manager to the terminal operator. The need for careful handling may increase as each process is repeated, or as more data or logic is applied. Instruction to terminal users is very unusual today and, in most cases does not exist.

## SECURITY CONSIDERATIONS

We do not have the luxury of contemplating a future use for advanced time-sharing and/or other network systems. In fact, we are already there. But our security is far behind our application of technology.

In terms of the technology described, US businesses are well advanced into timesharing, moderately into data base operation, and only starting to use distributed computing. Exposures exist because:

1.    At present, effective encryption systems are not available in most data centers. Few systems that process very sensitive data provide encryption via application software. Critical data is being transmitted over telephone circuits without encryption.

2.    Most systems do not provide positive terminal device identification, and few, if any, require identification via remote site call-back—a tedious but satisfactory method. As a result, data streams directed to certain terminals might inadvertently end up at others, or might be mischievously diverted. Since encryption is not used, an interceptor could receive clear-text data.

3.    Passwording and access control systems in use are woefully weak, or suffer from such poor maintenance that they become almost worthless. Very large networks have single-code access mechanisms in which the code has not been changed for months or years. Systems containing sensitive data have only one level of access management. Systems provided with access controls have no backup provisions; if the security systems fail, no redundant method is in place to maintain protection. These facts show that the proliferation of computer terminals provides many doors to stored information, and that unauthorized persons wishing access will have only the most shallow obstacles in their path.

Of special concern is the programming environment where on-line terminal program writing has become commonplace. Security and privacy requirements dictate that programmers be restricted access to only those those programs and test data files needed for their program development and testing. Access to live files should be prohibited. "Base case" test data packages should be provided to eliminate any excuse for accessing live files. Current practice does not usually provide these security measures.

4.    Many firms currently use vendor services in the processing of business information. This service may be in the form of time-sharing networks or commercial packages that process customer data on vendor computers. Most vendors necessarily provide security subsystems to prevent one customer's information from leaking to another customer. Some vendors offer optional security features (at extra cost). If a business is using vendor processing or services, a careful review of security features

provided by the vendor is in order. Further, the customer should make sure that optional vendor security features are used and properly administered by persons charged with operation.

5.    Effective management and administration of the security subsystems in many major data processing operations has not been provided for in basic system design and operation. To some degree, this flaw reflects the reluctance of many functional managers to accept responsibility for security, and to insist on security procedures and subsystems from their supporting systems groups.

6.    Realistic and effective contingency planning, in most cases, has been overlooked, is in its early stages, or is in a most rudimentary form. Since a computer network affects so many people and corporate functions, sudden loss of that service for an extended period due to a local disaster could be very harmful to business operation.

7.    Terminal security practices and terminal site security are ineffective and in most cases do not exist.

8.    The users of time-sharing services require special security direction. Instructions on how to recognize security requirements for outputs, how to achieve proper protection in the terminal environment, and how to mark and handle terminal outputs and displays should be prepared and given to users.

## PROTECTIVE MEASURES

System users, generally the organization sponsoring the data system or whose members are using the computer, should be responsible for the security of their information. Determining the level of sensitivity of the information being processed is the first and basic step in the information security process.

This sensitivity level sets an information value and determines the necessary protective effort. Managers of systems development, system maintenance, computer processing, and telecommunications services must provide a variety of protective mechanisms including appropriate measures from each of the four levels of protection, generally described as follows:

1.    *Physical protection*—access control; identification of restricted areas; monitoring the use of terminals; employee identification; etc.
2.    *Organizational and procedural security*—separation of duties; control over changes to systems, programs, and files; system installation procedures; programming management; etc.
3.    *Hardware and software security elements*—manufacturer-supplied system security features; special software packages; hardware separation and isolation methods; terminal identification; etc.
4.    *Encryption* of sensitive information as the final barrier if the other three levels are penetrated.

The variety of protective elements from the four concentric levels may be viewed as a menu of protective devices. Managers of systems development activities, in concert with the functional systems user (where appropriate the system user directly), must select from the variety of protective features to provide an overall level of protection for the system or operation commensurate with the sensitivity of the information being processed.

The following minimal security requirements are necessary to insure a basic level of protection:

- Encryption, via hardware, software, or both, for all sensitive information on magnetic media, or in transit via telecommunications.
- Control of access to information in computers through personal identification, authentication and individual authorization for specific action. Such a system limits access and activity to those duties required to perform an employee's assigned job. The multitude of direct and remote entry points require that such controls be at the central or data base site. Controls of access to and use of terminals enhance security but are insufficient in themselves.
- Hardening of data centers and terminal sites to control access and minimize the threats of theft and mischief.
- Management supervision that supports the previous requirements and, in addition, provides guidance to the many terminal users who may create or process business information.

# CHAPTER 24

## Will Computer Security Keep Pace?

Carl R. Armstrong, CCP
Security Product Developer
Goal Systems International

As computer hardware technology seems poised to enter a fifth generation, computer security software struggles to achieve a new level that seems, at best, third generation. In spite of this lag in development, management, users, and security administrators are more aware today than ever before of the need for some level of security in almost all computer environments.

One pressure that has helped change our concept of the need for security is the increase in on-line access to the data stored in business computers. This increase in access has resulted from the demand for more and more processing work to be done in "real time." In other words, business has come to expect to be able to act upon data as soon as they are available. Responding to information needs and making decisions quickly have become vital business capabilities. Thus, seconds count when several hundred or several thousand "data technicians" are entering data into terminal devices and awaiting responses.

Perhaps such a data technician is the clerk at your local department store who presses the "credit authorization" button on an electronic point-of-sale terminal. Or maybe it is a travel agent trying to find the best airline fare to Davenport, IA. It could even be you, getting extra cash from your checking account at the automatic teller. These and many similar situations require that requests for available data be acted upon immediately.

Our need for speed, coupled with the large volume of work usually present in business computer systems, prohibits the involvement of a human decision-maker in each data processing transaction. There is no time for anyone to make the "allow/don't allow" decision on access to data; the sheer number of transactions is too great.

Reprinted with the permission of the American Society for Industrial Security, from *Security Management*, April 1985, p 50.

At the same time, the requirements of such large systems demand ever more instantly available, on-line data.

A second cause of the growing need for security is the increased ability of data technicians to damage computer records through errors or unauthorized intrusions. As a society, we are just beginning to realize that these errors and intrusions can cripple a business. Great sums of money, important and critical information, and valuable ideas and concepts are routinely entrusted to computers. Improper access to these data can raise the stakes in the risk analysis of any computerized business. The extent of such risks tends to justify a larger expenditure of money, time, and overhead for security.

The computer is evident in all phases of our daily lives, performing services for a broad cross section of the population in ways we don't often think about. But we are entertained by popular television programs and motion pictures based on the premise that high-tech hobbyists can access large data processing centers with minimum effort and can accomplish almost any feat of data manipulation a screenwriter can imagine.

In truth, the actual risks are almost as spectacular as these fictional situations. The number of in-the-field terminal devices and portable computers in daily use by business and industry is expanding at a phenomenal rate. Soon the average home will be as likely to have a computer as two color televisions. Almost every secondary school in the country and many public libraries provide students and patrons with access to personal computers. All of these computers can be used as terminals for a large system when connected to the public telephone network.

## DIAL-UP ACCESS

On their end of the phone line, most medium to large computer centers are expanding their ability to accept dial-up requests for access via the switched network and packet carriers. Their reason for this expansion is the availability of the personal computer: many managers and data technicians are beginning to use personal computers or portable terminals to perform their duties. Often these employees must access the company computer center over the dial-up network. However, making it possible for authorized users to dial in can also result in unauthorized access.

For instance, in one large insurance company, the data processing staff was unable to convince management to install dial-up terminal support until the vice president of systems and data processing was assigned an IBM PC for his own use. Not long afterward, the switched network support appeared and the VP's teenaged son was the company's first unauthorized intruder. Fortunately his intentions were neither malicious nor hostile.

The fourth influence on computer security is the US government's demand for rigorous security standards: the government is the largest buyer of data processing products and services. The need for security is above question in government, and the mandate is unswayable. In addition, unlike most commercial computer users, the government writes its own contracts with vendors. As a result of their requirements, the government's standards usually have become industry standards.

Essentially government is a good influence, applying economic pressures to the mainframe vendors to implement and support rigorous security. This trend is bound to continue as the American public continues to support strong security in the public sector and privacy in computer record-keeping.

Finally, independent auditors, long the hired paranoids of business, are becoming much more competent in auditing computer-automated processes, and they have been appalled and shocked by the lack of checks and controls in most systems. Any competent audit of a computer system today will certainly record some comment about the degree of security provided. Such pressure by auditors is important because it supports and reinforces management's desire to protect the informational assets of a company just as forcibly as the company protects physical assets.

Computer managers have been relatively slow to react to the changing circumstances of computer security, frequently needing a poke from the auditors or a bitter experience with computer theft or fraud to goad them into action. Previously, few computers processed work requiring on-line or real-time terminals and even fewer were connected to the switched telephone network. Security in that environment consisted of watching who came into the computer room.

## A PARTICIPATORY EXERCISE

Today the average computer user is not in the computer center or even in the same building. A new approach to security is required, and those managers who have not kept up with the times do not understand the risks. But commitment from management is essential because good security is a participatory exercise, with users and data owners sharing the cost of security implementation. As the saying goes, there is no free lunch; the price for security is in ease of access (which must be sacrificed for the sake of identification), freedom of activity (since only acceptable actions will be allowed), and administrative overhead (someone must maintain the "rules").

Successful security must be mandated and supported from the highest levels of management, with refinement and implementation handled by the security administrator. In more and more instances, the responsibility for computer security is being assigned to security departments. This is an excellent solution since allowing security responsibilities to rest with data processing could seem like training the fox to guard the hen house.

However, users must be intimately involved with the security of a computer center. In most installations, users must identify themselves to the automated security apparatus and keep this identification confidential. If the users of a computer system do not believe in the importance of such security measures, it will be impossible to prevent unauthorized entry to the facility. Therefore, high-level management involvement and commitment to security is essential to motivate users to do their part in controlling access and use of the computer resources and data.

## SOFTWARE TECHNOLOGY

Another encouraging trend in computer security is that data owners are taking responsibility for governing the use and accessibility of their data. Data owners and data administrators are becoming more careful about who has access to their data and when the data can be accessed. Good security depends on the data owners wanting to define fully the acceptable and unacceptable uses of their data. As security practices become more a matter of habit, the general competence of the data owners and data administrators should improve. They also will demand better and more convenient tools to protect and manage their data.

Computer security software technology for IBM and IBM-compatible processors has progressed, but not as fast as computer security hardware. Except in government installations, automated system security for other mainframe computers is even more spotty. Instead we now have mainframe computers with multimegabyte memory and billions of characters of on-line data storage, with only rudimentary security facilities delivered with the operating system software. Smaller operating systems tend to have even less security support, having been designed instead for compactness, simplicity, and speed.

Early automated security systems were "add-on" packages that extended operating system facilities to provide a modest level of control. The basic flaw in these systems was an inability to tighten security beyond the primitive level inherent in the system itself—enforcing stricter standards would damage the operating system. The early systems also involved modifications to the operating system, sometimes extensive ones, and often introduced maintenance and reliability headaches. Another drawback to such software security systems was that they only concentrated on surveillance, collecting data so an improper act could be verified after it was suspected and fault assigned.

Security software today solves these early problems. The newest operating systems include basic security mechanisms, which can be extended to provide a tightly controlled environment. A variety of vendors now offer automated security support for mainframe computers, mostly for IBM and IBM-compatible processors. Market pressure encourages improvements in the generally accepted "basic" features of these systems, and has been responsible for the emergence of several packages that improve operating system security support. These software packages solve the problem of modifications to the operating system by integrating without user modifications.

This user-base support is essential if security software is to be both comprehensive and efficient. It allows current systems to offer active security, in which an individual's authorization to perform actions and access data is checked *before* permission is granted to proceed. In addition, the current packages continue to collect the surveillance data used to audit system security performance and to fine-tune the access and use rules.

Current technology in automated security support includes installation without system modifications, comprehensive and integrated software within the operating system, and support programs. This technology is a great improvement over the add-on approach, and greatly enhances the integrity of the computer system and the competence of the security subsystem. In addition to improving the reliability of the secured computer environment, the current software can be much more difficult for an unauthorized person to disconnect, bypass, or deactivate. The trend toward easily installed, comprehensive, high-integrity, yet efficient software is bound to continue.

## HARDWARE TECHNOLOGY

Despite improvements in security software, the most exciting advances in computer security are being made in the hardware arena. Currently, the accepted means of identification are something one *knows* (e.g., a password), something one *has* (such as a token), and something one *is* (an identifying feature). Hardware solutions to the problems of identification are appearing fast and furiously on two of the above fronts: token recognition and feature identification.

The science of token recognition has come a long way. Today commercially available systems use proximity sensing of tokens to track the token holder at all times. These tokens may be small radio transmitters or "intelligent" ID cards only slightly thicker than a credit card that use microchip logic to generate an encoded radio frequency signal. These RF signals are then read by tracking receivers. Soon it will be economical to use such systems to secure doors, elevators, and other equipment, in addition to computers and their data.

Feature recognition is heavily sponsored, and often required, by government as the most dependable security identification system. Current technology in this technique is delivering commercially usable retina scanners capable of identifying one person from a repertoire of fifty stored individuals, in just under two seconds, with an error rate of one in a million.

Similar work is under way on voice-print recognition systems, which compare the distinctive spectrums of voice. The outstanding problem of these systems is the rejection of a user who has a valid reason for an altered voiceprint, such as a cold.

Another hardware recognition system currently on the market recognizes the characteristic geometry of an individual's palm print for security authorization.

All of these feature recognition devices share the disadvantage of being relatively expensive. Their high cost results from their required special-purpose devices and the high research and development costs of their emerging technologies. These devices also require special nonstandard connections to the computer system.

Many pressures are acting on the computer security environment to hurry technology improvements. The growth in on-line capacities and capabilities, along with the growing availability of terminals, increases the risk of easy intruder access. This increase in risk contributes to a high motivation for tight security and improved management and user attitudes. And government pressure on vendors and auditor pressure on management ensure the continued education of both vendors and management.

In response to these influences, new hardware and software security technologies have appeared and are unlikely to decrease in emphasis. All signs point to a necessary increase in computer security—we must learn how to prevent unauthorized misuse of data while allowing proper and normal use of our growing computer power.

# CHAPTER 25

## Remote Controls for Computer Data: Data Processing Firms Offer Security Packages

Mary Alice Crawford
Staff Writer
*Security Management*

Few firms can survive in today's business climate without the aid of computers. In-house data centers are commonplace, and protecting this facility and the information it handles is fast becoming a standard duty of security professionals.

From time to time, however, firms must employ the services of outside data processing firms to bridge the gap in data processing services while new in-house computers are being installed, to increase the range of software packages available to users, to test new applications being considered for use, or to relieve the in-house data processing load. In these cases, the most well thought-out computer security program is compromised instantly if critical data is handed over to outside firms without the proper security controls.

Because such sensitive information as personnel records, inventory and pricing figures, and financial planning or modeling is stored and processed routinely at outside computer facilities, most reputable data processing firms are aware of the need for security. Many emphasize available security controls in their marketing strategies and corporate literature.

"Security is very important to our client companies and to us," says Paul L. Jones, vice president, operations for Comshare, a data processing firm headquartered in Ann Arbor, MI. "As a result, we have a very healthy security program. From the president on down, everyone is very aware of security, and designated people monitor the controls daily."

In general, three types of security controls are considered essential for data processing firms: software controls to protect client data; physical security to control

Reprinted with the permission of the American Society for Industrial Security, from *Security Management*, July 1983, p 66.

187

access to the data center and support facilities; and personnel screening to check out employees who handle clients' data.

When clients open an account with Comshare, for example, they are given a random eight-letter password that permits access to their data. The first time the data are accessed by the client, the password must be changed to a private code. "No one in Comshare has access to the passwords," explains Jones. "We don't even know what the passwords are."

Customers of Martin Marietta Data Systems each receive a unique account number and identification code that permits access to their files only. Martin Marietta uses the Resources Access Control Facility (RACF), a program produced by IBM for data security and control. At the direction of the client, RACF permits a further breakdown of users, either as individuals or as groups, with certain privileges based on a need to know. Thus anyone who gets into the files can be restricted in what they can do with the data: read only; read and write only; or read, write, and alter. RACF then builds profiles of the users based on the data they are allowed to access and what they can do with it—verifies users, checks assigned authorizations, and provides an audit trail of authorized and unauthorized access attempts. Customer service representatives from Martin Marietta assist clients in establishing and monitoring these restrictions and assign ID codes.

I. P. Sharp Associates in Toronto, Canada, has developed its own security software. "Users have no access to the operating system," explains William Apsit, data center manager. In turn, "we are not even aware of the types of processing clients are doing. We only log the number of times a particular data base is used, not who uses what."

The range of data security available to clients is "enormous," says Apsit. To gain access to client files, the user must enter a correct account number and a password. The system reacts to certain attempts to sign on whether or not they are successful. Through an "access matrix," the client controls which users can access what information and what they can do with it. The client can restrict who can add passwords, for example, or limit the time of day certain data is accessible.

"We have one government client who tightly restricts access to certain data most of the time," says Apsit. "But at noon on Thursdays, the information is available to anyone."

The security packages available to clients add no cost or only a small charge to the processing fee. Comshare insists that clients use minimum levels of security, namely passwords that must be changed periodically, and encourages clients to select other options for file protection. The client handbook describes what is available in a section on security.

Even though data security is optional for clients of Martin Marietta Data Systems, "we are not silent about it," says Charles M. Elliott, director, quality assurance, security, and safety. "When a new account is being established, a representative from Martin Marietta goes through a questionnaire on the service with the client. "One question asks, 'are you interested in the security package?' The user then must make a conscious decision about security." A user guide also describes all security procedures and how RACF can be used.

Even though clients can reject specific controls on data, they are generally quite interested in the physical security precautions used to control access to data processing facilities and to the data center specifically. "Access to our building itself is restricted after business hours," explains Apsit. At all times, "no elevators stop on the data center floor, and entry is permitted only through a controlled stairway leading down from the floor above." Another type of physical security control divides client data among many disc drives, so that even if an intruder gained access to the center and tampered with a disc, no single client would risk losing all their data.

Comshare uses "multilevel security boundaries" in their data center, with various access restrictions to the office areas, and others to the computer locations and data storage vaults. "No programmers are allowed in the data center," says Jones, "and access is controlled by me." Basically, a card entry system is used, supplemented by push-button locks. All doors are alarmed and monitored by a computerized system checked by a security employee. The software detects unsuccessful entry attempts as well as those that are legitimate.

Security for the primary Martin Marietta data processing center in Orlando, FL is controlled by a security officer who supervises a guard force on duty around the clock. The guards monitor fire and water detection equipment, environmental controls, intrusion alarms, exterior CCTV cameras, and microwave motion detection equipment used at access points not easily scanned by cameras. Location indicators at the central station pinpoint the source of an alarm.

In addition, guards monitor access points around the facility not controlled by electronic readers and cypher locks. A combination of photo ID cards, color-coded badges and access cards, and visitor badges identify authorized personnel and their access privileges. To minimize the problem of tailgating, turnstiles have been installed at critical access points—those leading to the computer center from the outside and from an adjoining building. Despite the many security devices installed at the facility, "security personnel are the backbone of the physical security system," says Elliott.

If employees at the Martin Marietta data center work with government classified information, they receive a DoD security clearance. Background checks for other employees are done on a "discretionary basis now," says Elliott.

Employees of Comshare who have access to the data center are all bonded, and reference checks are completed before they are hired. When an employee leaves, all internal passwords are changed. Also employees are required to collaborate on sensitive programming or access tasks involving client data.

Redundancy is also a cornerstone of the personnel security procedures used by I. P. Sharp. At least two employees must be involved in any transaction. For example, "an operator cannot send out information based on a request by phone without approval," explains Apsit. "All the controls on line are useless if someone can just get information by phone."

The company checks the references of employment candidates before they are hired, and personal history records are documented if gaps are found. "It's a good company to work for," says Apsit, and turnover is low. Most programmers have been with the firm for at least seven years, and employees in senior positions have been with the company even longer.

Data processing centers use other checks and balances to maintain the integrity of client data. Backup and recovery plans and off-site storage of disc and tape duplicates are essential so service can continue without interruption. Comshare keeps all printouts and tapes in a security vault within the data center and keeps backups in an off-site security vault.

Scrambling and encryption services are available as options to clients, along with other communication security features. Computers at I. P. Sharp, for example, accept data sent from clients directly; no conversion is necessary. Apsit feels those systems that must convert a user's code to a specific machine code are "inherently unreliable" and susceptible to security breaches.

Martin Marietta offers such communications software features as line character checking to ensure that what is received at point B is the same as what was sent from point A; communication network services to validate trunk usage by blocking and deblocking data transmission on the trunks; and network certification to verify that all network and host computer software is synchronized.

In addition, Martin Marietta has developed an internal risk management review program to continually identify, analyze, and manage in a cost-effective way the risk exposures to the data center and the information it handles. Adds Apsit of I. P. Sharp, "when we undergo a security audit, about six people are here for five days to look at all the aspects of our data security."

Despite the many controls available to users of data processing services, "most commercial clients do not use the security package," says Elliott. While he has noticed an increase in RACF use, Elliott feels the rise has been caused in large part by the increased attention to data processing security by a client's auditors.

"Customers always complain about the security procedures we use," says Apsit. "They set up a method of control, like not permitting hard copy printouts of certain data, and then try to reverse this decision because they lose the original. It's just not possible."

Perhaps because of this user apathy, tales of data security compromise continue to fill newspaper headlines. Still, the technology used to permit the processing of information at record speeds continues to offer ways to protect sensitive documents from unscrupulous users. "We're a part of a very dynamic industry," says Elliott. "Technology changes almost daily."

# CHAPTER 26

## Computational Cryptography Is an EDP Security Aid

William E. Perry
Executive Director
ACUTE

Herbert S. Bright
President
Computation Planning, Inc.

While the security of an organization's assets is gaining increased corporate attention, EDP auditors, security personnel and computer systems analysts alike are aware that no system is one hundred percent secure. In a data processing system, the objective of controls is to increase the cost and effort required to penetrate it, thereby discouraging such attempts. The use of modern computational cryptographic techniques for this purpose should be evaluated not only by security professionals but also by data processing and auditing personnel concerned with all phases of a firm's business activity.

In this article, we will evaluate the potential uses of cryptography, and emphasize recent developments in cryptographic methods. We will also give a proper perspective to cryptography in the security program of a data processing installation.

### MANAGEMENT'S ROLE

In spite of appropriate bars and locks on its segments, a computer system remains vulnerable if the information it handles is in a form that can be understood, used or damaged by unauthorized persons without such access being immediately evident to management.[1] Unauthorized access to information may be perpetrated for improper or malevolent purposes or may simply occur by accident. Avoiding errors and omissions in planning that might lead to this vulnerability is the responsibility of management.

Reprinted with the permission of the American Society for Industrial Security, from *Security Management*, Feb 1979, p 60.

Only the integrity of system constraints can prevent the loss of management control over sensitive information or operations.

When planning physical and logical configurations in hardware/software installations, management has some choice in selecting "appropriate bars and locks." Protecting the information itself using cryptographic technology provides an additional level of management control that can be relatively low in cost and high in effectiveness.

Elementary applications of cryptographic protection can include:

- User authentication (off-line)
- Terminal authentication (on-line)
- Data link protection
- Network protection
- File access protection

The basic concept of modern cryptographic protection for information is to limit access to properly authorized persons merely by protecting an information key.

## MODERN SYSTEM SECURITY HAZARDS

The incorporation of cryptographic techniques in a well-implemented system can significantly raise security effectiveness even in the presence of several modern computing features such as the following:

- The sharing of multi-purpose data bases;
- Concurrent operation of multiple unrelated or related programs;
- Remote access by many users (continuous, on-demand, or scheduled; batch or interactive);
- Distributed Processing (computers geographically dispersed with or without related functions being performed in parts at various locations);
- Distributed Storage (single- or multiple-purpose data bases geographically dispersed); and
- Economy of Scale (resource sharing in large systems).

## CRYPTOGRAPHY CONCEPTS

The transformation of discrete data into cryptographic elements prevents the data from being recognized, used or modified without these actions becoming obvious. We will consider only reversible crypto processes or those methods that are capable of subsequently reversing the encryption (decrypting) to recover the original text.*

---

*Irreversible or "one way cipher" transformations can be useful in system security procedures and in key generation.

Exhibit 26–1 shows the relationship between input data (the plaintext or cleartext); the encrypted data (the cipher or cipher-text); the data used to control encryption and decryption (the key); and the encrypt/decrypt operations. A system that uses the arrangement of elements shown in Exhibit 26–1 involves the simplest and most basic use of cryptography.

Many writers distinguish between encoding (conversion of message elements to a different form using a substitution process) and enciphering (transforming message elements using an algorithmic process). Enciphering transformations include both resequencing and in-sequence conversion.

C. E. Shannon, whose 1949 work is fundamental to much subsequent work,[2] separates the functions into the following categories:

- *Concealment Systems*, also known as steganography, in which the very existence of sensitive information is concealed;
- *Privacy Systems*, in which the physical form of information is transformed and reconverted by special equipment assumed to be accessible to unauthorized users; and
- *"True" Secrecy Systems*, in which the information is modified only logically. Unauthorized persons can be assumed to be aware of the information's existence and to have any equipment needed to decrypt it into plaintext except the key.

We assume that the algorithm(s) used for data transformation and all necessary systems information are completely public and that only the key is physically secure. The key is known only to persons authorized to access the information protected by cryptographic transformation. This assumption is consistent with the National Bureau of Standards' Federal Data Encryption Standard (DES).

The long key information can be retained as physically secure or can be generated from seed by using a short key which starts an appropriate random number generator.[3] Note that appropriate steps (such as block-skipping in the key stream) must be used to prevent "backtracking" to recover the seed of the random number stream.[4] If these precautions are omitted, the process would be vulnerable to "known plaintext attack."

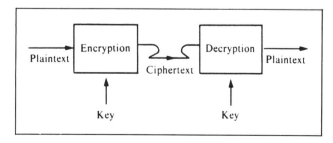

**Exhibit 26–1.**   Encryption and decryption.

## CONVENTIONAL SYSTEM SECURITY FEATURES

Practical encryption requires hardware/software that performs both the encryption and decryption functions. The vendor-supplied facilities provided to users of conventional general-purpose computers include a variety of control mechanisms. Among the most common are one or more of the following:

- *Access Control Algorithms*—special commands in control languages, which may or may not be in a "restricted mode." They may provide for entering/leaving such a mode, give special procedures accessing restricted address domains in memory, and establish user-level procedures for evoking such processes.
- *Access Control Hardware*—"key-lock" mechanisms for memory access control.
- *Nonchangeable Program or Control Storage*—Read Only Memory (ROM) and Programmable-Read-Only Memory (PROM), which may have contents written or changed only through unusual physical processes not normally available to users; Hard-Wired Logic in which components or assemblies of components perform fixed functions.
- *Encapsulation of Systems*—limitation of access to systems by isolating them physically or logically, or by providing barriers between sensitive information and the outside world. (One widely used aspect of encapsulation, especially in military classified systems, is the dedication of a machine to a single task and perhaps to local use only).
- *System Logging Features*—data recorded by executive systems, readable either by machines or by persons. These features provide a running journal of machine usage.

Several of these security methods might be fairly effective except that all require programs (including executive systems and applications) that must be "maintainable." Programs that are assumed to be imperfect in plan or construction must be capable of being changed periodically to correct errors and omissions. Thus, someone must be able to read and change programs and sensitive data, meaning that all security features must eventually be bypassed.

In general, the bypassing of such features merely requires an understanding of their characteristics and the ability to gain access to the system and the tools for change. This fact limits the extent to which systems such as those mentioned previously can be used in "modern" ways.

## BREAKING SYSTEM SECURITY

Most of the system security mechanisms listed previously represent elementary control algorithms which, once understood, can be bypassed readily by any of the following reasonably skilled computer technicians.

- *System programmers* are responsible for maintaining and updating system software. They are, of course, continually required to bypass system security features to perform their basic work. Consequently, not only do system programmers have the requisite information and skill to break security features, but they become practiced in the use of such techniques through frequent opportunity to perform the task.
- *System operators* have physical access to all local input/output equipment and to recorded data such as automatically-generated system logs and must be able to bring a system into operation from "down" status. Therefore, they have the skills and also the opportunity to use a system in a broad range of unauthorized ways. In conspiracy with highly skilled programmers, especially system programmers, a competent operator could perform many acts of malfeasance without detection.
- *Application programmers*, even without access to central system hardware and without special knowledge of system software and its maintenance methods, are able to break many kinds of safeguards. Because few installations include hardware memory-protect features, and fewer yet use them effectively, even the most sensitive system files may be invaded readily from remote terminals by using the elementary technique of "browsing" (dumping randomly chosen areas of memory to locate sensitive data). Sophisticated remote users may apply more advanced methods such as "piggyback" (intercepting and modifying legitimate messages), "trapdoor" (planting of unauthorized entries to a system), or "Trojan Horse" (including improper or unauthorized coding in service routines).
- *Users* of programs are persons or organizations that provide input data to existing programs and receive results. Unlike programmers, who produce or maintain programs, users have little opportunity to engage in computer malfeasance other than "fake payee" and similar data entry ploys, which are readily caught by conventional auditing practice. Thus, this largest group of people with access to computers does not constitute a hazard to system and file security.

Some other risks involve fringe persons who would not be expected to constitute a meaningful hazard: disgruntled employees or ex-employees, indignant objectors to some aspects of an organization's activities, or individuals with emotional concerns or other interests that do not involve a desire for personal gain through sabotage. Strangely enough, such persons constitute a significant fraction of all the cases of computer malfeasance detected to date.

According to Robert Courtney, a well-known IBM speaker on the subject of computer security, these cases are among the two or three largest sources of risk. Many of the recorded cases of this class of computer abuse involve violation of widely used physical security precautions, and we believe that most are detected promptly. Those incidents that involve information security violations, such as scratching backup tapes or writing over transaction history files, could be controlled through the use of crypto methods. Those cases that involve physical security violations, such as the manual degaussing of file tapes, would not be solved by cryptography.

## GROWING COMPUTER LITERACY

A 1972 report by the American Federation of Information Processing Societies (AFIPS), estimated computing technical employment in the United States as of about 1970.[5] Although the categories of employment used in the report do not correspond to the categories we used, the following estimates are meaningful:

| | |
|---|---|
| Systems Analysts | 150,000 |
| Programmers (all kinds and levels) | 210,000 |
| Computer Operators | 200,000 |

Total computing personnel, including clerical support workers, were estimated at one million. These numbers include those in the computer and related equipment manufacturing industry, who are competent although not necessarily employed in high risk situations, such as positions in fiduciary institutions. Educational levels for all programmers and analysts were summarized as about 0.5% Ph.D., 11% M.A. and M.S., and 58% B.A. and B.S.

These data were compiled early in the period of rapid growth of dedicated minicomputer application to business problems, which started in the late 1960's and continues unabated. Computing education and training, in related and unrelated fields in higher education, and even at the trade school level, constitutes a major specialty in teaching. Thus, ''computer literate'' people entering the work force continue to represent a significant percentage of the total.

## APPLYING CRYPTO TECHNIQUES

In opposition to the conventional system security features mentioned previously, cryptographic methods protect the information itself by transforming it into a representation that is meaningless to a person or program without proper decryption.

Encryption, using modern computational techniques, consists of applying a data element, the key, to plaintext or clear information (See Exhibit 26–1). The result of encryption is cipher or ciphertext which, in general, looks like a string of random numbers or characters. The cipher contains all the original information in disguised form. Decryption requires use of the reverse transformation under control of the same key to transform the cipher back into plaintext.

The invertibility of the reversible process is the first and most crucial requirement in the cryptographic procedure. An authorized user must be certain that the original information will come back correctly. Any cryptographic process should be tested exhaustively before release for use to insure its reliability. Furthermore, any soundly implemented encryption process, even a highly complex one, should permit encryption on one kind of machine and decryption on another.[6]

Second, for many uses a cryptographic process should be highly sensitive to small changes or errors in the ciphertext. If a cipher is transmitted, copied or changed from one medium to another (for example, magnetic tape to magnetic disc) any small error could result in largely or completely incorrect plaintext upon decryption.

This fact has both useful and hazardous connotations. On one hand, it provides a highly sensitive error-detecting mechanism; cipher errors become obvious upon decryption. Thus, apparently correct decrypted plaintext is likely to be free of cipher transmission error. But, any data segment containing an error is likely to be useless.

The modern approach to controlling data loss through ciphertext error is to perform encryption/decryption on data in blocked form so that any error affects only the block containing it.

A third requirement is that decryption without presentation of the correct key should be so difficult and costly as to discourage cryptanalysis (development of means for decryption by an unauthorized user).

A fourth requirement of useful cryptographic methods is that they should be economically acceptable, both in preparation and in use. Protection can be applied to existing applications without a major increase in complexity. Usage cost for software encryption/decryption in large systems can range from what we would call "high" (perhaps one dollar per thousand characters for DES emulation), to what we would call "low" (perhaps one dollar per million characters for a simple long key system). Usage on small quantities of data or with random access files may call for careful planning to assure low costs. In all, cost should not be a discouraging factor for use of modern cryptographic methods.

## CRYPTOGRAPHIC PROCESSES

Encryption changes the emphasis from protecting system-algorithm integrity (which is difficult and perhaps unrealistic to support) to physically securing key information (which might be as small as a single number or as large as any file to be encrypted). Thus, key generation and management become important issues in any crypto application.

The two elements of the cryptographic process are data preparation and the application of the cryptographic algorithm. Data preparation includes extracting and assembling data elements to be encrypted into appropriate segments. Such elements might be as small as one bit or might constitute long messages or large tables. In general, we recommend selectivity in encryption. All sensitive information and enough format and pointer information to make the information innocuous until decrypted properly should be encrypted.

Encryption methods include use of special-purpose hardware to execute DES or other algorithms. Because secret keys are used to control any encryption process, generating and managing keys is of central importance to the effectiveness of any cryptographic process. The primary performance requirement of key generation is the suppression of the memonic factors (birthdays, street addresses, any number visible in an office) that have always caused numerical combination locks to be subject to penetration by guesswork. Any key should bear no recognizable relationship to any other key or to any available number.

## MEASURING CRYPTOGRAPHIC SECURITY

Breaking a published algorithm (for which only the key is kept secret) could be as simple as finding an analytical solution for reversal of the algorithm. In practice, no algorithm that is subject to such solution by a presumed finite amount of mathematical effort would be likely to withstand serious scrutiny at the present time. Surprisingly, some computer users still use trivial disguises to hide sensitive numbers. Usually, the principal effect of such disguises is to call attention to the number, and to encourage some curious, and possibly competent, observer to uncover it merely as an intellectual exercise.

One still occasionally hears or reads the archaic term code breaking. In cryptographic parlance, "code" usually refers to a strict substitution cipher scheme involving replacement of a list of words or numbers according to a secret transfer table or code book. Such schemes are found most often in fictional spy stories and can be no more secure than the transfer tables.

Oddly enough, one recent paper commented, ". . . a sharp programmer can, with a little effort, break the code . . ."[7] In fact, no competent cryptographic process should be subject to such breaking, but essentially all password schemes, including the one described in the paper have precisely the weakness the author ascribes to encryption.

In spite of published rumors that it contains government-known trapdoor weakness, speculation about DES algorithm breaking has concentrated on brute force methods or on exhaustion procedures in which every possible key is tested until one is found that seems to work. For DES's key length of 56 bits, nearly $10^{17}$ tests would be needed to break the code. At a million tests per second, this process would take three thousand years; at a trillion tests per second, (a feat said to be possible by 1990 on a special-purpose machine[8]) it would take one day. Changing the key regularly can frustrate any brute force attack.

Only a few dozen persons in the US outside the military science community possess modern computer cryptanalytic skills. Even if, as we expect, many people become competent in use of cryptographic methods, we feel that the economic infeasibility of cryptanalysis of a competent crypto application constitutes an acceptable level of protection for many situations.

## COMPUTER SECURITY FALLACIES

Many people having management roles in organizations using computers believe that unusual skills such as those possessed by computer scientists and software engineers (persons who design and develop major executive systems) are needed to bypass the system security features in common use. We believe this idea is a fallacy. We feel some other common beliefs are *incorrect* and lead to unjustified management complacency. Some of these erroneous ideas are:

1.  *Password access controls in vendor systems are effective.*

This concept was refuted previously when we mentioned password vulnerability to simple browsing.

2.  *Locally-developed table control schemes can provide additional security.*[9]

These schemes are claimed to provide significant protection but are even less secure than a password. All that is needed to compromise the system is some information from the job card of an authorized user.

3.  *Locally-developed accounting controls (use of account numbers as controls) can add meaningfully to file security by limiting system usage.*

This precaution is ineffective because the tables of account numbers are readily available for perusal through the browsing method. In addition, the numbers are accessible to anyone who can use one of the more advanced methods of system invasion mentioned previously. Account numbers can also be copied from job cards or listings. These tables are very useful to a would-be machine time thief because they allow him to pick appropriate numbers for various kinds of fraudulent machine usage.

4.  *System-produced records constitute a credible audit trail of computer usage including access to sensitive data and programs.*

These records can be bypassed by anyone who can access certain elements of system programs or who can use the system in some "test" mode (for instance, an off-shift operator).

5.  *Keeping machine language or assembly language unavailable for user programming protects systems against misuse.*

This last statement can be bypassed in any installation with facilities and personnel to perform local software maintenance. Additional test versions of systems permit accessing and modifying programs which can be used to add or correct vendor-supplied system features.

In summary, management cannot justify complacency regarding the safety of sensitive files by saying that compromise would require rare skills on the part of a would-be malefactor.

Because cryptography offers potential for improved security, its benefits need to be evaluated by those persons responsible for controls in an organization. The merit of using cryptography in a specific corporation should be weighed carefully.

## REFERENCES

1.  This section is substantially reproduced from H. S. Bright and R. L. Enison, "Cryptography Using Modular Software Elements," Proc. NCC 1976, pp 113–123, AFIPS 1976. Used by permission.
2.  C. E. Shannon, "Communications Theory of Secrecy Systems." Bell System Technical Journal, October 1949, pp 656–715. (This paper contains the only mathematical proof of cryptographic strength ever published.)

3. H. S. Bright and R. L. Enison, "Cryptography."
4. See cryptopak™ Technical Description, 3/17/77 version, and HARD-NODE Technical Description, 3/31/77 version, Computation Planning, Inc., Bethesda, MD 20014.
5. B. Gilchrist and R. E. Weber, "Employment of Trained Computer Personnel—A Quantitative Survey," Proc. SJCC '72, AFIPS Press 1972, pp 641–648.
6. H. S. Bright, COMPLAN® TN-913–9 dtd 9/13/76, "Cross-Machine Encryption Testing."
7. R. Marsh, "Making Data More Secure," *Datamation* 22/10, October 1976, pp 67–69.
8. "National Bureau of Standards Workshop on Cryptography in Support of Computer Security," NBS, Gaithersburg, MD, September 21–22, 1976.
9. R. Marsh, pp. 67–69.

# PART VI

## Physical Security Issues

A key part of protecting computers involves measures designed to ensure the physical safety of the hardware and to limit unauthorized access to it. The articles in this final section deal with such considerations as the choice of site for a computer installation, special security concerns in open-plan offices, equipment selection for controlling physical access to the computer facility, and fire protection for computers. Four categories of computer hardware accessories that contribute to security are examined in a 1985 update on what is new in computer security accessories.

A related issue, the disposition of the input and output materials associated with computer use, is also reviewed since access to these materials can often provide valuable information to persons with less than honorable intentions.

# CHAPTER 27

## Seven Fallacies Confuse Computer Fire Safety

Robert V. Jacobson, CPP
President
International Security Technology, Inc.

Unquestionably, fire safety is an important consideration in prudent computer security management. Regrettably, however, many sources that purport to describe good practices for computer room fire safety, in fact tend to perpetuate a number of fallacies. This is probably a result of the mistaken notion that fire safety is simply a matter of common sense.

Just like any other profession, including security management, good fire safety practice depends upon the orderly application of methods and techniques carefully developed over the past hundred years by experienced fire safety engineers. Computer room managers would make a serious mistake to rely on anything less than fully professional advice on fire safety. Before substantial building alterations are made and expensive detection and extinguishment equipment are purchased, one would also be well advised to obtain solid professional advice. One should consult the authoritative publications of the National Fire Protection Association, including the provisions of the National Electrical Code.

The following seven fallacies are all based on misconceptions about fire safety I have heard expressed by data processing people. I present these fallacies in light of my own understanding of the basics of fire safety principles as they apply to data processing facilities.

### 1. COMPUTERS SHOULD BE INSTALLED IN FIRE-PROOF BUILDINGS

This fallacy is actually based on a slight deception. The fact of the matter is that the National Fire Protection Association forbids the use of the word "fireproof" in its

Reprinted with permission, from *Security Management*, Aug 1979, p 60. © 1979 by International Security Technology, Inc.

professional writings. It does so because the word has no useful meaning. *No* material and *no* building can be "fireproof." The notion that fireproof means the same thing as noncombustible is probably the source of the fallacy.

The fact that steel will not burn simply is not important. The important characteristic of steel is that at 1,800° F it begins to lose its structural strength. Thus, although the structural steel framework of a building may not be consumed in a fire, it may very well lose its strength and collapse. The most interesting demonstration of this effect was the fire at the Convention Center in Chicago a few years ago. The building collapsed in a fire fueled by the combustible materials in exhibits and display booths.

If the structure of the building is noncombustible, the structure itself will not contribute to the fuel. As a rule, the combustion of the contents of a building produces the heat and corrosive gases that do the damage. The important point to remember is that any material ceases to serve its function if heated to high enough a temperature. Perhaps the most dramatic examples of this is a burning bar (a tool used in bank robberies), which can burn through concrete.

This first fallacy teaches the importance of thinking of fire safety as the result of a number of actions taken together. It is not enough for the building itself to be fire resistant. Also important is controlling both the amount of fuel in the building and the number of ways to ignite it. In addition, one must think about the means of detecting and extinguishing fires.

Finally, one must ensure that the personnel in the building are trained to respond effectively should a fire occur. I will touch on all of these points later.

## 2. HALON IS AN IDEAL FIRE EXTINGUISHMENT SYSTEM

Most security managers are familiar with Halon, a fire extinguishment agent that has come into widespread use in computer rooms. Stored in the form of a liquid under high pressure (360 psig typically), it is released as a gas into the air of a room when a fire is detected by an independent fire detection system. Halon puts out fires by interfering with the chemical reaction of combustion. Assuming a suitable concentration of Halon is achieved, typically between five and seven percent,* it will extinguish open fires quite rapidly.

Being a colorless, odorless and inert gas, Halon, having extinguished the fire, can be ventilated from the room without causing any damage to the room's contents. Rapid response and absence of damaging side effects make Halon particularly ap-

---

*George C. Koth of the National Fire Protection Association comments, "Halon should not be used in concentrations of over 10% in places where there are people. People can stand a 7% concentration of Halon for five minutes and thus do not need a pre-discharge alarm. If the concentration used is 10%, a predischarge alarm would be needed as people can stand that concentration for only one minute. Systems using Halon are normally cross-zoned: detectors on two separate systems must be activated before the Halon is released to minimize false-alarm discharge."

pealing. Furthermore, Halon, being a gas, can work its way into hidden spaces water or dry chemicals cannot reach. Because of these and other characteristics, Halon is often described as an "ideal" fire extinguishment agent.

While Halon is extremely attractive as an extinguishment agent in rooms holding high value or critical items, one should be aware of some of its drawbacks. First of all, Halon is quite expensive. Typically, the cost of a Halon extinguishment system will be about four times that of an automatic sprinkler system, if installed during new construction. In the case of an existing building, Halon is often less expensive for protecting a relatively small area.

Once the Halon has been discharged, one must recharge the containers with a new supply, which will cost about 40% of the initial installation cost. As a consequence, operations people are rightfully concerned about the expense of an unnecessary discharge of Halon. Often substantial emphasis is placed on fire alarm response procedures, which include delaying the discharge of the Halon until the factual presence of a fire is verified. It would certainly be unfortunate to install an expensive fire extinguishment system and then have it rendered ineffective by a zealous operator overreacting to this part of the procedure.

The operation of the Halon extinguishment system depends upon a somewhat complicated chain of events. First the fire must be detected, either by an automatic fire detection system or by a human. Then the Halon control system is activated. In the typical installation, an alarm sounds indicating that the Halon will be discharged after a delay, usually of one minute. During the delay, air conditioning units must stop, ventilating ducts must be closed off, personnel must evacuate the area, and doors must be closed and secured. Then, the control unit must open the valves or, in some installations, rupture frangible diaphragms to release the Halon from the storage containers. Finally, the Halon must disperse into the room and an effective concentration be achieved at the locus of the fire. If any of these events fails to take place, the Halon may be ineffective in extinguishing the fire.*

Once the Halon has been released, one must then allow ample time for it to extinguish the fire effectively and for the fire location to cool below the ignition temperature. Then, and only then, can the room be ventilated. Of course, if the fire was not in fact completely extinguished, there is a danger that it may rekindle. If this occurs, one is faced with the difficult situation of having exhausted the primary extinguishment system. (In some installations, a dual supply of Halon is provided to overcome this difficulty. But this arrangement increases the installed cost by a significant factor.)

Finally, some evidence suggests that Halon is not entirely free of life safety hazards. Laboratory experiments indicate that Halon at relatively high concentrations, 12% or more, can cause arrhythmic heartbeat problems. If Halon does not extinguish the fire and is heated above 900° F, it tends to decompose into highly toxic compounds.

---

*"The Halon sequence is more complex than sprinklers, but sprinklers fail despite their simplicity. Look at the record. In twenty-five years of use, Halon 1301 has been failure-free in all fire incidences," notes Dr. Herbert S. Boden of DuPont Company.

While the gas is entirely inert under normal circumstances and at low concentrations, the difficulties just described *do* exist and need to be considered carefully by a qualified engineer when planning the installation and by management when developing alarm response procedures.

None of these points are intended to suggest that Halon is a bad extinguishment agent. Halon has an excellent combination of qualities for use as an extinguishment system under the raised floor in the computer room, in a tape-storage vault where difficult-to-replace magnetic tapes are stored, and in rooms in which telephone data communications or other complex electronic hardware is installed. Likewise, it seems ideal for use in a rare book room or other facility with irreplaceable contents. My point is simply that Halon, like any product, is not ideally suited to all situations. It must be matched carefully to the requirement at hand.

## 3. SMOKE DETECTORS MAKE THE BEST FIRE EXTINGUISHMENT SYSTEM

This is another "trick" fallacy. The alert reader noticed the reference to smoke detectors as fire extinguishers. Of course, smoke detectors do not extinguish fires. I include this as a fallacy because on several different occasions I have seen such a confusion made in writing. It seems unlikely that one can make wise decisions about fire safety if unable to distinguish between the meanings of the words detection and extinguishment. In a critical place like a data processing facility, prompt detection of fires plays an important role in skillful fire safety management. Products-of-combustion detectors, often referred to as smoke detectors, can provide such prompt detection. The important point is to distinguish clearly the function of each element in an overall, integrated fire safety program.

## 4. WATER DAMAGE IS THE MOST SERIOUS THREAT TO COMPUTERS

This fallacy is based on the curious line of reasoning that one should avoid using a fire extinguishment agent that will damage the source of the fire. A horrifying example of this fallacy occurred during the 1975 fire at the Browns Ferry Nuclear Plant near Decatur, AL. The fire burned for six-and-a-half hours before the plant manager finally permitted the local fire department to use water, which extinguished the fire in fifteen minutes. The plant suffered direct losses of $10 million, was closed for eighteen months and had to buy power from other plants at a cost of $200 million for fossil fuel.

Experience has shown over and over again that the most important objective in combatting any fire is to extinguish it as quickly as possible. As long as the fire continues to burn, it continues to do damage, some of it remote from the location of the fire itself. Major damage can be done to building contents, particularly delicate electronic apparatus, by the corrosive by-products of burning plastics used increasingly in furniture, interior finishes, and electrical apparatus. Many of these plastics include chlorine which, when it burns, forms highly corrosive compounds related to hydrochloric acid. While smoke damaged objects may have been completely unaffected by heat and flames, they are, nonetheless, often totally destroyed by corrosion.

Another example of this fallacy in action was presented by the devastating fire at the US Military Records Center in St. Louis, Missouri. This large, six-story, reinforced concrete building was designed specifically to store paper records of military personnel. The designers evidently felt that the installation of a sprinkler system would threaten the paper records with water damage! Consequently, they decided not to install any fire extinguishment system. Ultimately, as might have been foreseen, a fire started. The paper records provided ample fuel, and the heat was so intense that *portions of the reinforced concrete roof actually collapsed.* Had the local fire department been less effective than it was, the entire building would have been destroyed.

## 5. DRY PIPE SPRINKLER SYSTEMS ARE BETTER FOR COMPUTER FACILITIES THAN CONVENTIONAL WET PIPE SPRINKLER SYSTEMS

We should begin by explaining that the wet pipe sprinkler system is so named because, naturally, the pipes making up the system are constantly filled with water. When a fire breaks out and room air temperature rises to a specific level, typically 165°F, in the vicinity of a sprinkler head, a fusible link in the sprinkler head opens, allowing a plug to fall out of the sprinkler head. This permits water to discharge, striking a deflector, which distributes the water in a fine spray over an area twelve to fifteen feet in diameter.

Dry pipe sprinkler systems were devised to protect unheated buildings where wet pipe sprinklers would be damaged by the water freezing in the pipes. Water is prevented from entering the piping by a valve, which is held shut by air pressure inside the piping. When a fire causes a sprinkler head to open, the compressed air in the pipe escapes through the sprinkler head. This allows the valve to open. Water enters the piping, and is discharged onto the fire.

A dry pipe sprinkler system has two obvious disadvantages. The first is increased complexity. Secondly, because the pipes are not filled with water, a substantial delay occurs between the time the sprinkler head opens and the time water begins to fall on the fire. This means extinguishment action is delayed and we have already stressed how important a prompt attack is for successful fire extinguishment.

Despite these disadvantages, dry pipe sprinkler systems were evidently thought superior for computer rooms precisely because of the delay in initiating water discharge. This delay period could be used to assess the seriousness of the situation, and if the fire appeared not to be serious, the water flow could be stopped by closing the OS&Y (open stem and yoke) valve to avoid undue water damage. In some cases, it has been argued that computer rooms face a serious danger from having a sprinkler head mechanically damaged, causing it to open. Neither of these arguments is cogent in this situation. First of all, if a fire is hot enough to cause a sprinkler head to operate, the fire is going to do far more damage than the water would. Concerns about water damage should take second place. Too, sprinkler heads are quite rugged and must be treated *very carelessly* before they will discharge accidentally.

Another reason a dry pipe sprinkler system should not be used in computer rooms is that it is subject to substantially higher levels of corrosion in the piping. Thus, when water is discharged onto a fire, the initial supply of water will tend to be heavily loaded with scale which could block some sprinkler heads. This scale will contaminate the computer hardware and represent a serious clean-up problem after the fire. The relatively clean water from a wet pipe system falling onto the computer hardware would be preferable.

Pre-action sprinkler systems are similar in operation to dry pipe systems, except that water flow is controlled by a fire detection system. Thus, if a head is accidently broken, water is *not* discharged. For this reason pre-action systems are often recommended for computer rooms.

## 6. FIRE PROTECTION EFFORTS SHOULD BE CONCENTRATED ON THE COMPUTER ROOM

Two basic reasons justify striving toward a high level of fire safety in a computer facility. The first reason is to protect its valuable physical assets. In almost every case the organization's insurance manager will recognize this major loss exposure and will provide proper insurance coverage.

This means that the second reason, continuity of service, often is unrecognized as a major loss exposure. While the data processing function obviously cannot be performed without the computers, proper functioning also requires a supply of electricity, air conditioning, uninterrupted telephone service, the availability of master files recorded on magnetic tape, special preprinted forms such as checks and stock certificates and a host of other ingredients. In short, all of the constituents of the data processing facility, wherever located, must be carefully evaluated to assure that each is properly protected—not only against fire but against vandalism, sabotage, normal wear and tear, and any other factors that could interrupt the functioning of the data processing facility. The trap of concentrating all the fire safety (and security) attention on the computer room must be avoided.

A recent fire in Massachusetts illustrated this point most effectively. The data processing facility was located on the third floor of an unsprinklered, concrete-on-steel office building. A fire began on the first floor of the building. Evidently the fire was not major, as the fire department confined the actual flame and high temperature to an area approximately fifteen feet in diameter. However, corrosive smoke from the burning plastic insulation on electric wiring traveled up through an electric service chase and poured out into the third floor computer room. While the computers were not exposed to high temperatures, they were severely damaged by the corrosive smoke. Operating reliability, which had been in the range of 98 to 99 percent, slowly decreased over several months as individual circuit boards operated more and more erratically. Two computer systems were declared a total loss, severe corrosion damage was done to two more, and the fifth one, farthest from the source of the smoke, sustained minor damage. The total loss was estimated to be at least $5 million. (See NFPA #75, which requires the walls, ceiling and floor of a computer room to withstand fire for one hour.)

Had proper consideration been given to the exposure of the computer room to damage from fires in other parts of the building, *this serious loss would not have occurred.* The fire barriers between floors in the building had been breached in the electric conduit chase, a common problem in office buildings. When new electric conduits are installed, the contractor probably will not patch the hole made in each of the floor slabs. These holes, aligned vertically, serve as chimneys, which spread a fire or its smoke from floor to floor. At a cost of a few hundred dollars, the openings could be closed up, blocking the passage of the smoke and preventing the resulting damage.

## 7. FIRE EMERGENCY TRAINING IS UNNECESSARY: IF THE FIRE ALARM SOUNDS, THE PROCEDURE IS SIMPLY TO RUN

This ostrich-like approach to a serious problem has grave consequences. First of all, the absence of a properly thought out fire emergency management program may result in loss of human life. As an absolute minimum, a proper fire evacuation plan is essential complete with fire wardens, searchers, alternate exit routes, and rally points at a place of safety. Furthermore, fire drills must be held regularly. Fire drills should take place at least twice yearly in multi-story buildings, be unannounced, and evacuate all occupants of a floor into the fire stairwells. Particular care should be taken to see that handicapped personnel can evacuate the building safely. Plans could also be made to remove essential documents, magnetic tapes, disk packs and the like, provided the damage from a fire is not immediate.

Untrained employees cannot operate portable fire extinguishers correctly in an emergency, and probably will forget all about such extinguishers. This brings us to another vital aspect of fire safety. Experience has shown, time and time again, that fire damage often increases unnecessarily because overzealous employees will try repeatedly to extinguish a fire with portable extinguishers before notifying the local fire department. *The first and unbreakable rule of every fire response procedure should be an immediate call to the fire department!* Only then, if the employee can do so at no personal risk, should he attempt to extinguish the fire with a portable extinguisher. Of course, if he is successful, he may prevent serious damage and interruption to data processing functions. The alternatives if he fails to take that crucial first step and is unsuccessful with the extinguisher, may be tragic.

This brings us to the last point about fire emergency management. Often, relatively simple measures for damage control, planned in advance, can drastically reduce loss. The most common example of this is the use of plastic sheeting to protect computer hardware from smoke and water damage during a fire. Other possibilities include emergency controls for heating and ventilating systems to allow prompt evacuation of smoke and to prevent introduction of smoke; the availability of replacement windows, pumps, and other suitable materials to deal with the damage that can be caused by a fire; and storing duplicates of vital information in a separate location.

The objective of this article has not been to criticize any particular fire safety technique or extinguishment agent. Rather, I want to stress the importance of competent, professional advice when making decisions about this important element of data processing security. The well-rounded security officer will want to refer to authoritative sources to expand his own knowledge. When faced with important decisions about building design, construction and layout, and about fire detection and extinguishment devices and procedures, the security officer will seek professional assistance just as he does in dealing with other specialized security problems.

## ADDITIONAL SOURCES

*Editor's Note:* The following sources are recommended for anyone wishing further information about points made in this article.

*NFPA No. 75, Protection of Electronic Computer/Data Processing Equipment 1976* and NFPA 12A, Halogenated Extinguishing *Agent Systems Halon 1301 1977*, both published by the National Fire Protection Association, 470 Atlantic Ave., Boston, MA 02210.

Report published by Underwriters' Laboratories, Inc.: File NC535, Project 71NK8162, January 17, 1972, *Fact-Finding Report on Extinguishment of Class A and B Fires in Electronic Computer Rooms With Halon 1301*, sponsored by Safety First Products Corp., Elmsford, New York.

Chapter VII, "Fire Protection System," of *Standard Practice for the Fire Protection of Essential Electronic Equipment Operations*, published August 1978 by the US Department of Commerce, National Fire Prevention and Control Administration.

Report by a special review group, "Recommendations Related to Browns Ferry Fire," (NUREG-0050), published February 1976 by the US Nuclear Regulatory Commission.

"Fire Protection for Computer Installations: A Cost-Effectiveness Comparison," by Jack A. Wood, Viking Fire Protection Associates, Inc., published June 1971 in *Instruments and Control Systems.*

The following articles were published in the *Fire Journal* of the National Fire Protection Association:

"Automatic Sprinkler Protection for Essential Electrical and Electronic Equipment," by Dan W. Jacobson, January 1967.

"Water and Electronics Can Mix," by Donald J. Keigher, November 1968.

"Looking at Fire Hazards," May 1970.

"Browns Ferry Revisited," by Andrew J. Pryor, May 1977.

# CHAPTER 28

## Security in the Trenches

Charles H. Norris, Jr., PE
Manager, Structural/Electrical Systems Group
H.H. Robertson Co.

In today's "open plan" office buildings, which use large unobstructed interior spaces, the wiring for communication services and electrical power are usually distributed beneath the flooring. Telephone, computer intelligence, and power cables appear to grow out of the carpet. Gone are the old-fashioned "tombstone" outlets mounted above the floor line. The convenient in-floor outlets are widely distributed throughout the office in staggered patterns, making it possible to move work stations virtually anywhere on the floor quickly and inexpensively. Service is always close at hand.

To handle this need for mobility, cables linking computer terminals, word processors, telephones, and video displays pass through a system of parallel steel raceways within the floor. The raceways lead to covered steel trenches running under the carpeting throughout every floor of the building. The trenches, in turn, lead to secure service rooms in core areas of each floor, where facilities personnel control the services provided to specific office locations. Raceways carrying communications cables normally alternate with raceways containing power lines.

Designed specifically for new construction in structural steel frame or concrete frame buildings, these "in-the-floor" systems provide greater physical security than designs that run cables through the ceiling plenum, on the surface of the floor, or through a false plenum under the floor (see Exhibit 28–1). But even systems entirely within the floor are not totally secure. The same raceways often must serve both sensitive and non-sensitive departments located on the same floor of a building. Access to the cables inside the raceways is virtually unrestricted. Anyone can open an outlet and casually attach small electronic interception devices to cables carrying proprietary information. Obviously, the regular inspection of hundreds or even thousands of outlets in a large office building is impractical.

Another type of in-floor distribution system, however, offers a higher level of security by physically separating electrical power and telephone lines from cables

Reprinted with the permission of the American Society for Industrial Security, from *Security Management*, Nov. 1982, p. 35.

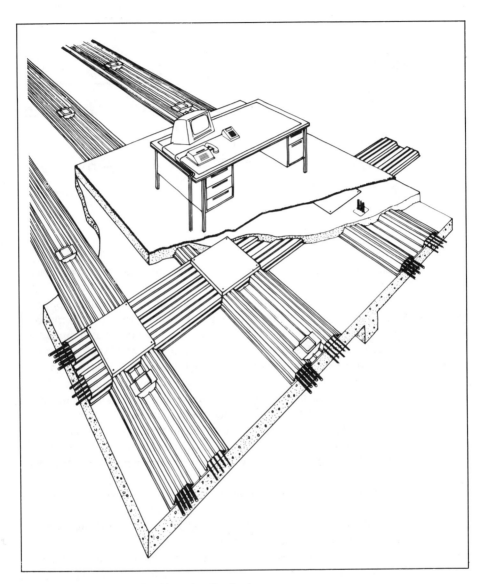

**Exhibit 28–1.**   ''In-the-floor'' service distribution system.

carrying sensitive information. In addition to its inherent security, the system provides electromagnetic shielding and increased capacity.

In this system, three steel raceways are used instead of two. One raceway houses electrical power wiring. The second contains low-voltage cable for non-secure telephone and other communications lines, such as those serving word processing networks. The third raceway—physically isolated from the other two—carries sensitive communications lines linking computers, visual display terminals, certain telephones, and similar information or communications equipment needing high security.

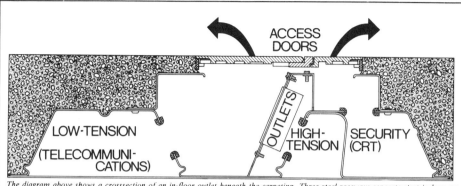

The diagram above shows a crosssection of an in-floor outlet beneath the carpeting. Three steel raceways separate electrical power and unsecured telecommunications lines from cables carrying sensitive information. This type of outlet would only be installed in secured areas of a building.

**Exhibit 28–2.** Cross section of an in-floor outlet.

Although the same in-floor distribution system serves the entire building, access to the third raceway is limited to those locations equipped with a specially designed in-floor outlet (see Exhibit 28–2). All other work stations are served by a standard outlet, preventing employees from getting access to cables in the third raceway. Penetration into the system involves drilling a large hole through a formidable concrete-and-steel barrier—a very noisy and dusty operation that could not be performed easily without attracting attention.

Isolating proprietary information cabling from ordinary telephone lines ensures a high level of corporate communications security without incurring the expense of installing redundant distribution systems on the same floor of a building. Routine telephone and electrical power service changes may be made without exposing the cabling for secure information.

Commercial property management experts cite outgrowing service distribution systems as one of the frequent reasons corporate owners/tenants abandon otherwise satisfactory buildings. Service distribution systems in older office buildings can be secured to some extent, but these systems frequently cannot be moved because of how they are secured. Yet studies have shown that the typical office work station may be relocated once every year. Constant reorganization and work station movement is a fact of life in modern facilities management.

Similarly, equipment is continually being replaced with more advanced, higher capacity, and cost-saving hardware. The in-floor distribution system must be capable of meeting the power and communications service requirements of all reasonable future equipment. Work stations are becoming more and more automated. Systems in many buildings constructed only a decade ago are already woefully inadequate. Once an office building is constructed, few options remain for the user who must expand available power or telephone service other than to move.

Increasingly, companies that lease office space in a building on a long-term basis specify the type and capacity of the in-floor distribution system to be used in a proposed new building—even paying a hefty premium to get what they need. Developers, too, are becoming acutely aware of the value of secure, high-capacity in-floor distribution systems capable of handling work station changes in attracting and retaining major corporate tenants.

When companies build new office space, designing a structure that can accommodate change without sacrificing communications security is a real challenge. Security managers should participate in the selection of in-floor distribution systems because architects and electrical consultants may not anticipate the effect of their planning on future security needs. Systems that meet other requirements may pose insurmountable security problems that can only be solved through costly attempts at retrofitting.

We live in a society characterized by the uninterrupted flow of vast quantities of information between individuals and organizations. Employees at all levels are communicating with each other at an unprecedented rate. The need to facilitate and safeguard information exchanged within the office complex itself is rapidly drawing the security specialist into new areas of consideration and decision.

# CHAPTER 29

## Scanning the Site for Computer Installations

### Richard H. Bessenhoffer
### Vice President
### Total Assets Protection, Inc.

The site chosen for a computer center must accommodate a number of different priorities, but strong security considerations should be high among these.

A computer center has to be accessible enough to handle high levels of traffic and to attract good employees. It must be situated close to adequate and reliable power sources and a flexible communications network, including land lines, line-of-sight microwave, and satellites.

Potential natural hazards also must be taken into account. Certainly, tornado alleys, sites on or near known earthquake fault lines and areas vulnerable to flooding are bad choices. The amount and type of real estate development at a proposed data center site is another factor. Dust, mud, broken water mains, severed power lines or power fluctuations, and accidental disruption of communications lines—inevitable results of development and construction activities—can seriously disrupt computer operations.

Selecting the right neighborhood is just as important in siting a computer center as it is in buying a home. Urban areas with a history of civil disturbances, older buildings with greater threat of fire, and industrial complexes that include hazardous materials or operations should normally be avoided. Determining the security posture of a computer center must also take into account the needs of the center's neighbors. In a building with many different occupants, the security plan may have to be adapted to accommodate the needs and desires of other companies. In leased spaces, the owner may dictate a security posture that significantly affects the plan that can be developed for the data center. Company-owned facilities, of course, have the advantage of allowing the security program to be designed around the unique requirements of the computer operation.

Reprinted with the permission of the American Society for Industrial Security, from *Security Management*, March 1985, p. 62.

Regardless of the location ultimately chosen, security planning should start at the outer perimeter of the building and grounds, not at the door of the computer center. For best results, the computer center security manager should coordinate security for the center with other tenants and the company security department.

## SECURITY ZONES

As a general rule, the application of a zone concept is helpful in planning security measures for a computer center. Application of this concept should also begin at the outer perimeter. Separate vehicle access points and separate parking facilities should be established for employees and visitors, and separate building entrances should be designated where possible. This approach permits controlled and efficient movement of persons and materials into and within the building, which can minimize the threats to the computer center.

Enforcing traffic patterns within the building can help preserve the integrity of the security plan. One way to achieve this is to compartmentalize the functional areas within the data center by creating zones. This division offers higher levels of security on a selective basis and organizes work-flow patterns around the computer center logically. Typically, these zones include data entry, input/output, telecommunications, storage, COM operations, and support system equipment rooms.

For security zones to work effectively, they must be developed during initial planning stages. Possibilities for future expansion must be identified and planned for, so that changes can be made later without compromising the level of security.

The way the movement of people and material between zones is controlled will be unique for each computer center. One way to make this movement flexible is to install a card access control system. Card readers are placed strategically to channel traffic through the zones. Further control can be achieved with the installation of a network of alarmed doors and gates. These should be placed at locations within and between zones that will not be used as routine traffic routes.

Several factors must be considered to make the zone system work. For one thing, the entire access control network, including alarmed doors, must comply with all life-safety code provisions regarding means of egress. Then, to make sure the proper door and frame hardware is specified in the facility design package, the security manager must work closely with the architect at the design stages of a computer center. Many architects are fond of glass and open planning, and the corporate image often supports their ideas. Security requirements are important, however, and some trade-offs may be necessary.

Closed-circuit television systems can play an important role in the security plan for a computer center. However, they may represent a significant dollar entry on the security design cost summary. Justifying this cost is easier if it is addressed as a cost-avoidance factor. In other words, if the cost is compared to the long-term costs of security personnel who would otherwise be required to monitor the computer center.

When a CCTV system is introduced, a careful balance must be established between camera placement and the corporate image. Cameras must be placed to allow effective security monitoring without hurting employee morale or offending visitors. Discreet installations and effective security can be attained through the combined efforts of the security designer and the architect.

Motion detection can also be employed to provide warning of unauthorized activities in remotely located parts of the computer center, such as storage rooms, stairwells, crawl spaces, isolated equipment rooms, and executive offices. Most systems available currently are readily adaptable to a number of applications, but again, discretion must be used in placement.

Lighting is an important planning element because of its effects on normal operations, employee safety, and the functioning of surveillance equipment. Interior lighting levels are fairly standard in most work areas, and outside lighting is often ''soft'' to satisfy aesthetics. However, when a CCTV system is in place, sufficient illumination must be provided for good video quality. If adequate lighting is not available in an area where CCTV surveillance is required, low light-level cameras may be required, which can add to the cost of the CCTV system.

## FIRE PROTECTION

Fires in computer environments are not common. However, the effect on the data center and the company as a whole when they do occur can be catastrophic. For this reason, fire protection should be a major element of the computer center design plan (see Exhibit 29–1). Walls must be designed to accommodate fire protection, security, and environmental controls. Most computer installations should have walls with two-hour fire resistance ratings. The walls of computer equipment rooms should also include vapor barriers to maintain the necessary controlled environment.

Glass should be avoided whenever possible because glass windows and doors do not offer sufficient protection from fire. In addition, glass usually increases data center visibility, reducing overall protection.

In addition to appropriate fire-rated construction, the fire protection design should be based on several essential factors: speed and accuracy in the automatic detection of fire conditions, speed and efficiency in extinguishing the fire, and the provisions for an effective alarm system for the safety of personnel.

The automatic detection system should provide the earliest and most effective warning of fire conditions within the protected environment. Ionization or photoelectric detectors are the most commonly used devices in computer centers, but these may be augmented by thermal or other special-purpose detectors at certain locations.

The detection system should be designed to interface with an automatic fire suppression system. A Halogenated suppressant, such as Halon 1301, is the most effective for most fires in computer areas because Halon is discharged quickly, penetrates computer component cabinetry, and rapidly extinguishes the fire. Another important consideration is down time caused by the discharge of a fire suppressant. Since Halon can be discharged in a gaseous form that is safe for humans, the post-

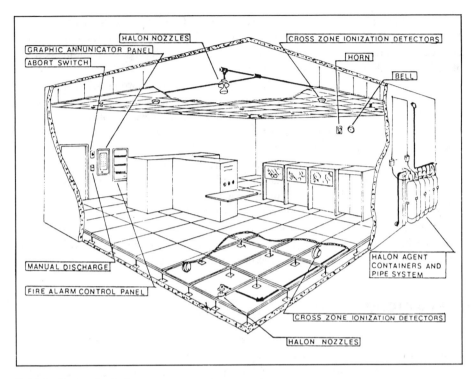

**Exhibit 29–1.**   Typical computer room fire protection system.

discharge down time is usually minimal. In the data processing world, down time translates directly to money—money spent for nonproductive work and money lost because of the inability of the computer system to support the company's requirements.

Water may be required as a fire suppressant in some jurisdictions or by some insurance underwriters. The pros and cons of water and Halon suppression have been widely discussed in the last ten years. We believe water and highly energized equipment do not mix, and that Halon is a more effective, although more costly, method of fire suppression. Where water sprinklers are required, pre-action systems should be considered as a backup to the Halon system. The combination of these systems provides a double-barreled protection capability: Halon for optimum protection of the contents, and water for saving the structure.

The fire alarm system must be distinct from all other alarms in the facility and should be designed to warn personnel of each stage of the fire condition so that appropriate actions can be initiated by fire wardens or other designated teams.

The last element of the fire-protection plan should be an employee training program that complements it. All occupants must fully understand the system and have no fear of its intent and operation.

Almost without exception, the design of any fire-protection system must be approved by the local fire department. Proper liaison with these agencies also ensures their knowledge of your system, as well as an accurate response to fire conditions. The fire department can also perform valuable services in the training of company personnel.

## COMPUTER SUPPORT SYSTEMS

Computers and computer center conditions are "driven" by a myriad of mechanical and electrical support systems. These include air-conditioning, chilled water, and special power-generating and distribution systems, among others. Advances in design and technology permit many of these systems to be located within the secured confines of the computer center. However, some or all of these components are often located outside the center—for instance, cooling towers, chilled-water condenser farms, transformer pads, etc. Since computer operations are totally dependent upon these support systems, the security design for the computer center must also cover these usually unprotected areas.

   An essential element of any security design is the ability to monitor and control the various systems, subsystems, and components that comprise the security, fire protection, and environmental monitoring networks. This monitoring can be accomplished through a central security console, which should be the termination point for all card readers, alarm sensors, CCTV cameras, fire protection systems, and other devices that require continual monitoring. From this console, trained security personnel can monitor the status of all systems, evaluate activities occurring in the protected areas, respond to emergency or out-of-tolerance conditions, and keep management informed of the security posture throughout the facility.

## SECURITY AWARENESS

Since security responsibilities are rarely stated in job descriptions, most employees do not have a good grasp of the subject. Thus it is vital that the overall security plan include an additional module—a security awareness training program. The underlying theme of the program should be that security of the company and its operations promotes employee job security. The program should also stress that both tangible and intangible assets have to be protected. The why, where, who, and how of the security program must be addressed to ensure a clear understanding of the general need for security by all employees and to solicit their continued cooperation and involvement. Many companies have discovered that a well-produced, hard-hitting, 20- to 25-minute audiovisual presentation can usually deliver the desired message in a cost-effective manner.

## SUMMARY

Security planning for new computer centers takes many avenues and involves many people in various disciplines. Site selection is a key step in the planning process since, in many ways, location of the center dictates the type and depth of internal security systems. Careful selection and placement of security devices must complement the business operations. Environmental conditions and fire protection systems require special attention because of the nature and criticality of computer operations. Security of mechanical and electrical support systems cannot be taken lightly, merely because they are often remote from the computer center. The focal point of security and protection is a monitor/control console to ensure optimum effectiveness of installed systems. Finally, when implemented, the security program will be only as strong as the employee base it is intended to protect; thus, the need for a security awareness training program is evident.

Like security for any other operation, security planning for the computer center must be built on a strong foundation to achieve optimum protection.

# CHAPTER 30

## Controlling Physical Access from a Central Location

Brian B. Austin
Programmer Analyst
San Diego City Schools

The control of physical access is an important aspect of computer security: individuals who come into contact with the data processing system should have a legitimate reason for doing so. A computer system protected by security guards and locked doors would be secure were it not for the fact that guards may be bribed, distracted from their duties, or physically coerced, while keys are easily lost, stolen, or duplicated.

An electronic access control system is an attractive alternative for the data processing manager who is seeking to improve physical security. Such a system is activated when the user presents a code, usually through a card reader or keyboard, at the point where access is desired. If the code is valid, the controlled door is opened by an electric door strike. The system may use independent readers at each door, with each reader being individually programmed to accept valid codes. If the code is compromised in some way, it is a simple matter to reprogram the readers and issue new codes.

More sophisticated systems, with which this article is concerned, make it possible to monitor physical access from a central location. A typical system consists of readers, expanders, a controller, and peripheral devices (Exhibit 30–1). The components may be connected by dedicated lines or by telephone lines.

The reader is the point at which the user presents his code for validation. Each reader may have a direct channel to the controller, or expanders may be used to permit several readers to share an input channel. The controller serves as the central processor for the system. The code entered at the reader is compared with authorized codes, which, typically, are stored in random-access memory.

The readers and expanders may share intelligence with the controller and function as remote processors. Authorized codes are programmed into memory through the

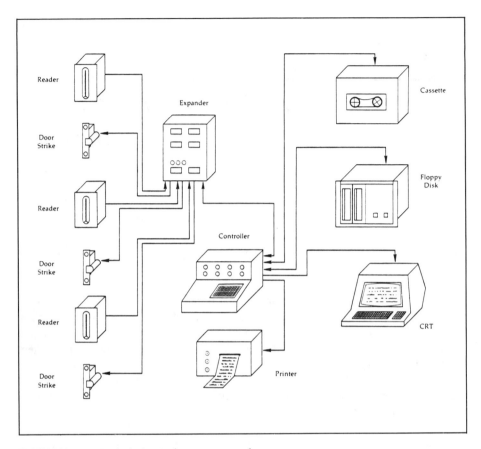

**Exhibit 30–1.**   Typical electronic access control system.

controller, and printers and CRTs may be attached to the controller to provide information about system activity. These centrally controlled systems are sometimes called
"on-line" systems, while those which use independently programmable readers are
called "off-line."

In 1979 a survey was conducted of firms that sell on-line systems; this was
updated in the summer of 1980. Most firms in the survey are original-equipment
manufacturers; to avoid confusion as to the source of the equipment to be described,
the term "vendor" is used to refer to all of the firms collectively. Exhibit 30–2 lists
the firms included in the survey, with their addresses and the model designation of
each system they sell. (*Editors' Note*: Additional firms that entered the market with
electronic access control products since Mr. Austin's survey are presented in Exhibit
30–3. The list is by no means intended to be all-inclusive. While reasonable effort
has been made to update vendor addresses, each one has not been verified for the
publication of this book.)

When intelligence is distributed throughout a system, the distinction between on-line and off-line systems becomes a matter of semantics; the criteria for inclusion in the survey were that the system be intended primarily for access control and that it be possible to program the system from a central location.

## USER CODE SYSTEMS AND METHODS

### Code Input

The term "code input" refers to the means by which the user passes his code to the system for validation. The most common medium for code input is a plastic card, which may also include the user's photograph or otherwise serve as a general identification badge.

Proximity systems use a sensor that both transmits and receives a signal over a range of radio frequencies. The code is entered by holding the card near the sensor; the circuitry in the card modulates the frequencies in a predetermined way, which the sensor translates into a code input.

Alternatively, the user might be required to enter a memorized code through a digital keyboard. If a code is compromised it is easier to implement a new memorized code than to prepare new cards. The disadvantage of a memorized code is that it may be forgotten or written down in an obvious place by the user. A higher lever of security is obtained by combining a card reader and a keyboard, in which case access is granted only if the two codes agree in some predetermined way.

A unique high-security device is the Identimat hand-geometry reader. For detailed information about this system see D.J. Sykes, "Positive Personal Identification," in the November, 1978, issue of *Datamation* magazine (Vol. 24, no. 11, pp. 179-86). The unique identifier is the relative length of the user's fingers. The advantages of using an identifier that cannot be misplaced or duplicated are obvious. (*Editors' Note*: Other systems based upon unique physical attributes have subsequently been introduced.)

### Encoding Method

If a card is used, the code may be contained in a magnetic stripe, an electronic circuit, or a magnetic core laminated into the card. The mag stripe card is the least expensive, but laminated cards are more difficult to duplicate. The code may also be concealed in a hidden pattern of optical filters embedded in the card, in which case the code is "read" by photocells rather than by an electronic circuit.

### Code Capacity

The memory size of centrally controlled systems makes it possible to obtain a high degree of security by assigning a personal code to each user. The capacity of the typical system ranges from 250 to 20,000 codes, usually available in increments of

| Vendor | System Name |
|---|---|
| A.P.D. Security Systems<br>24710 Crestview Court<br>Farmington Hills MI 48018 | Model 705<br>Model 710 |
| Cardkey Systems<br>20339 Nordhoff Street<br>Chatsworth CA 91311 | Interrogator 790 |
| Continental Instruments Corp.<br>70 Hopper Street<br>Westbury NY 11590 | CardAccess 100<br>CardAccess 150<br>CardAccess 200 |
| Stellar Systems, Inc.<br>231 Charcot Avenue<br>San Jose CA 95131<br>(formerly Identimat Corporation) | Identimat 3100 |
| Johnson Controls, Inc.<br>507 East Michigan Street<br>P.O. Box 423<br>Milwaukee WI 53201 | MG-7610<br>MG-7620<br>MG-7821 |
| Norton Door Controls<br>P.O. Box 25288<br>Charlotte NC 28212 | Identi-Logic 6002<br>Identi-Logic 6003 |
| Pyrotronics/Sentracon Systems<br>51 Morgan Drive<br>Norwood MA 10062 | Sentracon 650<br>Sentracon 660<br>Sentracon 670<br>Sentracon 678<br>Sentracon 690 |
| Robertshaw Controls Company<br>1701 Byrd Avenue<br>Richmond VA 23261 | PAS-4000 |
| Rusco Electronic Systems<br>1840 Victory Boulevard<br>P.O. Box 5005<br>Glendale CA 91201 | MAC 530<br>MAC 540 |
| Schlage Electronics<br>3260 Scott Boulevard<br>Santa Clara CA 95051 | SE/414<br>SE/732 |
| Toye Corporation<br>P.O. Box 729<br>Chatsworth CA 91311 | CRC-100<br>CRC-200<br>Telecentral |
| Vikonics, Inc.<br>23 East 26th Street<br>New York NY 10010 | TAC-1000 |

**Exhibit 30–2.**   Manufacturers and system designations.

**Exhibit 30–2.**    Manufacturers and system designations.

In addition to the firms listed in this table, other firms provide complete building-automation systems of which access control is an important feature. Honeywell, Inc., Honeywell Plaza, Minneapolis, MN, 55408 and Walter Kidde and Company, 9 Brighton Road, Clifton, NJ, 07015 provide such systems but were omitted from the survey because the access control portion of the systems are not available separately.

• A.P.D. Security Systems also offers a system, designated Safeguard I, which provides environmental control and video surveillance in addition to external and internal access control. A teleprogrammer is also available for programming card readers via telephone lines.

• The Continental CardAccess 100 system can be upgraded to the CardAccess 200 system. Monitors for copy machines and fuel dispensers are also available.

• The basic product in the Stellar/Identimat system is the Model 2000 stand-alone reader. Various versions of this device store the users' hand geometry in digital form on a mag stripe card or in a host mainframe system. The Model 3100 listed in the tables is an expander for use with the Model 2000 reader; by virtue of an optional lockout memory the Model 3100 expander gives the system the characteristics of an on-line system. Also available is a time-clock control system which uses hand geometry to assure that employees' time cards are not punched by unauthorized persons.

• The Norton Identi-Logic system uses the lockout approach. Keys are voided by means of patch cords, with a special extraction tool being required to remove the cords from the console. Two models are available: Model 6002 has a memory capacity of 1,000 codes and a lockout capacity of 100 codes; Model 6003 has a 10,000 code capacity with the capability of voiding 70 keys as well as individual doors.

• The Pyrotronics models 660, 670, 678, and 690 are minicomputers with nonvolatile ferrite-core memory. Models 670 and 678 can interface with the user's host computer. All systems are compatible with this vendor's Multialarm V building automation system.

• Robertshaw's PAS-4000 system is compatible with the PAS 4000-3 building automation system.

• The Rusco systems can also monitor copy machines and fuel dispensers. Also available is an employee time and attendance reporting system which includes workstation data collection. An auxiliary controller, designated the MAC 550, permits extensive file handling and CRT display.

• The Schlage systems are available with a host-computer interface. A single proximity sensor can be used to control both ingress and egress at each door. The Model SE/732 can accommodate up to three printers with independent reporting functions.

• The Toye Model 200 and Telecentral readers have self-contained memory. The Telecentral console is designed around a portable modem for programming the readers via telephone lines.

• The Vikonics system is able to monitor video surveillance cameras. Also available is the Viscan system, which includes building automation and employee time and attendance reporting.

In the months since Mr. Austin conducted and later updated his survey, a number of other firms have entered the market with electronic access control products. Should you wish to investigate the products they have available, the names and addresses of the firms are listed here.

Access Control Systems
2105 S. Hardy Dr.
Tempe, AZ 85282

Alarm Controls Corporation
Brandywine Drive
Deer Park, NY 11729

Del Norte
Box 696
Euless, TX 76039

Electronic Security Systems
P.O. Box 61403
Sunnyvale, CA 94088

Federal Signal Corporation
Security Products Division
291 Frontage Rd.
Hinsdale, IL 60521

Honeywell Inc. (Fire & Security Systems)
Honeywell Plaza
Minneapolis, MN 55408

Intercontinental Communication Services Inc.
1 Hiscott St.
St. Catherines, Ontario L2R 1C7
Canada

ITT North Electric Company
Power Systems Division
P.O. Box 688
Galion, OH 44833

Laminex
P.O. Box 577
Matthews, NC 28105

Mastiff Security Systems Ltd.
(distributed in US by Sterling Industries)

Plessey Communication Systems Ltd.
Beeston, Nottingham
United Kingdom NG9 1LA

Security Control Systems, Inc.
3007 Washington Blvd. Ste. 115
Marina Del Rey, CA 90291

Simplex Time Recorder Co.
Simplex Plaza
Gardner, MA 01441

Sterling Industries Inc.
Suite 545 Pleasantdale Business Ctr.
4029 Pleasantdale Rd.
Atlanta, GA 30340

Synergistics Inc.
Ten Huron Dr.
East Natick, MA 01760

Sygnetron
2103 Greenspring Dr.
Timonium, MD 21903

Systematics*
41 Colonial Dr.
Piscataway, NJ 08854

*As this issue goes to press, a tentative merger has been announced between Systematics and Cardkey.

**Exhibit 30–3.**    Addition to survey results of Exhibit 30–2.

1,000 or 2,000. Some of the firms surveyed also provide systems that interface with the user's main computer; such a system would, for all practical purposes, have unlimited code capacity.

### Reader Capacity

An additional advantage of centrally controlled systems is the ability to monitor usage by assigning a unique identifier to the reader at each entry point. Typical systems can identify from 4 to 256 readers in this way, usually in increments of 4 readers. Readers with self-contained intelligence are functionally independent of the controller; in this case the controller serves to monitor rather than to control system activity and the reader capacity of the system is unlimited.

### Access Levels

Since the system can identify individual users and individual doors it is possible to create restrictions as to when and where a user will be granted access. Security levels can be assigned so that, for instance, some users will be admitted to the computer room while others will be denied access. The minimal system configuration will have one access level (no restrictions); at the opposite extreme, each user may have his own access-level profile. The number of access levels available may therefore be as great as 64,000.

### Time Zones

Access restrictions may be implemented in time as well as in space. A number of time zones can be created, with each user assigned specific times of day during which he will be permitted to enter the protected area. Each work shift may be designated a time zone, with additional zones for weekends and odd shifts. The minimum system configuration will have one time zone (No restrictions); at the opposite extreme, each user may have his own time-zone profile. The number of time zones available may therefore be as great as 64,000.

## PROGRAMMING METHOD

All systems in this survey were capable of being programmed—that is, having codes validated and, in most cases, time zones and access levels assigned—from a central location. Programming is generally accomplished from a keyboard attached to the controller; this combination is called a "console."

An alternative approach is to use a digital keypad that can be stored away when not in use and attached to the controller when programming changes are required. This keypad is referred to as a "plug-in module."

A lost or stolen card is voided by removing the user's code from central memory. Some systems use a "lockout" approach: all codes remain in memory but invalid codes are flagged as being locked out of the system. Lockout is accomplished by making an entry from the keyboard or by plugging a patch cord into coded receptacles on the front panel of the controller.

### Console Security

Because an individual could use the console to make fraudulent changes to the parameters of the system, access to the keyboard is a potentially vulnerable point in these systems. The keyboard may be protected by a locked panel, or a key-operated switch may be used to activate the keyboard. A password may be required of the programmer, or the console might have its own card reader. The system might be protected by multiple levels of security: for instance, one level of security may permit an individual to view the contents of memory while a higher level is required to make actual changes. In systems that use a plug-in module, special measures should be taken to protect against the programmer when the module is not in use.

## PHYSICAL SECURITY CAPABILITIES AND CONSIDERATIONS

### Reader Override

Under special circumstances it may be desirable to override the system from the console to unlock doors, disable readers, or even lock all users out of the system. Reader override may be done manually or might be on an automatic schedule. It might be necessary, for example, to allow unrestricted access through certain doorways during heavy traffic periods, such as at the beginning and end of work shifts.

### Reader Temperature

The readers may be located out of doors and subject to severe weather. Some vendors provide a cold-weather pack for the readers, usually consisting of some combination of insulation, built-in heaters, and a protective covering for the reader slot. In the systems surveyed, the temperature range over which the reader will function normally varied considerably, from as wide a range as -40°F to +175°F, to as narrow a range as +50°F to +100°F. In systems with an optional cold-weather pack, the temperature range in the table assumes that the pack is in place.

### Elevator Readers

Special readers can be used to control access to floors that are reached by elevator. These elevator readers are designed to interface with the elevator controls, and in some cases the floor-selection buttons are incorporated in the reader.

### Tamper Alarm

All of the systems surveyed are able to generate an alarm if there is an invalid access attempt. The addition of a tamper alarm will increase the security of the readers: such an alarm is activated if the reader faceplate is removed or if the internal circuitry of the reader is damaged.

### Duress Alarm

A useful option with keyboard readers is the duress alarm or hostage alarm. This option will generate a silent alarm if an authorized user is forced to enter the protected premises against his will. A special hostage code entered at the keyboard will open the door in the usual fashion but the remote alarm will be activated.

A significant advantage of electronic systems is that their capabilities extend far beyond simple access control. A number of options are available, as discussed in the following paragraphs.

### Anti-passback Capability

The anti-passback capability is of particular use where the system is used to control turnstiles or parking lots. The purpose of anti-passback is to prevent the user from entering the protected area and then passing his card back for someone else to use. The access point must have separate readers for entry and exit; the system will not permit two successive entries on the same card without an intervening exit. A useful consequence of this feature is that management can determine which users are on the premises at any given time.

### Guard Tour Monitoring

The card readers also provide a convenient way of monitoring the progress of a security guard as he makes his rounds. A tour schedule may be programmed into the system, specifying the time at which the guard should arrive at each reader station. If the guard does not enter his code at or about the given time, the system will generate an alarm.

### Single Use Restrictions

In some cases, such as where a cafeteria is provided for the use of employees, it may be desirable to restrict each user to a single entry during a given time period. In systems with this option, selected readers can be designated "single use" by the programmer, and subsequent entry attempts by the same user will be refused.

### Buddy System Restrictions

The buddy system is the electronic equivalent of mechanical locks which require two or more keys. The controller is simply programmed to require that two or more codes be entered before access is granted by designated readers.

Because of the crucial nature of access control, it is necessary to provide for the possibility of a failure of communication lines or of the power supply. The following options deal with these concerns.

### Auto-degrade

In systems with the auto-degrade, or fail-soft capability, any malfunction in the communication lines will cause the readers to revert automatically to off-line operation so that some measure of access control is still available. Unless the reader has its own memory, the ability to check for individual codes is lost when communication with the controller is disrupted. In the degraded mode, however, the reader will accept only cards bearing a special facility code; this code is the same for all authorized users but is unique to the system.

### Console and Reader Battery Backup

Backup power to the controller is important: if power is lost, not only will the controller not function but (except in the case of systems that use nonvolatile core memory) the contents of memory will be lost.

The auto-degrade capability requires the use of backup batteries for the readers and door strikes. Electric door strikes are designed—in accordance with building codes—to remain open if their power supply is cut off. If the controller, readers, and strikes have standby power, on the other hand, the entire system will function normally in the absence of utility power.

### Audible and Visible Alarms

Some of the situations previously alluded to, such as invalid access attempts and entry under duress, imply the need for alarm indicators at the central monitoring point. The indicator is usually an audible tone or a flashing light on the front panel of the console. Alarm conditions may also be highlighted on the system printer.

### Contact Condition Monitors

In addition to the alarms already mentioned, the controller may have alarm contacts that allow for monitoring of non-access related events in the protected area. Any kind of sensor that changes state in response to an external event—a fire detector or intrusion detector, for example—may be connected to the system. This arrangement is known as contact condition monitoring.

For some applications it may be desirable to operate remote switches in response to a change-of-state signal. The controller might, for instance, turn on an air conditioner in response to a rise in temperature at a remote location. Devices with this remote-switching capability are known as environmental monitors or building automation systems.

## SYSTEM REPORTING OPTIONS

Most of the systems in this survey have LED's or some other provision on the console for reporting events as they occur. Additional information may be displayed on a printer or CRT.

### Printer

The printer is usually fifteen to forty columns wide and may be incorporated in the console. A standard 132-column printer may be attached to some systems. Alarm conditions may be highlighted, such as by being printed in red ink or marked with an asterisk, or the user may choose to have only alarm conditions printed and normal transactions suppressed.

### Memory List

The system may be capable of printing out summary reports relating to system activity, and in some cases may be able to answer detailed queries: the user might, for example, request a list of all ID numbers stored in memory, or the names of card holders currently on the premises, or the number of the last card used at a specific door. The most extensive memory-list capabilities are found in those systems which include floppy disk or cassette drives. Most systems which lack this sort of peripheral storage have a recall buffer in which the most recent transactions are stored. The capacity of the buffer is typically from 16 to 128 transactions.

### CRT Display

Some of the systems in the survey are available with CRT display in addition to, or in place of, a printer. The CRT provides essentially the same information that would be produced on a printer.

## PRICE

Each system is available in so many combinations of code capacity, reader capacity, and assorted options, that it is difficult to assign an "average" price for any system. To provide a frame of reference for the reader, however, the respondents to the original survey (1979) were asked to estimate the costs of the two hypothetical systems.

The first system had a code capacity of five hundred, with four readers and a printer. No time zones or access levels were required. Five estimates were received, ranging from $6,000 to $20,808, with an average price of $11,517. The second system had a code capacity of one thousand, with ten readers, a printer, four time zones, and four access levels. The five estimates for this system ranged from $18,000 to $53,370, with an average of $29,726.

The estimate included only the price of the controller, readers, printer, and necessary expanders. Other items, such as data lines, batteries, cards, and door strikes, were not included. The prices given above therefore represent an absolute minimum cash outlay, particularly when it is considered that the systems specified are relatively small in terms of the many options and the high capacities available.*

Under any circumstances, a centrally controlled system for monitoring physical access represents a substantial investment for the average buyer. In justifying such an expenditure to management, it should be stressed that the system not only protects the computer hardware but also reduces the possibility of loss to the firm due to theft, fraud, and espionage directed against the data stored in the system. The cost benefit aspect of a reduction in the size of the security force must not be overlooked; most of the surveyed systems can be run by one person. The psychological benefit of presenting a security-conscious image to employees and to the public should be emphasized.

---

*Prices as of 1986 can be expected to have been affected by inflation, competition and declining costs in computer components.

# CHAPTER 31

## What's New in Computer Security Accessories

Sandy Evans
Freelance Writer

The computer is a standard fixture in offices today—one that becomes the responsibility of security personnel across a variety of industries. While this equipment brings with it many advantages, it also poses unique problems, such as the question of information as an asset and the importance of protecting this information along with the hardware that houses it.

The market for computer security accessories is changing dramatically, striving hard to catch up with the exploding technology of the equipment it seeks to protect. As competition increases and more manufacturers get into the game, systems are perfected, new technology is developed, and prices come down. This chain reaction is evident in the types and ranges of hardware now available to protect computers.

When designing a computer security program, many firms rely solely on hardware that physically restrains the computer—bolts, steel encasements, cables, and locks that make it extremely difficult for someone to come in and walk off with the equipment. Protection is important. In addition, however, other hardware devices protecting access to information should be considered when possible.

Computer security hardware systems offer special benefits. A major plus is that they block entry—an intruder cannot even tie up expensive computer time or ramble through various programs. Also, because hardware devices are largely independent, the same piece of equipment is compatible with most computer systems. This feature gives the user flexibility and often greater protection at less cost.

Basically, hardware available to protect computers falls into four categories: encryption devices that encode information as it leaves the terminal to travel across the phone lines and/or via satellite, decoding the message only at the authorized destination; call-back programs that refuse access to unauthorized users calling into the system; biometric devices that block entry into the system through identification procedures; and hardware that secures the physical equipment from theft.

Reprinted with the permission of the American Society for Industrial Security, from *Security Management*, Jan. 1986, p 36.

## ENCRYPTION DEVICES

Encryption devices, often cited as the best type of protection since it makes the information useless to the thief, is also one of the most expensive. However, the cost figures are changing rapidly.

"Two years ago, a company would have had to spend about $2,500 per terminal for a good encryption device," explains Glen Horback, director of marketing services, LeeMah DataCom Security Corporation, Hayward, CA. "Today, (Nov. 1985) that same quality is available for $1,200 to $1,800 per terminal."

Alan Brandt of Alan Brandt & Company Distributors, NY, notes that simple encryption add-on boards for personal computers are now available for as little as $90 to $290 per terminal, though he cautions these systems are hardly fool-proof. But the technology is definitely moving ahead, and new developments—and competition—are making prices more realistic for many potential users.

Michael Sobol, president, MIS Training Institute, Framingham, MA, strongly feels encryption is the best security method. "You can secure computers and equipment in your own building," he comments. "But once the information leaves the building—over telephone wires, via satellite—it's out of your control. Encryption is the only way to protect it.

"As competition continues to heat up in this technology, we'll see prices come down further," he continues. "Just this past year, vendors offering encryption devices have literally doubled."

Encryption hardware involves a well protected box that sits between computer and modem, scrambling data as it leaps across the phone lines. In addition to cost, critics of the technology point out these devices add to processing time; since all the information must be coded, transmission time slows down. Also, in a large company the procedures established to manage the code that makes the devices work—for example, rotating the code frequently enough to keep the process tamperproof—"can be a real nightmare," according to LeeMah's Horback.

An alternative to making the information unreadable, he suggests, is to keep people out of the information through a call-back system.

## CALL-BACK SYSTEMS

Call-back systems are the major recent technological advance in computer security hardware, believes Jack Bologna, president, Computer Protection Systems, a consulting firm in Detroit, MI. Sobol from MIS agrees. "The biggest problem with computers in companies large and small is unauthorized entry," he explains. "The industry must institute more control methods to keep unauthorized people out. The call-back systems do just that."

Adds Nancy Paton, marketing communications specialist, TACT Technology, Philadelphia, PA: "Call-back systems provide a real solution to one of the largest problems facing computer owners—unauthorized access. It's so easy to break into a computer system over the phone lines—that's a key spot to protect. Even if the intruders don't steal data, they can wreak havoc simply by manipulating or changing information within the programs.''

Call back devices work with dial-in ports or host modems, intercepting the call before it reaches the modem to check authorization. After intercepting the call, the program waits for the caller to enter an access code, searches its directory for authorization, and disconnects the line. If the caller is an authorized user, the system calls that person back at an authorized location.

These steps provide double security—even if someone discovers the proper access code, he or she must actually be at the authorized location to hook up with the modem. At the same time, the authorized user learns his or her access code has been discovered when the line rings unsolicited at the authorized location.

Most call-back systems offer three modes of operation—and three levels of security. The highest level of security is through the call-back mode described previously. Most systems also offer variable call-back, an option that allows the caller to feed in different call-back phone numbers, giving the user more mobility; and pass-through, a password process that allows the call to connect once the access code has been verified. This third alternative offers the least amount of security.

To maintain the flexibility of the pass-through mode and improve the level of security, the leading manufacturers in this field have begun offering a key decoder device that creates a random access code, personalized for the particular user and used in tandem with the password. "It's a personal ID, and must be used with the access code," states LeeMah's Horback. "It makes it virtually impossible to break into the system." Harback also says call-back systems generally run from $500 to $650 per host modem, adding most companies have eight to sixteen host modems or dial-in ports.

## IDENTIFICATION DEVICES

A more esoteric aspect of computer security hardware includes devices used to control access by various identification methods. In addition to the more standard methods of magnetic cards or key inserts, passwords, and code names, this category includes such biometric technologies as fingerprinting, signature recognition (signing on to the computer terminal with an electronic pen), palm printing, and eye retina reading.

Another identification technology involves radio transmission. Mastiff's terminal protection system uses a miniature radio transmitting token worn or carried by the computer operator. When the token-wearing operator is in front of the computer, he or she has access to the computer and can operate it normally. When the operator leaves the computer, no one can use it or gain access to its information.

Jack Bologna of Computer Protection Systems adds other technologies to this category, such as devices that lock a user out of the computer system after a certain number of consecutive log-on errors, and time operable systems that only allow use during certain predetermined hours. But Bologna suggests caution when considering these options: "People tend to be paranoid when it comes to protecting their information," he theorizes. "You've got to be careful not to spend more money on security systems than the information being protected is worth."

Cost can also be a factor with identification devices. For example, one of the most time-tested and reliable systems, based on verifying identity through fingerprints, costs $3,500 per station for the hardware, backed up by a onetime software fee of $5,000. One bright spot: a station can serve up to eight terminals.

Still, for a good-sized company that deals with extremely sensitive material, biometric technologies can provide a viable option.

One particular system, manufactured by Fingermatrix, White Plains, NY, extracts data from the user's fingerprints and stores the information. That file is called up when the user wants to enter the system through an access code, which opens the file and allows access if the person is who he or she claims to be. "This check serves as a second line of security," explains Emily Ginsberg, vice president, Fingermatrix. "The user must have a valid code just to get the machine to scan. Then the fingerprint must match up with a file on record." A multilevel security system, the Fingermatrix system requires user identification as often as the company deems necessary. "Users might be scanned every time they log on, or only when dealing with financial transactions or when seeking entry into certain data bases," Ginsberg says.

One particularly high-tech entry in biometric identification devices is a unit that scans eye retinas for positive personal identification. Manufactured by EyeDentify, Inc., Beaverton, OR, the device uses a low-intensity level, harmless infrared eye retinal scan technology. Its manufacturer claims the internal structure of the eye cannot be counterfeited or altered, making false acceptance one in a million. As a result, the retina scan can be an expensive but worthwhile investment for companies needing extremely high security.

Another option in the biometric category blends hardware and software in one package. An example is the CyLock, manufactured by Cytrol, Minneapolis, MN, which combines a password within an access key. Each user has a personal key and each key has live memory—the password is not in any system; it is actually stored within the key. The system provides individualized security: keys can be programmed for access to different levels of files needed by a particular user.

A detailed audit trail is created automatically as the user works. Each time the user logs on and off, the time spent within each file is recorded automatically. If the user attempts to gain access to an unauthorized file, that action is recorded in detail as well.

"The CyLock is cost-effective even for just one terminal," says Alan Brandt, president, Alan Brandt & Company, NY, distributors of CyLock. "It's priced at $540 per station." Currently, the CyLock only works with IBM PCs and compatible systems, but Brandt notes adaptions to other systems are relatively simple and will certainly be developed down the road.

## BACK TO BASICS

Certainly the category most often purchased by users of computer security accessories includes hardware that physically secures computers and similar equipment. Steel encasements, bolts, and special locks provide the first step toward computer security for most companies.

Some of the offerings in this category include equipment that steel-bolts computers to a heavy-duty locking plate, and bonds that plate to a double-faced adhesive mat attached to a desk or countertop. Steel rods may then be inserted to interlock the locking plate with a steel plate bonded to the adhesive mat. Two pick-resistant locks threaded into the locking plate completes the virtually burglarproof system. A special key and extractor tool allows users access within minutes.

Mastiff also markets an electronic tracker, which is secured to the computer at the AC power insert point. While the computer is plugged in, it operates normally. If the power cord is removed from the wall or the tracking unit, a coded transmitter sends a signal that can activate an alarm or camera, reporting a unit may be leaving the premises. According to Geoff Dear, Mastiff's manager of technology, the tracking device is especially suited to companies with many computer terminals.

Another option is a steel encasement, which literally fits over the computer to secure the equipment. Usually constructed of heavy gauge welded steel, one system consists of a dual key-locked removable front door that secures the keyboard and terminal. A lock is available for disk drives as well.

Leaders in this category include Anchor Pad International of Ventura, CA and FMJ Inc., distributed through Seagull West in Sherman Oaks, CA.

Corner bolts and special locks are inexpensive methods of battening down equipment. These accessories become more important as micros become lighter and more portable, points out Sobol of MIS. "If someone walks away with your micro, they walk away with your hard disk, too," he points out. "You can lose a lot of information that way—in addition to the loss of equipment."

No matter what a company needs in computer security, sources can supply the hardware required—be it easy to install and maintain corner bolts or dramatic eye-scanning equipment. And one fact is certain in the changing world of computers: just as computerized information becomes more sensitive and computers become more sophisticated, computer security systems will grow in complexity and effectiveness. Companies can no longer ignore the onslaught of more creative—and more elusive —data pirates.

# CHAPTER 32

## Destruction of Input and Output Materials

Megan Jaegerman
Staff Writer
*Security Management*

Your mission, should you choose to accept it, is to destroy all documentation on XYZ Corporation's alpha beta research project. Research notes, formulas, and product specifications must be destroyed beyond recognition, to preclude reconstruction in whole or in part. This tape will self-destruct in twenty seconds.

The state of the art in "destruction technology" hasn't quite caught up with Hollywood, or with "Mission Impossible's" self-destructing tape machine. Destruction on demand may be tomorrow's answer to classified waste disposal, but for now other less dramatic methods will have to do.

Nearly every business, industry, or organization has a built-in cache of classified materials. In the normal course of product research and development, manufacturers and engineering firms generate masses of research data, test records, product formulas, and design specifications. If these materials fell into the hands of a competitor, the company could lose millions.

Businesses also have information in their files that should be safeguarded and destroyed when no longer useful. Contracts, mailing lists, prospect files, market studies, and even cancelled invoices could provide a company with just the edge to undermine a competitor's business. Simply by stealing a price list, a competing manufacturer could underbid another firm and steal its customers.

Personnel records must be carefully guarded against theft or accidental disclosure. Right-to-privacy regulations and equal employment laws prohibit disclosure of information about employees, including records of hiring decisions, discrimination charges, disciplinary action, demotion, termination, and pre-employment test records. Release of this material could result in costly lawsuits and heavy financial penalties.

Reprinted with the permission of the American Society for Industrial Security, from *Security Management*, Sept. 1981, p 44.

Accounting files also contain highly sensitive information that should be carefully disposed of when no longer needed. Bank statements, payroll registers, corporate financial reports, cancelled checks, and cancelled stock certificates should not be accessible to outsiders.

Every firm should set guidelines for safeguarding and disposing of all sensitive material. A records retention schedule should be established to set time limits on the storage of classified materials and obsolete company records. As a general rule, the quantity of classified material on hand at any one time should be kept to an absolute minimum to limit risk and avoid excessive security requirements. Disposal should be accomplished on schedule, by appropriately cleared employees, and in a manner that ensures total destruction. In general, the volume and form of classified material and the degree of destruction required should determine the disposal system that best suits a company's needs.

Two or three decades ago, burning was by far the most common means of disposing of defunct or classified records and documents. Eventually, however, the general uproar about environmental pollution led to strict regulations and emissions standards, which greatly restricted the use of incinerators. Users and manufacturers of incinerators were required to make costly modifications to their equipment and submit to stringent emissions tests administered by the Environmental Protection Agency (EPA).

Beyond the emissions restrictions, incineration has always posed a transport problem. Since incineration is generally carried out away from the offices generating classified waste, the security of the material was open to compromise during transport and transfer from truck to incinerator.

Although emissions standards and transport problems have led to a general reduction in the use of incinerators, some facilities have successfully overcome both obstacles.

In 1977, officials at the Pentagon were faced with a gigantic disposal problem. Of the millions of highly classified documents that were being generated by the Department of Defense each day, about ten tons were considered so sensitive that recycling by any means was too great a security risk. Burial of the documents was also deemed far too risky, and incineration of the material was sure to be blocked by the EPA.

The solution was a custom-made liquid-fueled incinerator built to meet emissions standards, and situated on Pentagon property. Not only did the incinerator pass EPA tests, but its heat was harnessed to provide power to supplement the Pentagon's heating plant. An article in a December 1977 edition of the *Washington Post* hailed the incinerator as the solution to a "twenty-year-old secrets disposal problem for the Pentagon. It provides nearly twenty-five percent of the heat and hot water for more than 22,000 Pentagon employees, and will save the Defense Department an estimated $250,000 a year."

Only a stone's throw away from the easternmost side of the Pentagon, the incinerator virtually eliminates storage and transport problems. The *Post* article continued, "The incinerator is already a roaring success with Defense officials. The EPA checked it, and it far surpassed their greatest expectations." In technical terms, the incinerator produces about .08 grams of particulate matter per cubic meter of flu gas, which is well under the EPA ceiling of .18 grams.

The Pentagon's "trash-to-heat" system was engineered by a firm that builds incinerators capable of converting trash and garbage into steam power or electricity to produce heat, hot water, or even air conditioning.

In all, the Pentagon incinerator cost about $300,000 (in 1977)—equal to the cost of hauling and commercially incinerating its classified materials for one year. In addition, by cutting the Pentagon's coal consumption by five tons a day, the incinerator saved the Defense Department about $50,000 per year.

The trash-to-heat system may have been a dandy solution for the Pentagon, but it is clearly not feasible for every firm or facility. Most companies don't generate the volume of classified materials produced by the Defense Department, nor do they have the financial resources of the US government to foot the bill.

## THE SHREDDER BOOM

In the early 1970s, when energy conservation became a matter of necessity, incineration was increasingly criticized by energy conservationists and the EPA. Gradually, firms that for years had relied on incineration to destroy classified materials began switching to paper shredders. Today, there is a shredder made for nearly every size, form, and quantity of classified waste material. For small firms, which generate relatively little classified information, there are table-top shredders and shredders made to fit over wastebaskets or in compact, sleek, unobtrusive cabinets. For firms with a higher volume of classified waste, there are heavy-duty shredders capable of destroying up to a ton of paper per hour, paper clips and all.

In general, each shredder model is designed to handle a certain type and/or volume of material. Some models are designed for computer printouts, others are made specifically for microfilm. Some shredders can handle only standard office bond paper, while others can shred all three materials with equal ease. The range of capacities available is tremendous. Some of the smallest office shredders can shred only ten sheets of bond paper at one time, while others can handle up to 120 sheets at one "gulp."

Shredders also vary somewhat in the kind of cutting action they provide. Slitter type shredders are the most common in use today. These have meshed, rotating, disc-shaped blades that cut material into strips ranging in width from 5/64 of an inch to one-half inch and equal in length to the original document.

Crosscut shredders are designed for greater security, or more complete destruction, than slitter-type shredders can achieve. Using specially designed cutting blades, they slice material both horizontally and vertically, reducing documents to particles as small as 1/35 of an inch by 3/8 of an inch. Few facilities or businesses require such total destruction, but for those that do, crosscut shredding is the rule. US military security regulations, for example, require that documents classified "cryptographic" or "comsec" (communications security) be shredded to 1/32 of an inch in (too small for a single typewriter character to emerge intact), and crosscut width (too small for a single typewriter character to emerge intact), and crosscut to a maximum of 1/2-inch in length.

The capacity of crosscut shredders, or the quantity of paper that will pass through the cutting mechanism without jamming or stalling the machine, is considerably lower than that of most slitter-type shredders. Thus, while the additional cuts enhance security and reduce the bulk of the shredded material, they reduce the shredder's output per hour as well. This principle applies more broadly to all shredders: narrower shred width tends to reduce both the capacity of the shredder and the velocity of the paper passing through the cutting mechanism. Consequently, it is generally accepted that a shredder can offer either extraordinary security (very narrow shred width) or high capacity, but not both.

Operator speed and efficiency also affect the capacity of a shredder. If an unskilled operator feeds more material into the machine than it is equipped to handle at one time, the shredder will jam and a large electrical current inrush will occur. For this reason, most shredders are equipped with circuit breakers, which interrupt abnormally high current flow to protect the motor and other electrical components from damage. The circuit breaker switch contains a bi-metal element that, in response to the heat produced by high current flow, opens the circuit, interrupts the current, and stops the machine. When this occurs, a cooling-off period is required before the machine can resume operation.

To avoid repeated shutdown, most heavy-duty shredders are equipped with an automatic overload cut-off feature, which responds to changes in cutter speed rather than current flow. When cutter speed is reduced, signalling an impending overload, the shredder automatically turns itself off. Because no heat buildup is involved, no cooling-off period is required to restart the machine.

Other specifics to consider when purchasing a shredder are cutting width, blade quality, and voltage requirements. Cutting width, sometimes called throat capacity, is determined by the width of the internal cutters. Choice of shredder should be based on the width of the majority of the material to be shredded.

American-made machines generally feature cutter widths made to accommodate the most common document and computer printout sizes. In general, cutter width should be about ten to fifteen percent wider than paper width, to permit rapid feeding of documents, which are often dog-eared and fed in out of alignment. Typical cutting widths range from ten inches to seventeen inches, and up to nineteen-and-a-half inches on heavy-duty models.

If imported shredders are being considered, remember that European-made models are generally based on standard European paper sizes, and may not be compatible with your firm's classified materials.

Cutting width should not be confused with *funnel* width, which refers to the width of infeed funnels, a feature of some shredders that permits them to accept materials wider than the throat opening.

Cutter quality depends on the kind of steel used to form the cutting blades. Cutter discs that are fully hardened, as opposed to surface-hardened, are preferable.

Surface hardened cutters can be damaged by paper clips and staples, and tend to wear more rapidly. Fully hardened cutters rarely need sharpening, and can handle staples, fasteners, and paper clips. Most shredders on the market today have *knurled* and hardened cutters, which have serrations, or teeth, that grip and pull material into the cutting discs.

Voltage requirements are of extreme importance in selecting a shredder. Shredders with motors under 1 1/2 horsepower are suitable for 120-volt, single-phase outlets, which are standard in most offices. Higher capacity and heavy-duty shredders, with over 1 1/2 horsepower motors require three-phase, 220-230-volt electrical service. Even though most office photocopy machines operate on 220-230-volt *single*-phase current, few offices have equipment requiring three-phase service, and some don't even have access to a three-phase power source. In a large office building, where three-phase service is usually provided for elevators and air-conditioning systems, shredders exceeding 1 1/2 horsepower can be accommodated without electrical modification. If no three-phase power source is available, alternate wiring configurations or phase conversions are required. For this reason, the exact electrical power available at the proposed installation site should be determined before a shredder is purchased.


## RECYCLE YOUR SECRETS

Pollution and the energy crunch aside, there is a distinct advantage to shredders over incinerators: shreds are worth money. Unlike smoke and ash, the by-products of incineration, shredded waste paper can be recycled. Many firms that have switched from incineration to shredding have offset equipment costs by recycling shredded material.

AT&T Long Lines, for example, recently purchased eighty-eight shredders to provide its southern region facilities with on-site document destruction capability. According to Jim Sheats, records supervisor for AT&T, shredders were selected because they provide greater security and efficiency, and are less costly than incineration or landfill disposal. "Last year eighty-six tons of paper were recycled from our main facility," said Sheats. "That represents an equivalent savings of 217 barrels of oil or 1,468 trees. Our cash return for the shredded paper was $1,300."

Owens-Corning, a Toledo-based fiberglass manufacturer, switched to shredders when its natural gas allocation—half of which was used to power an incinerator—was cut back eighty-five percent. Other factors made incineration even less practical. Abe Webb of Owens-Corning recalls the days when outdated and confidential company records were burned in company incinerators. "In addition to the gas costs, we had to clean out the ashes and load them into 55-gallon drums. Then we had to water them down and store the ash for three weeks before paying someone to take it away. The shredder eliminated the cost of natural gas, cleaning the incinerator, and hauling away the ash. Instead, we sell the shredded paper to a paper mill. And we're saving two or three thousand dollars a year in pickup charges alone."

## FOR THE ROUGH STUFF . . .

Clearly, shredders suit the document disposal needs of most firms. All shredders can destroy paper, some can shred microfilm and even cardboard, and most will accept an occasional staple or paper clip. But some firms generate classified materials that a shredder simply can't handle effectively. Others require greater security than most slitter-type shredders can provide. For these firms, security disintegrators may be the best choice.

Disintegrators, which resemble oversized industrial vacuum cleaners, can't compete with shredders for sleekness or compatibility with office decor. But disintegrators can destroy materials that would probably wreck the inner workings of a standard shredder. Most security disintegrators can chew up bound manuals, unburst computer printouts, credit cards, crumpled paper, metal offset plates, microfiche, and microfilm—reel and all.

Disintegrators utilize rotating cutting blades enclosed in a perforated, screen-like confining drum. Material fed into them is repeatedly sliced by the cutting blades until the particles are small enough to pass through the perforations of the drum. Most disintegrators incorporate an industrial grade vacuum, which pulls the particles through the screen and into a storage bag chamber or external container.

Paper comes out of a disintegrator looking like so much cotton fluff. Disintegrated microfilm resembles tiny flecks of mica, some reduced to silvery-black dust. Metal offset plates emerge as crumpled, misshapen, silver beads, none much larger than the head of a pin. Reconstruction of original material is absolutely impossible, even with the most patient, experienced particle pasters.

Noise and cost are the two basic drawbacks to disintegrators. In addition to the ear splitting roar of the motor, the industrial-grade vacuum included in most models contributes to a noise level that would be intolerable in an office environment. Small units with special sound enclosures are available for offices, but most models are too large, noisy, and, well, ugly for an office.

Sound enclosures can be purchased as accessories for most large model disintegrators, as well. In general, however, these machines belong in a basement, sound-proofed machinery room, or in an industrial setting where a high noise level is acceptable.

In price, disintegrators vary according to size, design, and capacity. The smallest unit manufactured by one firm, for example, is an acoustically treated office model, with a base price of about $3,000. Accessories add another $700 to the total bill. The company's maximum capacity, heavy-duty disintegrator sells for about $30,000; spare parts and accessories cost an additional $15,000.

Electrical requirements vary but most disintegrators require three-phase, high voltage power. Although some offices don't have access to a three-phase power source, manufacturers can usually rewire disintegrator motors or install phase converts at the installation site.

## CLASSIFIED PULP

Pulping, a process often confused with disintegration, is a less popular alternative to shredders and disintegrators. A pulper employs a grinding mechanism resembling a commercial garbage disposal, which grinds wetted paper to a thick pulp. An auger device packs the pulp into a perforated chamber, compressing it until most of the water is discharged through a drain. The end product is thick, packed pulp. The contents of documents destroyed in this manner can be considered lost to the world forever.

Pulpers are expensive, and are generally only practical where extreme security requirements justify the relatively high cost of the equipment and the necessary plumbing modifications.

## MOLTEN MICROSECRETS

If a firm stores most of its secrets on microfilm, and puts relatively little classified information on paper, a melting system might be the best answer to its disposal needs. A low-volume microfiche disposal system, capable of melting up to ten sheets of microfiche at a time has been developed by a leading manufacturer of shredding equipment. The microfiche are rolled and inserted in a disposable aluminum tube, which fits into an electrically powered heating unit. The heating cycle lasts for about five minutes; an internal fan then cools the system for fifteen minutes. At the end of the cooling period, the unit shuts off automatically. The sealed, disposable tube, containing a semi-solid plug of melted microfiche, can then be removed and tossed in the wastebasket.

No article on document destruction equipment is complete without a mention of the famous Watergate shredder—the one that made headlines during the dark days of a past administration. Today that shredder sits quiet, all but forgotten, on the showroom floor of Whitaker Brothers Business Machines in Washington, DC. Crammed among forty or fifty disintegrators, coin counters, change sorters, and paper shredders, the only sign of its illustrious political past is a faded, peeling, red-white-and-blue decal that probably once read, "Now More Than Ever."

When J. T. Whitaker, president of the company—once dubbed the dean of Washington paper shredder salesmen—discusses his machines, he speaks earnestly, scientifically, and with all due seriousness. Approaching the Watergate shredder, however, a grin breaks through. He can't resist demonstrating the famous machine in action. Tossing a stack of typewritten papers on the conveyor belt, he presses the red button. Inside of a second, the pages are transformed into a mangled heap of spaghetti-like strips. The Committee to Reelect the President can rest easy—this machine leaves hardly a shred of evidence.

# CHAPTER 33

## Conservation and the Destruction of Classified Waste Material

Gerald A. Straccia
Security Officer
Westinghouse Electric Corporation

Each day, Americans are inundated with a steady stream of news, mostly bad, concerning the energy crisis. During the past several years, we have experienced shortages in everything from sugar to gasoline. Recently, the *Pittsburgh Press* and *Post Gazette* daily newspapers printed their editions on yellow paper because of a shortage of normal newsprint.

The security industry is responsible for the disposition of a valuable renewable resource—classified waste materials. Thousands of organizations in the United States are faced with the task of destroying classified, sensitive, and proprietary information in accordance with corporate guidelines and government regulations. These organizations have employed methods including burning, mutilation, disintegration, and shredding to dispose of these materials. But in a time of energy crisis, the environmentally preferable method of destroying classified material is recycling.

Paragraph 19a of the Department of Defense (DoD) Industrial Security Manual (ISM) directs government contractors to establish ''a program for the review of classified materials for the purpose of reducing to an absolute minimum the quantity on hand at any given time.'' Contractors are further directed to destroy classified material ''as soon as practical after it has served the purpose for which it was released by the government, developed or prepared by the contractor, or retained after completion of the contract.''

By direction, then, government contractors are required to have an ongoing program of destruction, not only to rid their facilities of excess documents, but to ensure that documents used are kept to a minimum. Throughout the life of a government

Reprinted with the permission of American Society for Industrial Security, from *Security Management*, June 1980, p 84.

contract and beyond, contractors are continuously burning, disintegrating, and shredding classified waste materials.

Paragraph 19c of the DoD ISM sets forth guidelines contractors must adhere to in implementing a program to destroy classified material: The material is to be destroyed beyond recognition so reconstruction of the classified information in whole or in part is not possible. Methods of destruction other than burning, and the equipment used for each must be approved by the cognizant DoD security office. If classified material is removed from the contractor's facility for destruction, it must be destroyed the same day it is removed. The equipment and methods used to destroy classified material must be inspected each time they are used to ensure minimum requirements approved by the cognizant security office are met. The destruction process must be witnessed by two of the contractor's employees who possess appropriate security clearances.

Several companies with government contracts have developed recycling methods for destroying classified waste that meet all of DoD's requirements for destruction. One use of this method is outlined in the following paragraphs.

Classified waste is collected daily from designated, approved burn barrels at the contractor's facility. The material is packed in boxes, sealed, and clearly labeled to indicate classified contents. These boxes are stored in a designated area of the company's vault-type storage room, which has space for about 150 cartons.

About once a month, classified waste is transported to a pulping mill by two properly cleared employees using a rented truck. The rear door to the truck has a standard door lock and a padlock to keep the door from jarring open in a minor collision. The truck is loaded only with the contractor's classified waste, and the drivers take a direct, non-stop route.

In destroying classified waste by pulping it, the following procedures are followed:

1. Classified material removed from the contractor's facility is destroyed the same day it is removed.
2. The contractor is the sole user of the pulper during the destruction period.
3. Appropriately cleared employees of the contractor are the only personnel authorized to perform the destruction.
4. Only appropriately cleared employees of the contracting company transport and escort the material to be destroyed from the contractor's facility to the pulping mill.
5. The contractor's employees call the contracting company to report the safe arrival of material at the pulping mill.
6. Pulping mill employees are denied access to the classified material and to the area where it is being destroyed.
7. After the material has been destroyed, appropriately cleared contractor's employees examine the destruction equipment and residual waste to ensure the classified material has been destroyed beyond recognition and cannot be reconstructed in whole or in part.

The total time from unloading the boxes at the pulping mill to destruction of the materials is about thirty minutes.

This method of recycling classified waste materials has been approved by both the Department of Defense and the Department of Energy. The program was also approved as a preferred method of disposing of the contracting company's corporate proprietary information.

The recycling program has been in operation for about a year. During this period, minor problems have occurred which required slight adjustments. Initially, the double-wrapped boxes had a plastic inner wrapper, which caused a filtering problem with the pulping machinery. The problem was eliminated through the use of paper liners. Also, although at least two cleared employees *had* to be used for the destruction process, three proved necessary. The pulping mill had agreed their employees would not enter the area during the destruction process, but they did not station anyone in the area to monitor their personnel. The solution was to have one of the contractor's employees act as a monitor, while the other two unloaded the vehicle. The monitoring job was rotated among the three employees during subsequent trips.

The pulping mill agreed to pay twenty dollars a ton for the waste materials delivered. They offered to pay more if the materials were separated (computer cards in one box, etc.). For general recycling, the contractor found separating materials preferable, as money earned was increased and the procedure is more acceptable to the pulping mill. However, such separation is not practical for classified waste materials.

Research into pulping facilities showed that most are extremely cooperative and willing to agree to a system for destroying classified waste such as that described. Allowing a government contractor to be the "sole user" of their operation simply accounts to instructing pulping mill employees to leave the general area while the contractor's personnel dump the materials into the pulper.

Pulping mills and paperboard companies are located throughout the United States. Local offices of environmental groups and recycling organizations can often provide a list of such facilities in their areas.

Although the government contractor described here has experienced minor inconveniences in pulping classified material, the rewards are great. Not only are they receiving twenty dollars a ton for materials delivered, but they are turning what was a non-renewable resource into a significant asset. In 1979, the three organizations which have adopted this method so far accounted for the recycling of approximately one thousand tons of classified waste materials that previously would have gone up in smoke.

# PART VII

## Software Controls

Security that makes assets unusable is obviously unacceptable. For computers to be of value, they must be accessible to those who are intended to use them. The objective then, must be to allow access only to that information each individual is authorized to see and to permit only certain people the capability of entering or changing specified information in the system. To accomplish this selective access, security features must be built into operating software or special security software controls must be added for use in conjunction with the computer's other operating software.

Advice on how to select and implement a data security product is contained in this group of articles. A model for screening computer users is offered as an example of a computer system access program, and the technical aspects of access controls are examined.

# CHAPTER 34

## How to Select and Implement a Data Security Product

Robert E. Johnson
Manager, Data Processing Security
Phoenix Mutual Life Insurance

Selecting and implementing a computer system usually involves only a single business function and frequently does not significantly affect the overall office environment. Even so, the decisions and learning involved in choosing a system make this a complex process. Introduce a data security product, which can affect all users of a system and often does affect the overall office environment, and the selection and implementation process becomes even more difficult.

More than ten data security software products are marketed for IBM systems alone. In addition, there are many hardware enhancements on the market. Which of these should you consider? Should you be using one of them? Is one enough? Proper selection and implementation will result in an efficient security tool accepted by employees, rather than one that is circumvented at every opportunity.

To achieve an effective data security system, you must be fully informed about the options available, as well as your company's needs. What information needs to be controlled? What are the differences between centralized and decentralized administration? Should you implement automatic data security or data security only when requested (default versus declared security)? What about auditing and control of persons with sensitive authority and capabilities?

Can an organization lacking traditional computer security controls successfully implement a data security product? Which controls are most critical? Which should be done first? Which individuals' involvement will improve the possibility for success?

Reprinted with permission from *Infosystems*, January, February, March 1984. Copyright © 1984 Hitchcock Publishing Co.

## PLANNING AHEAD

In most companies, the typical approach to selecting a data security product is to wait until the need for one is evident. Then the company evaluates available offerings, resulting in a recommendation and selection. This method is wrong. The selection process should start *before* the need is perceived. This permits those responsible to perform an objective evaluation without the pressure of immediate need snapping at their heels.

An effective advance selection process will accomplish many things. It will identify your current security posture, revealing its strengths and weaknesses. Where practical, it will identify appropriate corrective action and alternative measures. All related job functions should be studied to determine what should be done to improve their support of security.

Often, the greatest security problem is lack of management support as perceived by the general staff. Letting employees know in advance that a security system is being planned can correct this misconception and better prepare everyone for the day when a specific product is introduced.

## CONTROL IS IMPORTANT

One of the biggest problems encountered in the data security market is making the user understand that a specific product is not the sole solution to an organization's security problems. Without satisfying basic types and principles of control, a secure environment for processing data cannot be ensured. Three types of control are applicable to the use of computers—administrative, physical, and logical—and four basic principles of control—accountability, responsibility, separation of duties, and auditability.

1. *Administrative controls* are often referred to as the bureaucracy. When consciously applied, they greatly enhance the overall security of data. Administrative controls include publishing standards and procedures, requiring written requests, having a formal approval process subject to review, and separating responsibilities. Other administrative controls include logs of various activities and balancing.

One administrative control often overlooked or looked upon as negative is the process of built-in delays. Too often the emphasis on service and responsiveness to users precludes their effective use. Many crimes today are crimes of opportunity. Processes that include built-in delays dramatically reduce this exposure.

2. *Physical security* employs more traditional and familiar controls. Nonetheless, these must not be overlooked. Data security software controls will do you little good if the data can be walked out the front door on a printout or magnetic tape. Typical security controls include locks, guards, surveillance, restricted access, and physical separation.

3. *Logical controls* are those enforced by computer software. Specific examples

include a monitoring process that records or logs designated events. The identification process that includes authentication of the person logging onto the computer is a logical one. Validation of input through evaluation and processing separation or specifically separating processes are other examples.

An effective yet frequently overlooked logical control is threshold alarms, which are a logical extension of the monitoring and recording process. When a given event occurs a specified number of times, this software will trigger another event. For example, when someone violates a rule five times, his or her authority to continue processing is automatically terminated.

1.  *Accountability* establishes who is responsible for actions on the computer. Who did it? Who approved it? Who reviewed it? When? Where? Logs and authorization processes are most frequently used to establish accountability.

2.  *Responsibility* must be affixed and involve supervisory personnel. A quality assurance control function is often of great help here. The most important element of responsibility is management followup. That is, when problems arise or events occur that warrant a review, periodic management inquiry assures everyone that management is involved and concerned about the matter.

3.  *Separation of duties*, depending on the size of the organization, can be one of the most difficult principles to support. Note that the function of separation has appeared in the three basic types of control and now appears as a basic principle. Its importance cannot be overemphasized. Just as good accounting controls require checks and balances in the handling of monies, so does data security. Wherever practical, duties should be separated.

One simple method of evaluating whether separation is adequate is to evaluate what happens when an error occurs. If the process followed results in resolution of the error and documentation is present to establish clearly what has happened, then the controls are adequate.

4.  *Auditability* is that element of control that determines whether everything else has been done correctly. When a process is auditable, it is said the pieces can be connected, somewhat akin to putting a puzzle together. When the pieces are put together, what do they show? And, can the auditor do it alone? If not, then the process is not truly auditable.

The most significant elements in making a process auditable are that (1) authorizations must never be verbal and (2) all functions must be documented. When exceptions to the authorization process are granted, these also must be documented.

In expressing the need for a particular data security package, I like to use the following formula:
DACI = MS (C + A + R + E).
DACI means data access controls installed; MS, management support; C, concern; A, accessibility; R, risk; and E, expense. If this formula will help you drive a point home, feel free to use it.

## WHO'S IN CHARGE?

A major controversy lies in the administration of data security products within a company. Frequently the issue is whether it should be centralized or decentralized.

A strong case can be made for centralization, which can dramatically reduce the span of control and supervision. This type of administration also makes it much easier to measure the impact of changes and lowers the need for training significantly.

Furthermore, when problems arise, there is no question as to who must take corrective action.

Among the negative aspects of centralized administration, the first is staffing. Except for larger installations, administration of data security products on a centralized basis requires less than one person full time. Thus, other persons must be trained to perform the backup responsibilities, and responsiveness to user needs begins to suffer. Communication time from a requestor to the central administrator is greater. During periods of peak load, it is often difficult for the central administrator to satisfy all requests on a timely basis.

Decentralized administration tends to be more responsive since localized administrators report within the same management structure as the people they support. Although in this arrangement, security is still only a part-time responsibility, these administrators are more responsive to requests for service and can better understand the impact of delay.

Decentralized administrators are more difficult to supervise and training requirements are greater, however. Backup of the individual administrators becomes the responsibility of each division. But when these administrators are out of the office, problems are minimized because only one department is without their services rather than an entire organization.

Many organizations are setting up a modified form of administration in which some functions are decentralized and others are centralized. Control of critical items is retained centrally, while others of greater sensitivity to user needs are placed in the hands of those users.

## DEFAULT VS. DECLARED PROTECTION

Another issue of great concern, particularly when discussing data security software, is automatic protection (referred to as default or closed) versus manual protection (referred to as declared or open). The question here is whether all datasets should automatically be protected or whether only those identified as requiring security should be protected. The pros and cons on both sides are many. However, every product that offers one as a feature also offers some variation of the other.

When all points are scored, automatic protection must always win. The processing rates of today's computers remove any concern for performance. It is far better to have over-protected 100 datasets than to have left a sensitive one inadequately controlled. The most effective way to accomplish this is to establish a minimum level of control (security) for all company datasets. This minimum level is delivered to all who do not request special controls. Such a doctrine effectively establishes that all corporate information is important and deserving of protection.

## KNOWING WHO THE USERS ARE AND WHAT THEY ARE DOING

Another element often discussed is the authorization process. Once a product is brought in to enforce the controls automatically, it often seems the authorization process exponentially lengthens. In most instances, this is unnecessary and the former process can be continued—assuming the former process supports the basic principles of control.

Authentication is quite another issue. Do not lose sight of the purpose of authentication: to establish without doubt that individuals attempting to get into the computer system are who they say they are.

Since different individuals have different levels of responsibility, when someone attempts to use the computer system, it is vital to ensure they are who they claim to be. This can be ascertained by asking for information known only by that person, as in the case of a password. Or it can be done by what you possess, such as a driver's license. A third method could be by what you are, as in the case of your fingerprints.

Some products will support any of these forms of identification. However, the only one practical for implementation by most firms is what you know—the often maligned password.

Often, password administration is confused with security administration; it should not be. The process of authorization is distinctly separate from password administration.

Also, it is important to distinguish today's password administration problems from those of yesterday. In the past, it was customary to establish a single password for authorization of a particular activity. Everyone performing that activity used the same password. With this method, the password had to be changed every time a person changed responsibilities or was fired.

In today's environment, passwords are used to verify that individuals are who they purport to be. Once they are authenticated, their authority to perform specific activities is validated on the basis of who they are, rather than what they know. This distinction is critical to understanding the transformation that has taken place in the way passwords are administered.

Three methods for individual authentication are possible today: centrally issued, locally issued, and individually chosen. The primary problem associated with both central and local issue is that someone other than the individual knows the password. This opens the door for the claim that employees are not responsible for everything performed on the computer in their names because others have knowledge of or access to their passwords.

For passwords to be effective, they must be changed periodically. When passwords are centrally or locally issued, dissemination of the new passwords is a problem. Some automatic password generation processes install the new passwords and produce a mailer to deliver the password to the individual. But this method adds to the administrative process.

The entire hassle of password administration can be virtually eliminated, however. Many available products support the concept of individuals choosing their own passwords. For those companies that prefer a more random method of authentication, the system selects the new password and informs the individual of the password chosen. This is normally done on a frequency specified by the firm. The advantage is that the only person who knows an individual's password is the individual—providing the system precludes anyone from looking at the password chosen. This arrangement makes individuals responsible for all activity conducted under their identification.

More and more firms are finding it practical to derive passwords from individual employees' names. Pride and responsibility increase when people know their work bears their names. Errors tend to diminish rapidly.

Auditability is another important factor to consider when choosing a data security product. Your first concern should be whether the product provides the tools needed to ensure it is performing as intended. These tools are usually used by the data security officer to monitor the product and the administrators. Your second concern is whether the product provides tools that enable the internal and external auditors to review the results of the product's implementation.

If these tools are available, it raises the question of whether providing these tools makes those who use them so powerful that fresh controls must be developed for them. An auditor can become a very powerful individual if the ability to observe is not properly controlled. Are the audit trails automated in such a manner that manipulation or alteration is readily detectable?

Other persons to be concerned about include the data security officer, the systems programming staff, and any decentralized administrators of security. A good product will provide a system of checks and balances that will ensure transgressions by any are observable by others. It is true that in each system there must be one "all powerful" person. Some products, however, provide the vehicle to ensure that even this individual is properly monitored.

## INTEGRATING A DATA SECURITY PRODUCT WITH EXISTING CONTROLS

One of the biggest concerns regarding acquisition of additional security products is integrating these with existing controls. All too often, this problem is ignored. But the best use must be made of each control, including the security product. Many controls that contribute to a secure environment are accomplished by products overlooked in the initial evaluation of a company's data security situation. A closer look at these elements of your operation sometimes reveals that the means for achieving the desired control level are already at your disposal:

*Tape management system.* In spite of the fact that most major tape management systems can be interfaced with available operation system data security products, many data centers successfully operate without such a system. However, the interface would provide a greater level of control for tape libraries sometimes numbering in the thousands of volumes.

*Automated scheduler.* Automated schedulers provide information about the jobs they initiate. First, the jobs have met some standard for acceptance. Second, they are more frequently the primary source for production tasks. Can it be said that all jobs initiated by the automated scheduler are production and that access to test data is not allowable?

*Job accounting (expense management).* Including effective job accounting within an operating system ensures that staff members do not have unlimited access to computer time without management review. You can install the best security system money can buy, but given the time and resources, someone can always defeat it.

*Output distribution control.* You don't have any? What good are software/hardware controls if all of the information is available from hard copy?

*Data center access.* Access to the data center, particularly the computer room, must be effectively controlled.

*Program library management.* Programs are the vehicles used to update and alter your data. If they are not controlled, virtually any protection installed can be circumvented.

*Data backup for recovery and data archives.* Properly managed data backup and data archives will minimize any damage caused by a prankster or disgruntled employee who successfully circumvents the controls. To assume invulnerability as a result of a good security program is like assuming your car will never run out of gas because it has a gas gauge.

*Access control to the tape library.* For most organizations, data backup is on magnetic tape. If access to and accountability for these tapes are not maintained, all of the on-system controls may be in vain.

*Control of libraries.* Libraries other than the program library are used to direct processes. These contain parameters, data base definitions, and procedures. In addition, special versions of these libraries are often established for reruns and oneshots. If these concepts are not present, they will be necessary to ensure the separation of production and test.

*Transaction/command naming standards.* Many products offer controls by transaction/command name. Some go on to offer these generically. To take advantage of generic specifications (all transactions beginning with the characters RUN, for example), you must have standards that ensure no overlap. Inability to use generic authorizations greatly increases the workload of the administrators because all transactions must be defined.

*Other software products.* Often, before a data security product has been selected, other software products have already been installed or planned for acquisition. It is important to identify all of these and to determine whether the interfaces provided are acceptable. Such products may be a data communications manager, a database manager, a disk space manager, or other products that offer specialized services.

*Standards for names.* There are resources you may wish to control. Candidates include datasets, programs, jobs, terminals, and disk volumes. Just as with transactions, the effort it takes to control access to information in the computer is intensified when naming standards that permit generic references are not present.

Some of the controls discussed may not currently be employed within your operation. If they are in your future, however, and the data security products you are considering interact with any of them, it is important that you consider that interface during your selection process. You do not want to find yourself in the position of having to change data security products a few years from now due to a lack of foresight. Nor do you want to limit your choice of the particular specialized software (e.g., automated scheduler) you need.

No doubt you can implement most available products without the forestated controls. However, in many cases implementation will be more arduous, and some objectives are unobtainable without them. You can make the transition from a lack of controls to good controls far simpler and less painful if you define the controls needed and their parameters—if not their specifics—before implementing data security products that will interface with them.

## WHO SHOULD HELP SELECT THE DATA SECURITY PRODUCT?

It is imperative that the right individuals participate in each phase of the data security selection process from evaluation through maintenance. The participants will vary by company, the products being considered, and the phase. Candidates should include the security director, the data security officer, database manager, auditor, operations manager, director of MIS, and staff knowledgeable in technical support and applications systems. Other, less obvious candidates would be staff from purchasing, law, corporate management, user management, personnel, corporate communications, and expense management.

This latter group is often overlooked, yet staff in these positions can play a significant role in one or more phases of data security implementation. Because of the number of products now available, it may be necessary to involve purchasing to satisfy policies regarding competitive bids. The legal department should review and negotiate any changes to the contracts. Corporate management should be involved in the implementation of products that affect the whole company in order to demonstrate their support to the entire corporate community. User management involvement in the selection and implementation processes is essential to obtaining their support and later, that of their subordinates.

Personnel may need to be involved if a data security product crosses departmental lines. Special forms regarding responsibilities of individuals may be required, and personnel often has some voice in these matters. The public relations department can be very helpful in supporting the implementation of data security through articles in the company newsletter. Expense management should not be overlooked either to assure proper budgeting.

## CHOOSING THE RIGHT PRODUCT FOR YOUR COMPANY'S NEEDS

Identification of candidate products is no longer the difficult process it was even two or three years ago. The competition is keen and all are frequently advertised in the trade journals and exhibited at the trade shows. Comparison articles are seen frequently, and products' implementations are discussed at conferences and seminars.

Previously, it was difficult to find users willing to discuss their experiences with data security products. Today this is no longer a problem. Frequently, a few inquiries within your local data processing community will identify one or more firms in your area using the products you wish to consider. Do not lose sight of the fact, however, that other products exist that may do a better job for you.

Developers of security products identify a market, then develop and introduce their solutions for that market. In this article, many available products are discussed and sources of additional information are described. Not surprisingly, of the twenty-four products mentioned, twenty-two support the IBM mainframe market. Several of the twenty-two also support virtually any computer that functions in a dial-up environment.

Fifteen of the products address IBM mainframe operating systems or subsystems. All are software driven. Exhibit 34–1 identifies each of these products and the primary areas they service. Seven of the remaining nine, shown in Exhibit 34–2, focus on securing dial-up lines. The last two offer security either for the IBM personal computer or the DEC VAX series. Encryption products are not included in this article.

## SECURITY FOR IBM MAINFRAMES

The following software products support IBM mainframe operating systems/subsystems:

**ACF2** is designed to improve the security of the IBM MVS or VSI operating systems. The basic philosophy of ACF2 is to protect all data by default. Based on this, no one except the owner can access a data set until the owner, the security officer, or a specifically designated agent enters an access rule into ACF2 specifying to whom and under what conditions access authority will be given. Each user's authority to access the operating system, user-defined addressable resources, and data sets are established at job initiation or at log-on/sign-on during password verification.

**ACF2/VM** is the VM version of ACF2. Introduced in 1983, it is currently the only product available to enhance the security of VM. It follows the same philosophy as ACF2, security by default. In addition to controlling access to the computer, it also controls access to data residing on the system and to other defined resources. Initial

| Product | Features | | | | | | |
|---------|------|------|------|------|------|--------|------|
|         | MVS | VS1 | DOS | VM | CICS | IMS/DC | TSO |
| ACF2 | X | X |   |   | X | X | X |
| ACF2/VM |   |   |   | X |   |   |   |
| CA-Sentinel |   |   | X |   | X |   |   |
| COPS |   |   |   |   | X |   |   |
| COSS |   |   |   |   | X |   |   |
| Guardian |   |   |   |   | X |   |   |
| Protect-CICS |   |   |   |   | X |   |   |
| RACF | X |   |   |   | X | X | X |
| SAC | X | X | X |   | X | X | X |
| Secure | X | X |   |   |   |   | X |
| Secure/CICS |   |   |   |   | X |   |   |
| Secure/IMS |   |   |   |   |   | X |   |
| Surveillance |   |   |   |   | X |   |   |
| Top Secret | X |   |   |   | X | X | X |
| UPDU |   |   |   |   | X |   |   |

**Exhibit 34–1.**   IBM main-frame security products.

controls include user log-on and verification, user links to mini-disks, CMS file control options, and controlled access to OS data sets.

**CA-Sentinel** is the younger of the products offering protection for the DOS environment, having been introduced in 1983. In addition to validating users, CA-Sentinel protects all standard resources in batch and CICS. To provide the desired level of protection and security at the lowest possible overhead, verification of access is only performed for protected resources. Other features include flexible administration, complete logging and reporting, controls by date and time, and terminal control.

**COPS** is a veteran product, which exclusively addresses the enhancement of CICS security. It is totally on-line, requires no application program changes, and offers centralized or decentralized control. COPS maintains user accountability and provides automatic application menu display and unattended terminal sign-off. These features and many others have led to its reputation as one of the three ''anchor'' CICS security systems.

**COSS** addresses CICS security exclusively and has been in the marketplace for more than a year. It was developed to provide security under UFO, a sister product, as well as to CICS and works best in that environment. Administration is centralized or decentralized and is supported by "fill-in-the-blanks" screens. Installation time is minimal, and no modifications to CICS or the operating system are made. COSS offers an extensive logging and reporting facility, while minimizing the effect of security on performance.

It is a product of Oxford Software Corp., Hasbrouck Heights, NJ.

**Guardian** is another of the veteran products that exclusively addresses CICS security enhancement. Frequently referred to as the Cadillac of CICS security packages, its features and methodology are unique. Guardian is driven by an English language compiler that makes the rules and schemes readily auditable by nontechnical management or auditors. It is flexible and allows security to be phased in gradually. Impact on system performance is not measurable, and the logging/reporting facility is extremely flexible.

**Protect-CICS**, one of the newer security products, addresses CICS exclusively. It attempts to address the shortcomings of CICS "native" security and provides improved file security and an audit trail of security violations. It also dramatically increases the available number of security keys. One of the less expensive products, its price varies depending on operating system (DOS or OS) and number of terminals in the network.

**RACF** features both data security and resource control. With it an installation can specify access disciplines under which computing system resources are made available to users. RACF access control is based on an installation's definitions of users, groups of users, and resources, and on the attributes and authorities assigned them during RACF installation.

Ownership of each entity is established during the definition stage. From these definitions, profiles are constructed for each user, group, and resource.

The profiles contain information for user identification and verification, authorization checking, and system management facility (SMF) logging. User, group, and resource profiles are stored on a RACF data set. Special time sharing option (TSO) transactions are provided to allow users and managers to add, delete, modify, and list the profiles.

**SAC**, the veteran protector of DOS, is the only product that protects DOS, MVS, and VSI. It addresses the three major areas of logical security: system entry, data set, and auditability/accountability.

SAC provides security through a matrix of rules that control resource and data set access. Flexibility is offered through masking and character substitution. It uses the SMF for logging and provides an extensive set of reports.

**Secure** is a data access and integrity system that controls and audits access to protected information. It is designed to enhance the standard IBM password facility provided as a part of the operating system. With Secure, jobs and users must be specifically authorized to access protected data. Access authorization is provided by an access identification string, which is internally generated and maintained by Secure.

Control is passed to the Secure system during open processing for each protected data set. Under control of installation-specified algorithms, Secure automatically assembles the password from information present in the job control language or TSO log-on procedure. This technique prevents unauthorized disclosure of passwords, since they do not exist outside the system. It minimizes the interface between users and the system, as access to protected data sets is allowed or refused automatically by Secure.

**Secure/CICS** features a technique of automatic access authorization that controls access to CICS/VS by operators and terminals. It also restricts use of sensitive resources such as transactions, programs, and files according to levels of protection specified by the installation.

The third CICS exclusive security product, this package is frequently referred to as one of the veterans. It features an automatic audit trail, decentralized administration, on-line security updating, and multi-level access control.

**Secure/IMS** is an additional fee enhancement to Secure that extends Secure into IMS/DC.

**Surveillance**, another of the newer CICS exclusive security products, resides in the CICS region as a set of user transactions and programs. Requests for various CICS services are trapped to ensure that only those authorized have access to a protected resource. The use of generic resource definitions eliminates redundant terminal activity. Audit trail logging allows tracking of unusual occurrences. Batch report programs list detailed information about each security violation.

**Top Secret**, a security package for MVS, protects facilities, resources, and data by controlling user access to them. The youngest of the MVS software security packages, Top Secret protects access to all resources and facilities. Violations are reported to the SMF log and/or on-line audit file.

An extract utility with flexible selection criteria is a feature. It is possible to have selected users operating in "fail" mode and others in "warn" mode without compromising the security of those facilities and resources requiring "fail" mode protection.

Top Secret also offers centralized or decentralized administration. Utilizing the MVS "always call" feature, it either provides default security or allows data to be secured on a declared basis through the selective activation of the file security bit.

**UPSU**, a security product for CICS, focuses on the Copics DL/I Manufacturing Data Base Architecture, while retaining the ability to protect "conventional" CICS as well. It is sometimes referred to as the Volkswagen of CICS security packages, as it is a product without frills and of modest cost.

A unique feature it delivers is the ability to construct a custom menu for each user that lists only those transactions the user may execute.


## OTHER DATA SECURITY PRODUCTS

Products designed to protect dial-up facilities are similar to operating system data security products. Their objective is to provide an initial level of validation and control prior to encountering the sign-on protocols of the computer. They differ primarily in how sophisticated they are at providing this initial screening. Exhibit 34–2 lists these products and their key features. It indicates whether the product has pass-through or call-back authentication and if it provides an audit trail.

| | Authentication | | Audit Trail | Remarks |
|---|---|---|---|---|
| | Pass Through | Callback | | |
| Computer Sentry (IMM Corp.) | X | | | Single line, modest cost |
| Defender II (Digital Pathways) | X | X | X | 48 plus line capacity |
| Digilink II (Bakus Data Systems) | X | X | X | 6 line capacity |
| FOX-FONE (Fox Marketing) | X | | | Single line low cost |
| Lineguard 3000 (Western Datacom) | X | X | X | |
| Secure Access Unit (Lee Mah) | X | X | | Single line, modest cost |
| Secure Access Multiport (Lee Mah) | X | X | X | 32 plus line capacity |

**Exhibit 34–2.**    Security products for dial-up lines.

Pass-through authentication is where access is allowed as a result of offering the required password. Call-back authentication provides that, in addition to presenting the proper password, the caller must be at a designated telephone verified by the security device, which calls back before connection to the computer is allowed.

**PC Lock II** is a security product for IBM microcomputers (i.e., IBM-PC, XT, or compatible personal computers running DOS 2.0). It provides read/write controls and ensures that borrowed data on diskettes or other media cannot be processed in another PC that does not have PC Lock II installed. Each PC Lock II is unique as a result of the user selected key.

**Rabbit-4** is a security product for Digital's PDP 11/44, 11/70, VAX 11/750 and 11/780 computers.

Addresses for the data security products mentioned in this article are contained in Exhibit 34–3.

**ACF2 and ACF2/VM (Access Control Facility)**
The Cambridge Systems Group, Inc. (US & Canada)
24275 Elise
Los Altos Hills, CA 94022
415/941-4558
and
**SKK, Inc. (other countries)**
10400 West Higgins Road
Rosemont, IL 60018
312/635-1040

**CA-Sentinel**
Computer Associates
70 Jericho Turnpike
Jericho, NY 11753
516/997-8800

**Computer Sentry**
IMM Corporation
100 North 20th Street
Philadelphia, PA 19103
215/569-1300
800/523-0103

**COPS (CICS On-Line Protection System)**
TelTech
39 Broadway
New York, NY 10006
212/921-0250

**COSS (CICS On-Line Security System)**
Oxford Software Corporation
174 Boulevard
Hasbrouck Heights, NJ 07604
201/288-1515

**Defender II**
Digital Pathways, Inc.
1060 East Meadow Circle
Palo Alto, CA 94303
415/493-5544

**Digilink II**
Bakus Data Systems
1440 Koll Circle, Suite 110
San Jose, CA 95112
408/279-8711

**Fox Fone**
Fox Marketing
4518 Taylorsville Road
Huber Heights, OH 45424
513/236-3591

**Guardian**
On-Line Software International
2 Executive Drive
Fort Lee, NJ 07024
201/592-0009

**Lineguard 3000**
Western Datacom

5083 Market Street
Youngstown, OH 44512
216/788-6583

**PC Lock II**
MPPi, Ltd.
2200 Lehigh Avenue
Glenview, IL 60025
312/998-8401

**Protect-CICS**
Tech Products
7700 Leesburg Pike
Falls Church, VA 22043
703/448-9025

**Rabbit-4**
Taxco Inc.
6520 Powers Ferry Road
Suite 200
Atlanta, GA 30339
404/955-2553

**RACF (Resource Access Control Facility)**
IBM
1133 Westchester Avenue
White Plains, NY 10604
914/696-3043

**Secure Access Unit/Secure Access Multiport**
Lee Mah Telecommunications
729 Filbert Street
San Francisco, CA 94133

**SAC (Security Access Controller)**
Electronic Data Systems Corporation
Software Products Division
7171 Forest Lane
Dallas, TX 75230
214/661-6215

**Secure, Secure/CICS, Secure/IMS**
Boole & Babbage
510 Oakmead Parkway
Sunnyvale, CA 94086
408/735-9550

**Surveillance**
Tower Systems International
19782 MacArthur Boulevard
Suite 365
Irvine, CA 92715
714/752-8263; 800/851-7551

**Top Secret**
CGA Software Products Group
960 Holmdel Road
Holmdel, NJ 07733
201/946-7550; 800/237-2057

**UPSU (User Profile Security Utility)**
Scott-Kennard Assoc
814 Blossom Hill Road
San Jose, CA 95153
408/281-0432

**Exhibit 34-3.** Data security products discussed.

# CHAPTER 35

# A Technical Approach to Computer Access Control

Eugene F. Troy
Stuart W. Katzke
Dennis D. Steinauer
National Bureau of Standards
  Institute for Computer Sciences
  and Technology
Computer Security Management Group

Data processing resources are often so valuable, sensitive, or private that it is imprudent or even illegal to allow indiscriminate access to them.

System and data access controls are designed to prevent unauthorized access to information resources. Their origins date back to early computer systems, where it was necessary to protect system software (the operating system) from being destroyed or overwritten by the system's single user. As systems matured, to permit multiple users to share a computer, protection mechanisms were needed both to maintain isolation between the operating system's and users' processes and to provide for controlled sharing of system resources among users.

Continuing changes in computer system architectures have resulted in today's time-shared minicomputers and large host mainframes. Both require sophisticated hardware and software mechanisms for restricting a user's access to authorized system and information resources.

Access control encompasses defining the rules governing access privileges to system resources, implementing automated technical mechanisms to enforce these rules, and establishing administrative practices and procedures for effective and secure operation. Access controls allow management to control interactions among people and named system resources, since the privilege of accessing a resource can be selectively granted to or withheld from individual users or groups of users. Requests for

Reprinted with the permission of the American Society for Industrial Security, from *Security Management*, Oct. 1985, p 169.

access—say to read a data file or to execute a specific program—can be mediated by one or more system security components to verify the authorization of an individual before a requested action is performed.

An access control mechanism should, to the degree needed and specified by management, enable

- only authorized users (or processes acting on their behalf) to perform . . .
- only those functions they are authorized to perform . . .
- only on those data to which they have authorized access, using . . .
- only those hardware and software resources they are authorized to use.

In general, the principle of "least privilege" is usually recommended. The less a person using the system is allowed to do—consistent with the work the person is required to do—the safer the system's other users and the individual's own processes and resources.

Access controls provide a particularly effective solution to a significant portion of the intrusion problem. If used and administered properly, they are effective in assuring that directly or remotely connected users of a computer system cannot read, copy, modify, destroy, or use any information resources unless they are authorized to do so.

## USER ID AUTHENTICATION IS CRITICAL

It is important to remember that access control enforcement is based on the identity of the requesting user and the user's privileges. Consequently, the process of user identification authentication is critical. An individual masquerading as a legitimate user will be permitted the same access privileges as the legitimate user if the identification/authentication process can be fooled or subverted. Many of the break-ins we have read about have resulted from inadequacies in the user identification and authentication process, the access control mechanisms, or both.

While the primary objectives of access controls are to prevent unauthorized disclosure and to maintain the integrity of information resources, access controls can also be used to provide the following:

- allocation of limited resources among a user community competing for their use, by defining and enforcing the conditions under which the resources may be used;
- collection of information about resource use for billing and accounting purposes—who, what, and for how long;
- separation of distinct organizational entities, by restricting the access of groups of users to certain groups of data based on their job functions—the principles of "least privilege" and "need to know" apply here;
- control and monitoring of patterns of computer use to achieve efficient and effective use of resources; and
- specific implementation of local or organization-wide computer security policies and requirements.

## USER IDENTITY VERIFICATION

Verifying the identity of a user is essential if access to information resources is to be controlled on the basis of user privileges. Furthermore, users cannot be held accountable for their actions unless they (or processes acting on their behalf) are positively identified. Identity verification usually involves a two-step process:

*Identification*, which occurs when the user provides an identifier—the name by which the user is known—to the system. The user's identifier is unique, is unlikely to change, and need not be kept secret. It is used for access control, for security journaling, and for other purposes such as accounting and billing.

*Authentication*, which occurs when the individual passes some further test that "proves" the user is actually the person associated with the identifier.

There are three basic techniques by which an individual can "prove" identity. The individual can present for verification

- information, such as a password, numerical combinations, or other information known only to the user;
- objects, such as a magnetically encoded card or a key for a lock; or
- physiological, behavioral, or morphological attributes such as signatures, fingerprints, voiceprints, or palmprints.

Of all three techniques, passwords are the most commonly used automated method of verifying a user's identity. If password generation and distribution are effectively administered and if passwords are adequately protected by users and by the system, then passwords can be used with a degree of reliability adequate for most systems. When necessary, passwords can be used in conjunction with other methods to obtain a higher degree of reliability.

Of all the methods, passwords are the least expensive. The National Bureau of Standards is currently working on a federal standard for using passwords, which specifies management and technical requirements for password systems. The Department of Defense Computer Security Center is developing a specific password standard for use within the DoD community.

For systems with very stringent security requirements, the principle of "mutual distrust" should be used. In other words, not only should a system user authenticate himself or herself to the host computer, but the computer should be able to verify its own identity to the user.

## FUNCTIONAL MODEL FOR ACCESS CONTROLS

The following model identifies seven major components of the access control process.

1.  *Subject*, an entity that initiates access requests and possesses access privileges. Examples include individual users and the programs they execute on their behalf.
2.  *Object*, a resource resident in or constituting the computer system, to which access is restricted for purposes of protection or controlled sharing. Common

examples include data files, the records or fields they contain, programs, and hardware devices.

3.  *Mode of access*, the operation to be performed on the requested object by the requesting subject. Examples include the "read," "write," and "execute" functions.

4.  *Decision criteria*, the data and algorithm used to decide whether an access request should be permitted or denied. The three primary components—subject, object, and mode of access—must enter into the decision. Other useful criteria include time of day, content of requested data, passwords, and context in which a program is invoked.

5.  *System response*, the action taken by the system when an unauthorized access attempt is detected. Examples include termination of the session, notification of the offending program or terminal, and notification of security personnel.

6.  *Security log*, a journal that includes events of relevance to access authorization. Of interest are events that could trigger a log entry and the information that an entry should contain. Examples of events that should be logged are all requests and denials for access to sensitive objects.

7.  *Control of the authorization data*, a policy or procedure for managing the authorization data, particularly data governing the assignment and revocation of access privileges. Information about subjects, objects, and the privileges that hold between them must be stored within the system, and facilities must be provided for entering, reviewing, updating, and protecting this information. These facilities may be centralized—used by one or a few designated individuals—or be distributed throughout the user community.

## IMPLEMENTING ACCESS CONTROLS

A variety of strategies can be used to implement elements of the model. Consider the relationships presented in Exhibit 35–1. Four major system components—the hard-

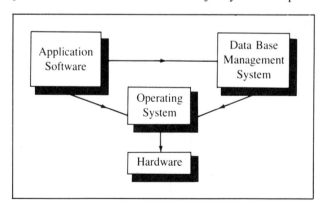

**Exhibit 35–1.**   Basic access control components and dependencies.

ware, operating system, data base management system (DBMS), and application software—are pictured. The arrows show potential dependencies of one component on another. While each of these components can implement access controls within its domain of protection, the access control mechanisms of higher level components usually depend on the mechanisms of lower level components.

## Hardware

Hardware protection mechanisms are needed in time-shared, multi-user mainframes and minicomputers to isolate user processes and to support rapid switching in the execution of user processes. Privileged instructions, process state switching, memory mapping, and bounds registers are but a few of the hardware capabilities used to maintain physical separation between users. Machines that lack hardware protection mechanisms (for example, microcomputers and personal computers) do not provide a firm base for protection mechanisms at higher levels of the system.

## Operating System

Because of its position as the principal interface between applications software and the underlying machine, the operating system (OS) is ideally placed to provide logical separation between users. Users—and the processes that execute on their behalf—are considered logical entities, because they are represented by a number of cooperating software components. Using the physical protection mechanisms of the hardware, the OS is able to control the scheduling, initiation, and execution of user processes to ensure efficient sharing of system resources—such as main memory, input and output devices, mass storage, and communication lines—as well as to provide logical access controls that enforce controlled sharing. At this level, subjects may be individual users or processes (executing programs), objects may be data files or software programs, and modes of access to objects include reading, writing, and executing.

Because the level of access control protection provided by vendors in their operating systems varies considerably, numerous add-on products have appeared in the marketplace to enhance the security of vendor-supplied systems. While these products improve a system's ability to enforce controlled access, adding on security is not comparable to designing and implementing a secure system.

Application software and the data base management system (DBMS) are dependent upon fundamental access controls provided by the OS. Consequently, the integrity and trust of the OS are of prime importance when implementing controls in these upper-level software components. Significant developments in the theory and construction of trusted systems have occurred over the past few years, culminating in the establishment of the Department of Defense (DoD) Computer Security Center and the publication of the center's Trusted Computer System Evaluation Criteria.

With regard to access controls, the criteria are derived from a basic statement of objective: the desired systems will control access to information so that only authorized individuals will be permitted to use specific system resources or to read, write, create, or delete information managed by the system's security controls.

The following basic requirements are needed to meet this objective:

- a well-defined security policy and model;
- a method for formal specification and verification of the system to ensure correct implementation of the security policy; and
- a security kernel, which is a small, centralized, and highly protected portion of the code in the OS, whose main function is to perform authorization checking. Since the kernel implements critical portions of the security policy, its formal specification and verification are essential.

If the DoD Computer Security Center is successful, trusted operating systems that form a secure base for computer applications should become commercially available. These will reduce the degree of trust that must be placed in application systems.

### Data Base Management Systems

These systems provide individual users and user applications with the ability to store, manipulate, and retrieve data. When access to information maintained by DBMS software must be controlled, the DBMS can provide powerful and effective enforcement capabilities. Examples of such capabilities include the following:

- Restricting user access to a user-view or subschema of the data base. Some DBMSs allow the data base manager to define the portions of the data base that users need to do their jobs and enforce access to that subset of data. From the user's point of view, the data base appears to contain only the data related to the job that has to be done.
- Password protection of specific files, records or fields within records. Many DBMSs, such as those following the CODASYL model, permit attaching passwords to individual data items, such as files, and permit access to those items only if the user knows the correct password. These passwords are different from, and in addition to, those required for user identification and verification at log-in.
- Query modification. Used in some relational DBMSs, query modification involves appending additional conditions onto a user's query to the data base. Before a response is given to a user's question (for example, ''Which employees have had psychiatric care?''), additional conditions are evaluated to determine if the user has a right to the information (for instance, ''Is the user an employee in the health unit, and is the user a medical doctor?'').

In most cases, the DBMS is viewed by the operation system as an executing process that must be scheduled, isolated from other processes, and protected. Ensuring the integrity of the code, directories, dictionaries, and other working files of the DBMS is primarily the responsibility of the OS. Other processes executing on the same machine must not be permitted to access data managed by the DBMS. The ability of the DBMS to maintain access controls over its user community cannot be ensured if the integrity of the OS cannot be guaranteed.

### Application Software

Application programs, like DBMS, depend on the OS to protect their data from other processes executing on the same machine. These programs can also control their users' access to application data. For several of the following reasons, access controls might be needed in application software:

#### Inadequate OS Controls

When operating systems provide little or no access control facilities, supplementary access control mechanisms can be placed in the application software. However, if the OS cannot be trusted—if it contains flaws that can be exploited to obtain system and user data—then application software controls will not provide a high degree of protection. This is typically the case with personal computer OS. Use of other technical anti-intrusion methods, such as cryptography or port protection, may have to be used in this case.

#### Restricted User Interface

As an analogue to the concept of user-views and subschema found in DBMS, application software can limit the type of actions a user may request of the application system. For example, based upon the user's identity, the application may allow the user to invoke only the specific subset of transactions needed to do the job. This technique is particularly effective when the user is constrained to interface only with the application software during the log-in sequence, is terminated from all system activity at log-off and is not permitted to escape from the application software while executing authorized transactions—for example, escaping to OS command mode.

#### Known Subjects and Objects

When the entities that comprise the subjects and objects are known only at the application level and not by the OS or DBMS, responsibility for access control rests with the application program. For example, clerks in a regional office (subjects) may be entering data transactions (objects) of a payroll application. From the application perspective, clerks and transactions are known entities. However, from the OS view, the application software process is a subject and the application data files are objects. Because the level of granularity of clerks and transactions is inappropriate for OS control, access must be controlled at the application program level.

Application software can use the capabilities of a DBMS for storage, manipulation, and retrieval of application data. When this occurs, access controls at the application level may supplement, complement, and depend upon those implemented in the DBMS.

# CHAPTER 36

## A Model for Screening Computer Users

Charles Goodroe
Safety and Health Officer
Fort Valley State College

Every day thousands of computers operated by governments, businesses, academic institutions, and individuals are involved in tasks ranging from designing the next generation of microcircuits to allowing multinational corporations to control and record thousands of daily business decisions and operations. By all indications, the scope of computer applications is destined for continued, explosive growth, as more users join the technological revolution and new computer uses are discovered.

The matter of protecting the machinery (hardware), the programs (software), and the data—collectively called "the computer"—from theft, alteration, or destruction is the most important challenge to security professionals today. In many cases, the security professional involved with the protection and control of computer systems is quite familiar with effective, direct access control measures for hardware, printouts, and on-site personnel. However, these same professionals may be unfamiliar with control techniques to prevent off-site penetration of these systems.

Recent disclosures of tampering by criminals and curious amateurs show the cost of this inexperience is high. National defense information, sensitive government files, vital scientific research, and confidential corporate data are all only a telephone call away from the unauthorized user. The protection of this information can depend on how well off-site system control is developed and maintained. As a result, the security manager must develop an understanding of access control techniques and constantly monitor their use in his or her installation.

This article will present one example of a computer system access program and provide a step-by-step description of the logic and functions involved in the control process.

The key to computer systems security is accountability. This observation has nothing to do with computers per se; instead it involves the most crucial aspect of the

From *Security Management*, Aug. 1984, p 61. Copyright © 1984 Charles Goodroe.

control system—the role of management. Dial-up controls are inconvenient, and many authorized users may lobby for a less complete system in the name of easier employee access. Management may also request a "golden key" that will enable certain executives to bypass the controls and access the computer system directly. Nonetheless, these encumbrances are a fact of life and the first job of the security professional will be to explain the need for an effective, comprehensive control program. Such a program not only ensures fairness to all employees and a uniformity of procedures, but also simply makes common sense. If the protective screen is too easy to get through, it is of no real value. If short cuts are designed to allow the controls to be bypassed, sooner or later those short cuts will be found and exploited.

A comprehensive approach to controlling access can limit the opportunity for exploitation. Should an intrusion be attempted or actually occur, the control program can assist in reporting the problem and determining the responsible parties. If, on the other hand, a weak spot must be included because of company policy or executive concern, the monitoring of this weak spot should be factored into the system's auditing procedure.

## LIMIT SECURITY PROGRAM KNOWLEDGE

While a security screen is being developed, overall knowledge of the program design must be limited to the smallest possible group. The program development team will require a representative of management who can authorize the system design, a systems analyst to perform the design mechanics and suggest technical options, and a security staff member. This security person should have a knowledge of computer programming and white collar crime or have accounting experience. This person must make certain the program is designed to protect the computer system against unauthorized penetration.

The employment status of those under consideration for inclusion on the development team should be examined. An employee may have superior professional credentials. However, if loyalty to the firm is questionable or if an employee has shown signs of being susceptible to alcohol or drug abuse, living beyond his or her income, or engaging in illegal activities, that person must be excluded. If this exclusion means you have to bring in outside consultants, do not take their stated qualifications at face value. In this case, requiring a background check of the consultant or the company is warranted, along with an updated background check on current employees being considered for the team.

Once the design parameters have been established by management and the team has been assembled, the development process can begin. The control program must be able to verify the user's identity, provide the user with the limit of his or her access, and prevent and report any attempts to penetrate the system. To accomplish these objectives, the program described in this article relies on a multi-level access design. This approach allows the user to take a comprehensive but unwieldy code, like **T421AR9YPAROICFAIE2791(*J = W),** and divide it into modules that are easier to remember and protect. The logic used in this approach is diagrammed in Exhibit 36–1.

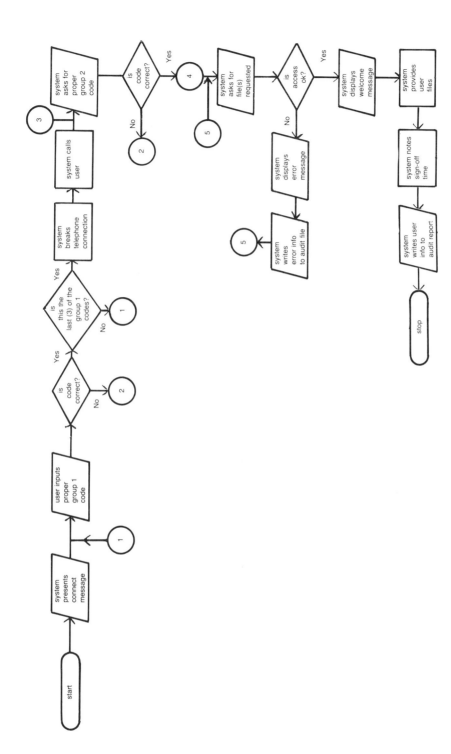

**Exhibit 36–1.** Flowchart of the logic used to develop the example control program.

277

To begin, consider the dial-up process. When a user at an off-site location calls the company computer, his or her terminal blinks to life and displays a message. For the sake of demonstration, let's say this message reads, "Welcome to the Grandarcher Aerospace Company computer network. Financial Data Analysis, Section 1. Please enter your account number now."

Such a message is quite informative, and if the person on the other end is a hacker, you can rest assured your network's telephone number and any other information the intruder can obtain about your system will race across every electronic bulletin board in the country. Then, instead of a single curious individual, dozens of "wizards" become intent on breaking into your system. Even if your access control program is foolproof, this open invitation presents an unacceptable risk. To prevent this breach, modify your announcement so those who are authorized will know what they are looking at, while the uninvited get only a minimum of information. For example, "G.A.C. computer network, F.D.A.-S1?" After the question mark, the first account number is entered and the program proceeds.

## FOUR POSITIVE RESPONSES

The sample program described in this article is designed to require four positive responses for an operator to enter the main computer network. These codes are divided into two groups. The group one access codes consist of a telephone verifier, personal identification, and access level code. The telephone verifier is an alphanumeric code —for example—T421-AR9Y—consisting of the larger, master code with a dash added. The alphanumeric code is not an actual telephone number; rather it is a symbolic code for a telephone number already entered into the computer's memory. When the user enters this code, the control program searches its memory for a match. When the computer finds that T421-AR9Y stands for (915) 555–6174, the proper notation is made and the next code request appears.

The personal identification code is a short, straight line code made up either of all numbers or all letters. For example, **PAROIC** could be the symbolic code for Randall Smythe, vice president of operations. Notice this code does not contain a dash and is a different length from the first access code. These features can help make the total access sequence harder to break by a sophisticated code attack program.

The last of the group one codes establishes the access level of the user. This code is structured differently from the first two. In this example, the third code is **FAIE/2791**. The grouping of letters and numbers separated by a slash serves as a code protection feature and can also be structured to serve other ends. For example, the FAIE could represent a code that would allow access to the research files, and 2791 could serve as another user identification.

The access level code can also be modified in a number of ways to control both the type and number of files accessed in one call. If the response is correct, a proper notification message is given to the user and the computer breaks the telephone connection. Now, instead of the user calling the computer, the computer calls the user, an added safeguard. The telephone number verified in the first code is called and only for a predetermined number of rings. This control prevents the codes from being stolen and used to admit an unauthorized user since, without the actual telephone, the codes are useless.

When the computer link is reestablished, the group two codes come into play. The first of these codes verifies that the original user is at the telephone by requesting an encryption code—in this case, (*J = W). This code serves as an "ace-in-the-hole" for the system. In your main memory, all the information can be encoded into a nonsensical arrangement that only this code can unlock. Without it, even if access to the system is gained somehow, the attacker cannot understand the information. This technique has been in use for many years in government, and now several computer firms are producing encryption controls for business systems. Using encryption devices that scramble the electrical impulses between your terminal and the main system is also an effective way to defeat transmission monitoring.

The final control feature asks the user for the name(s) of the file(s) he or she wishes to use. To answer correctly, the user must have specific knowledge of the existing files. When the user inputs a file name, it is compared against his or her access level (FAIE/2791 in this example). If the individual is not cleared for these files, access is denied and the reason for the denial is displayed on the screen. If the user wishes to create a file, the new file is automatically classified to his or her level of access, and a copy of the new file name is added to an audit file. Depending on the employee, a copy of the new program or information may also be sent to security to check for system abuse. A sample of an off-site daily activity report generated by the control program is shown in Exhibit 36–2.

Before going on to the next segment, let's wrap up some loose ends about code structure. As we discussed earlier, the codes should be random groupings, nonsequential and not designed to match personal initials, titles, birthdays, social security numbers, or any readily identifiable or logical sequence. This improves the basic structure of the total code and lessens the chance one algorithm could be designed to defeat it.

## CHANGING THE CODES

The codes should be changed on a regular basis, but here a new set of non-technical problems surface. If you change the codes too often, users may start writing down the codes to remember them and that paper could be lost or stolen. But what happens if you never change the codes? Maybe nothing, but individual codes could be discovered and used in tandem by the authorized user and the intruder. An alternative might be to change only one or two sections of the code at a time. The multiple access level approach makes this solution possible and practical.

When the last access code is entered successfully and before any information is released, a message similar to the following should be displayed:

Welcome to the computer network of the Grandarcher Aerospace Company. Please note: the information contained in this system is the proprietary information of the com-

Grandarcher Aerospace Company
Off-Site Computer Activity Report
June 12, 1984

| Name | Time-On | Dept. | Files | Cd-v | Time-Off |
|------|---------|-------|-------|------|----------|
| Kile Jackson | 10:03 a | Research | Analy (1) e | Y | 1:30  p |
| | | | Pro-nxt    e | Y | |
| | | | Datamix   n | Y | |
| Lamar Anson | 10:21 a | Legal | Colnam    e | Y | 11:01 p |
| Charles Bruce | 11:39 a | Business | Budget    e | Y | 1:00  p |
| | | | t/loss       n | Y | |
| | | | co-tem    n | Y | |

**Key:** a = am; p = pm; e = existing file; n = new file; Y = code verified with no problems. Note that employees Jackson and Bruce accessed and created files.

**Exhibit 36–2.**   Grandarcher Aerospace Company off-site computer activity report, June 12, 1984.

pany. Unauthorized access, removal, alteration, destruction, release, or other unauthorized use is a criminal offense punishable by imprisonment, a fine, or both. Grandarcher will also seek to recover all damages in civil court, and should employees of the company be found responsible for any intrusion, those employees will be immediately terminated.

This simple notice can prove invaluable in any criminal or civil action because it sets the record straight up front. The user is told bluntly that the information is exclusive property and unauthorized use is a crime. The penalties are clearly stated, and no one can say he did not know the company intended to protect its assets.

In each of the code examples, this illustration assumed the input was correct. But what happens if an invalid entry is made? The defensive controls in the program are diagrammed in Exhibit 36–3.

With each code entry, the user is allowed two tries. If he or she misses both times on any entry level or a total of three times during the sign-on procedure, the computer breaks the telephone connection. Every incorrect answer is recorded in a special file for review by security. This check can help spot an employee who may be "fishing" for information to subvert the control program or using the system while under the influence of alcohol or drugs. In either case, the advance warning could save a lot of work down the line.

If an unauthorized user continues to call, he or she can jam your telephone number with calls. This keeps authorized users out of the system as effectively as if the criminal changed the locks on the building. To prevent this form of abuse, several aggressive defenses can be employed.

The control program is designed to invoke aggressive defenses when five incorrect responses are recorded in a certain number of tries. Rather than turning off, the computer generates a new message on the screen disguised as a "help" feature. The message might say, "Control program overload. Please stand by." For the next five minutes at regular intervals a short wait message reappears. While this message is being displayed on the screen, another message is sent to the security desk and the company official on call.

This procedure allows the company to decide on its response. The intruder is still on the line and, depending on the potential for damage, you may elect to have the call traced. The complicated process of tracing calls deserves careful attention and planning before the fact. Before choosing this approach, get in touch with your telephone company business office and find out exactly when and how a trace can be used and the steps necessary to actually have the trace performed.

To allow more response time after the first waiting period has elapsed, a second message should appear. The attacker could receive another wait message or be shown a dummy file. If you opt for the red herring, include a warning before the file is shown. This warning can be a simple message stating the computer network is private property and unauthorized use is a crime. Display of this warning gives the caller proper notice and a chance to sign off. If the individual chooses to continue, he or she is asking for everything he or she gets.

The fake file can be constructed either to convince the unauthorized user nothing worth looking at is in the file and get him or her to hang up from boredom, or you

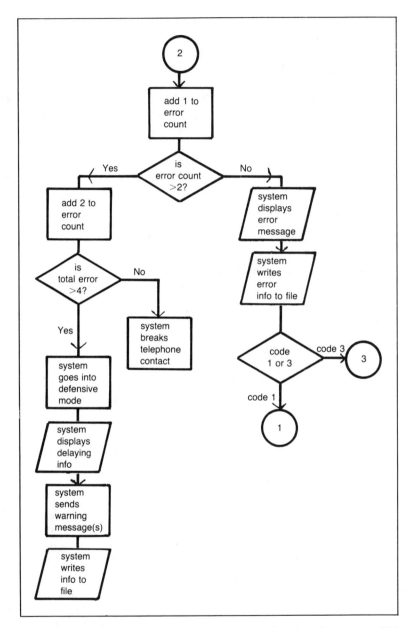

**Exhibit 36–3.**   Flowchart of the logic used to develop the sub-program which monitors the errors and controls the defenses.

could provide a dazzling array of meaningless data and keep the caller on the line. The latter approach gives you more time to run a trace and gather information to demonstrate criminal intent and establish the identity of the intruder.

Traps such as those just described should exist at every level of the access process and should demonstrate enough subtle, creative effort so your unwanted callers never know they're being had. These defenses can also be designed to allow employees using the system under duress to summon help but keep their actions from damaging the company. This kind of covert counterattack could also be the last thing an intruder expects, especially if this is his or her first call. Like the log-on procedure, all activity performed in the trap mode should be recorded in a specific file for reference at a later date.

## DIVIDE PROGRAMMING TASK

When your design work is completed the system's analyst should divide the total program into subgroups and assign each subgroup to an individual or small team of programmers. Through this procedure, total knowledge of the control process is limited to your planning group. Once the actual programming is completed and tested for effectiveness, a copy can be made of the subgroups to allow separate, independent firms to test for hidden, detrimental instructions that may have been inserted into the program. If no problems can be found with the copy, compare it line by line to the original for a final integrity check.

When you are ready to begin operations, use the copy as the control program and save the original as the master. The master, all copies, and the supporting documentation should be classified immediately and, except for the operations copy, kept in a secure storage area. The original will not simply gather dust, however. At least once per quarter, the master or another secure copy should be compared against the working copy to check for tampering. Attempts to gain access to the master or any secure copies, even for regular audits, should also require a well documented, deliberate effort supervised by a top security official and a ranking member of management.

The operations copy of the program and all of the working documentation should be restricted from almost everyone except the maintenance programmer, and the security audit personnel. This limit controls physical access, but another open door still needs to be closed. The control program will be interacting with other programs in the company's computer system. These programs can be designed by dishonest individuals to perform a normal business activity (a profit and loss report for example), but also covertly capture your control program and alter its function. To prevent this ploy, all programs must be inherently suspicious about other programs they work with. This process is delicate and difficult. However, only by protecting your programs in this way can you prevent such attacks. You may consider using a separate computer system—a business personal computer with sufficient memory, for example—to handle your control and audit programs and build in an audit gate that checks the incoming programs and prevents an unauthorized change or release of data. A sample of a daily incident report showing unauthorized activity is shown in Exhibit 36–4.

Even with these careful, calculated efforts of control program design and protection you may never feel your system is invincible. Remember the people on the other side are just as creative and hard working, and they do not have any company policies or other rules to constrict their activity. Anything is fair and anything is what you should expect. As a result, you must constantly audit software design and function, check personnel, change passwords, update procedures, and keep up with the advances in the rapidly growing computer security field. When it comes down to brass tacks, the computer, however sophisticated, is merely a tool. Its proper use and protection depends on creativity and intelligence.

## Grandarcher Aerospace Company
### *Security Action File ** Unauthorized Computer Activity*
### June 12, 1984

| Name | Time-On | Activity | Trace | Emp-stat | Cpy-act | Time-Off |
|---|---|---|---|---|---|---|
| George Lette | 11:00 p | CD1(m)<br>CD2(m)*<br>CD3(m) | na<br>na<br>na | Research(c) | N | 11:06 p |
| UA | 1:04 a | UEA | yes | n-emp | Y | 2:51 a |
| Frank Colak | 1:09 a | CD1(m)*<br>CD1(m)*<br>CD1(m) | na<br>na<br>yes | Business(t) | Y | 2:00 a |

**Key:** a = am; p = pm; CD = code; the following number denotes the code sequence: CD1 is code 1, the telephone verifier; (m) = missed; (m)* = missed twice; yes = trace was conducted; (c) = current employee; (t) = terminated; N = no copy of the activity other than this report was made; Y = a more detailed account of the intrusion was made on one of the defensive subprogram printouts; n-emp = not employed; UA = unavailable; and UEA = unauthorized entry attempt.

Note that employee Lette called up late and had trouble getting the access codes correct. This fact and the short amount of time he spent trying to get on line could suggest a potential problem. A hacker tried to break into the system at 1:04 am and had his call traced. Employee Colak was recently terminated and tried to gain access to his computer accounts by using his old access codes. It's a good thing you remembered to remove his access codes from the system.

**Exhibit 36–4.** Grandarcher Aerospace Company/*security action file**unauthorized computer activity*/June 12, 1984.

285

# PART VIII

## If a Crime
## Is Suspected . . .

The fact is sad but true that a great proportion of the security precautions taken by organizations are the result of having suffered a loss. Particularly in light of the rapidity of changes in the computer field, it seems likely that many computer abuses will occur before adequate security is implemented. In the event an abuse is suspected, a careful investigation will be needed to pursue legal recourse. How to conduct an investigation into suspected computer abuse is a subject that would require a book in itself. One aid that might be overlooked in the effort is a questioned document examiner. The article that follows suggests how such an expert might best be used to assist the investigator.

# CHAPTER 37

## The Role of the Questioned Document Examiner in Computer Crime Investigations

### Dr. David A. Crown
### Examiner of Questioned Documents

Crimes involving computers have been with us since the computer was introduced to the business world. The criminal activity involved can range from unauthorized computer access to fraudulently issued checks generated by a computer.

Although the function of a questioned document examiner does not change when involved in computer crime investigations, his work approach must. Non-computer investigations may involve just the investigator or attorney and the questioned document examiner, but computer crimes can be much more complex. Detailed knowledge of computer operations is normally beyond the ken of a questioned document examiner. In a complicated matter, a team will be required, possibly an investigator, an auditor trained in computer operations, and a computer programmer, in addition to the examiner.

The most effective use of the time and talents of the questioned document examiner takes place when the team leader in an investigation breaks the problem down into discrete units. Rather than presenting the total problem to the examiner, the case is separated into a series of issues. The examiner then looks at the materials involved in each issue, and the other team members determine the significance of his findings as they relate to the problems in the case.

The issues to be examined by the questioned document examiner could relate to a specific matter within the following categories:

- employee screening and hiring
- determining access to the computer
- examining computer inputs and records relating to access
- examining computer outputs, printouts, checks
- examining documents resulting from computer output

Reprinted with the permission of the American Society for Industrial Security from *Security Management*, June 1980, p 42.

Examples of matters amenable to document analysis are as follows:

1.   Examination of signatures on sign-in sheets to determine if specific signatures are authentic or forged.
2.   Comparison of handwriting and typewriting on a program change authorization to determine the authenticity of the change and the approval for the change.
3.   Examination and comparison of IBM keypunch cards to determine which keypunch machine was used to input certain data.
4.   Determination of whether a computer printout was prepared on a dot matrix, teletype head, ball head, daisy wheel, chain printer, drum printer, laser printer, or ink jet printer.
5.   Comparison of two printouts to determine if they are from the same printer.
6.   Identification of the tape head used to produce a magnetic tape by examination of the striated markings on the tape.

The procedures for utilizing a questioned document examiner in computer crime investigations involve a series of steps. First, and most important, select an examiner who is fully qualified. Members of the American Academy of Forensic Sciences, the American Society of Questioned Document Examiners, and Diplomats of the American Board of Forensic Document Examiners have had their professional qualifications approved by their peers in the profession. In addition to the above ''screens'' for selecting an examiner, it would be well to select someone with experience in handling computer problems. Not all competent questioned document examiners are equipped to handle the involved problems engendered by the computer.

After delineating each issue in the investigation, try to evaluate each problem in terms of its importance to the whole investigation and the possibility of a positive reply from the examiner. Some issues may have a low priority for examination because the conclusions are expected to be of limited use to the outcome of the investigation. An example of this would be comparing a signature on an ancillary document with the writing of over one hundred individuals. Such an examination would be very time consuming, hence expensive. If the anticipated identification would not contribute directly to the solution of the issue, the necessity for such an examination should be carefully reviewed.

Documents submitted to the questioned document examiner should be the originals, if at all possible. On occasion, an examiner can work from photocopies, but the best evidence rule is applicable here: The better the evidence, the better the chance of a definite conclusion. Comparison exemplars must also be located. They can be either request exemplars or course-of-business exemplars. The investigator must make arrangements to collect exemplars from specific persons or from specific input/output devices if needed. The extent and number of exemplars to be collected should be discussed with the questioned document examiner. Too limited a selection of exemplars would hinder the examiner, and too extensive a collection would place a heavy burden on the investigator.

Documents signed or accomplished in the ordinary course of business can also be used for comparison. The problems of legal custody should be covered by establishing a chain-of-custody for each item of evidence expected to be introduced at a trial. In the case of exemplars, the basis for using the item or items as exemplars must be established.

If the questioned document examiner requires further exemplars, the investigator will be so informed. Inadequate exemplars and poor copies of questioned documents are some of the most frequent factors causing an examiner to give qualified rather than definite conclusions. Unless the evidence is completely conclusive, the examiner must give a qualified conclusion using terms of probability to express the degree of certainty.

Normally, a competent questioned document examiner will give the reasons for a qualified conclusion and a statement as to the possibility of a definite conclusion if certain steps are taken or conditions met. In some cases a definite conclusion is not possible and additional exemplars will not be of assistance in changing a qualified conclusion to a definite conclusion.

A questioned document examiner usually provides a written report of his conclusions with a description of all items examined. The only exception to this will be when the requestor specifically states that a written report is not wanted. If it is expected that the case will go to court, adequate time should be provided for exhibit photography and illustration of the evidence. In the ordinary course of events, this would be a matter between the attorney involved and the questioned document examiner.

Examinations requested of an examiner can be divided into unilateral examinations and comparative examinations. Problems concerning document preparation—such as determining the sequence of writing; deciphering erasures, obliterations, overwritings, or indented writings; or determining the age of a document—are normally unilateral examinations and do not require comparative specimens. Determining the make and model of a typewriter, input device, or output device is also a unilateral examination and is dependent upon the specimen collection and reference files of the examiner. Identifying the work of a specific output device or writer is a comparative examination and requires adequate exemplars of the suspect device or writer for comparison.

Not all types of evidence can be definitely identified. Inks and papers normally have class characteristics, *i.e.*, they can be broken down into very narrow classes, but not into a class of one, and they cannot be connected to a specific pen or a specific ream of paper. An exception is the torn piece of paper, which can ultimately be connected to the piece from which it was torn. The potential of each item of evidence in a computer crime investigation should be discussed with the questioned document examiner, so there are no expectations beyond the scientific potential of the evidence.

A paper trail will exist when ''(1) fictitious data is prepared for input to a computer system or when otherwise authorized input data is improperly altered or destroyed; (2) when otherwise correct reports, files, or other outputs are mislabeled, mispresented, altered, or misdelivered so as to affect a fraud or coverup; (3) by the development of improper programs or segments of programs or by the subsequent alteration of once-acceptable programs; (4) when files are directly changed with file utilities or improper programs; or (5) deliberate misoperation of the computer system, such as using the wrong programs, data files, or transactions, interruption of normal program processing or destruction of outputs or results.'' The questioned document examiner is most effective in assisting to reveal the truth in a suspected computer crime when he or she is part of an investigation team.

## BIBLIOGRAPHY

Crown. "Choosing a Questioned Document Examiner." *SECURITY MANAGEMENT* (Nov. 1979), p. 72.

Allen. "The Menace of Computer Fraud." *The Office* (Aug. 1979), p. 74.

# INDEX

Abstraction, levels of, 29–30
Abuse, computer, 131–144. *See also* Crime,
    computer-related
  availability of data on, 138–139
  case file of reported, 134–135
  definitions of, 133–134
Abuser-friendly computer systems, 13–14
Access control, 29, 178, 267–273
  algorithms, 194
  to computer center, 259
  electronic, 221
  functional model for, 269–270
  hardware, 194
  implementing, 270–273
  levels, 227
  physical, 221–232
    capabilities and considerations, 228–
    231
    cost of, 232
    programming method for, 227–228
    system reporting options, 231–232
    user code systems and methods, 223–
    228
  software for, 36–37
  to tape library, 259
  technological advances in, 174–175
  user ID authentication, 36, 175, 257–258,
    268, 269
"Access matrix," 188
Accessories, security, 233–37. *See also*
    Technological advances
Accountability, 255, 275–276
Accounting
  automated, 159–161
  controls, 199
  human resource, 55
  job (expense management), 259, 260

ACF2 (Access Control Facility), 261, 262,
  266
ACF2/VM, 261–262, 266
Administration
  controls, 5, 15, 100, 254
  of data security products, 256
  of passwords, 21, 257–258
  of system logs, 21
  technological advances and, 176
  *See also* Management
Alarms, 229–31, 255
Algorithm(s)
  access control, 194
  DES, 198
American Bar Association (ABA) survey, 9–
  11
American Institute of Certified Public
    Accountants (AICPA), 11, 44
American Society for Industrial Security
    (ASIS), xiii
Anti-passback capability, 229
Application programmers, 195
Applications security, 6
Apsit, William, 188, 189, 190
Army Logistics Management Center, 24
Assets
  analysis of, 67–69
  obligation to protect, 43–45
  software and data as, 51–55
Assignments, changing of, 116
AT&T, 243
Attorneys, 20
Audible alarms, 230–231
Audit committee policy, 44
Auditing, 32, 255, 258
  considerations concerning, 44
*Auditing Computer-based Systems*, 161

Auditors, EDP, 20
  data security and, 119
  independent, 183
  recovery of DP function and, 161–162
Authentication, user ID, 36, 175, 257–258, 268, 269
Authorization, user, 36, 175, 257
"Authorization tables," 162
Auto-degrade (fail-soft) capability, 230
Automatic data processing (ADP) security, 87
Awareness, security, 219–220

Backup facilities, 22, 230, 259
Baseline security controls, 150
BASIC, 25
Batch processing, remote, 169
Battery backup, 230
Becker, Jay, 143
Biometric devices, 233, 235–236
Bologna, Jack, 234, 235–236
Bolts, 237
Bonding of employees, 116
Brandt, Alan, 234
Browns Ferry Nuclear Plant, 206
Buddy system restrictions, 230
Business information security program, 85–86

Call-back programs, 233, 234
Care, standard of, 41
Carroll, John, 124
CA-Sentinel, 262, 266
Caulfield Institute of Technology, 142
Centralized administration, 256
*Chatlos Systems, Inc. v. National Cash Register*, 41
Chief executive officers (CEOs), 19. *See also* Management
Chubb Group of Insurance Companies, 148
Classified information
  debriefing, 110
  disposal of, 247–249. *See also* Destruction technology
Closed-circuit television (CCTV), 216–217
COBOL, 24, 25
Code breaking, 198
Code input, 223

Codes, user, 21, 223–228
Colleges, community, 24–25
Communications, 91, 101–104. *See also* Telecommunications
  controls, 5–6, 22, 162–163
Computer Abuse Research Project, 131–144
*Computer Capers* (Whiteside), 128
Computer center
  access control to, 259
  systemic view of, 58
  technological advances in, 169–170
  *See also* Physical security
*Computer Crime, Criminal Justice Resource Manual* (publication), 46
Computer crime. *See* Crime, computer-related
Computer personnel-security personnel gap, 27–33
Computer Security Center (DoD), 271–272
Computer Sentry, 265, 266
Computer systems
  abuser-friendly, 13–14
  countermeasures, 15
  views of, 124–130
  *See also* IBM and IBM-compatible systems
Comshare, 187, 189, 190
Concealment systems, 193
Confidentiality agreement, 110
Conservation, destruction technology and, 247–251
Contact condition monitors, 231
Contingency planning, 6–7, 16–17. *See also* Disaster recovery plan
Control(s)
  accounting, 199
  administrative, 5, 15, 100, 254
  against computer-related crime, technology for, 14–15
  baseline security, 150
  communications, 5–6, 22, 162–163
  of data/information, 21, 99
  data security products and, 254–255
  forms, 22
  logical, 254–255
  output distribution, 259
  personnel, 100, 115–117
  programming, 118
  user, 118–119

valuation of information assets and, 51–55
    *See also* Access control
Cookie-jar view of computer systems, 126–127
COPS (CICS On-Line Protection System), 262, 266
Copyright Act (1976), 49
Corporation, "shadow," 127
Corporation management, 260
COSS (CICS On-Line Security System), 262–263, 266
Cost/benefit analysis, 15
Cost(s)
    of disaster recovery plan, 16–17
    of encryption, 177
    hardware, 168–169
    of identification devices, 236
    of physical access control, 232
    replacement, 67
    of risk analysis, 84
Countermeasures. *See* Control(s)
Courses for training, 24–25
Courtney, Robert, 12, 195
Crank (computer group), 125
Crime, computer-related
    ABA survey of, 9–11
    AICPA survey of, 11
    degree and nature of, 139–142
    employees and, 11–14
    environment and, 123–124
    examples of, 45
    fraud, 11, 46–47
    investigation of, 287–292
    legislation on, 10, 48–49
    losses due to, 45–46
    PCIE study of, 11–12
    prosecuting, 46–47
    technology for controlling, 14–15
    traditional crime vs., 46–48
    *See also* Abuse, computer; Theft, computer
*Crime by Computer* (Parker), 123
Criminals, computer, 20
    types of, 123–130
CRT displays, 232
Cryptography, 191–200. *See also* Encryption of data
    applying techniques of, 196–197
    concepts, 192–193

conventional system features, 194
    management and, 191–192
    measuring effectiveness of, 198
    processes of, 197
    threats to security and, 194–195
Curriculum
    for data processing personnel, 25–26
    for security personnel, 24–25
CyLock, 236

Data base. *See* Data/information
Data base management system (DBMS), 270, 271–273
Data base processors, 172, 173–174
Data communications. *See* Communications
Data Encryption Standard (DES), 162, 176, 193, 198
Data/information, 5
    as balance sheet assets, 51–55
    classified, debriefing and, 110
    control of, 21, 99
    destruction of, 114
    disclosure of, 114
    encryption of, 36, 103, 162, 178
        cost of, 177
        preparation for, 197
        services providing, 190
        technological advances in, 176–177
        *See also* Cryptography
    insurance against loss of, 155–157
    magnets for erasing, 135
    modification of, 114
    outside the office, protecting, 105–107
    in retailing industry, 113–119
    security products for, 253–266
        administration type and, 256
        controls and, 254–255
        integration of, 258–260
        protection type and, 256–257
        user characteristics and, 257–258
    sensitivity levels of, 179
    storage of, 102
        off-site, 155–157, 164
Data processing committee, 22
Data processors, 132–133
Dear, Geoff, 237
Debriefing employees, 109–111
Decentralized administration, 256
Decision base results, 85

Declared vs. default protection, 256–257
Defender II, 265, 266
Dennis, F.W., 123
Department of Defense (DoD)
  Computer Institute, 24
  Industrial Security Manual (ISM), 247–248
Deposits, bank, 135
Depreciation of information assets, 52–53
Destruction technology, 239–245
  conservation and, 247–251
Dial-up access, 182–83, 278
Digilink II, 265, 266
Disaster recovery plan, 16–18, 22, 100. *See also* contingency planning
  maintenance of, 164
  outline for, 151–153
Disclosure of classified information, 114
Disintegrators, 244
Disposal of classified information. *See* Destruction technology
Distributed processing, 169
Documentation, risk analysis and, 65
Documentation security, 5
Dual vendor approach, 98
Duress alarms, 229
Duties, separation of, 117, 255

Electronic data processing (EDP), 3–7
Electronic data processing (EDP) security program
  features of, 5–7
  implementation of, 7
  layering of, 15–16
Elliott, Charles M., 188, 190
Employee(s)
  bonding of, 116
  changing assignments of, 116
  computer-related crime and, 11–14
  control objective in hiring, 116–117
  debriefing, 109–111
  immediate separation of, 116–117
  mandatory vacations for, 116
  separation of duties of, 117, 255
  *See also* Personnel
Encapsulation of systems, 194
Encasements, 237
Enciphering, 193
Encoding, 193

Encryption of data, 36, 103, 162, 178. *See also* Cryptography
  cost of, 177
  devices for, 233, 234
  preparation for, 197
  services providing, 190
  technological advances in, 176–177
Environment
  computer-related crime and, 123–124
  programming, 178
  storage, 156
Equity Funding, 129
Examiner, questioned document, 287–292
Exception, security by, 27–28
Expanders, 221–222
Expense management, 259, 260

Fail-soft (auto-degrade) capability, 230
Failure, computer, effects of, 160
Fairyland view of computer systems, 128–129
Fallacies, computer security, 198–199
Family, protecting information outside office and, 106
Feature recognition, 185
Federal Computer Systems Protection Act, 49
Felony theft, 47
File(s)
  backup, 22
  protection of, 31
  *See also* Data/information; Software/programs
Fingermatrix, 236
Fire protection, 217–219
  emergency training, 209–210
  fallacies about, 203–210
Florida Computer Crime Act, 48–49
Foreign Corrupt Practices Act, 51, 161
Formalized analyses, 151. *See also* Risk analysis; Threat(s); Vulnerability(ies)
Forms control, 22
FOX-FONE, 265, 266
Fraud, 11, 46–47
Freedom of Information Act, 59
Fund transfers, electronic, 47, 49

General Accounting Office (GAO), 143, 161
General Electric (GE), 97–100

Ginsberg, Emily, 236
Guardian (security package), 262, 263, 266
Guard tour monitoring, 229

Hackers, 3
Halon, 204–206, 217–219
*Hancock v. State*, 46–48
Hardware
  access control, 194
  costs, 168–169
  maintenance, 30
  security, 185–186, 233, 271
Hayakawa, S.I., 29
High security facilities, 156
Hiring procedures, control objectives in, 116
  –117
Horback, Glen, 234, 235
Human resource accounting, 55

I. P. Sharp Associates, 188, 189, 190
IBM and IBM-compatible systems
  security for, 261–264
  software security for, 184
Identification
  of terminal devices, 178
  of threats, 74–81, 148–149
  user, 36, 117, 175, 269
  of vulnerabilities, 74–81, 148–149
Identimat hand-geometry reader, 223
Ignorance as source of protection, 27–28
Incineration, 240–241
Industrial Security Manual (ISM), 247–248
Information. *See* Data/information
Information processors, 172, 173–174
Information System, Office of (OIS), 35–37
Input controls, 162
Insurance against data loss, 52, 155–157
Integrity function, 174
Interdisciplinary approach to security, 20
Internal mail handling, 103
"In-the-floor" service distribution system,
  211–213
Inventory, 157
Investigation, crime, 287–292
  training for, 20–21
*Investigation of Computer Related Crime*
  (publication), 46

Job accounting (expense management), 259,
  260

Jones, Paul L., 187–188, 189
Justice Statistics, Bureau of, 46

Keyboard protection, 228

Land-of-opportunity view of computer sys-
  tems, 125–126
Law
  on computer-related crimes, 10, 48–49
  risk assessment methodology and, 60–61
Layering of security program, 15–16
Legal department, 260
Liability, judging, 41–49
Library
  EDP, 21, 118, 259
  program, management of, 259
Life cycle of information assets, 53
Lineguard 3000, 265, 266
Lists, memory, 231
Literacy, computer, 196
Locks, 237
Log(s), system, 118, 194
  administration of, 21
  research, 110
Logical controls, 254–255
  technological advances and, 173–174
Loss exposure analysis, 149–150
Luggage, securing, 106–107

Machine time, 117
Magnets for erasing data, 135
Mail, first class, 103
Maintenance
  hardware, 30
  of recovery plan, 164
Management
  cryptography and, 191–192
  expense, 259, 260
  gap between security personnel and com-
    puter personnel and, 32–33
  protection plan and, 93, 95
  risk assessment and, 66
  support from, 183–184
  user, 260
  *See also* Administration
Management and Budget, Office of (OMB),
  87, 161
Martin Marietta Data Systems, 188, 189,
  190

Mastiff, 237
Media, computer abuse research and, 132–133
Melting systems, 245
Memory lists, 231
Messages. *See* Communications
Message systems, electronic, 103
Microcomputers, 4
Military Records Center (St. Louis), 207
Minicomputers, 107
"Minimax," 148
Modification of classified information, 114
Momentum of sets, 30–31
Monitors, contact condition, 231

Naming standards, 259–260
National Bureau of Standards, 148
National Center for Computer Crime Data, 143
National Computer Centre, 142
National Fire Protection Association, 203
Networking systems, 170–174. *See also* Technological advances
New York Stock Exchange, 44
*Northwest Airlines, Inc. v. Glen L. Martin Company*, 41

Objective of security, 33
Office buildings, "open plan," 211
Off-line systems, 222–223
Off-site storage of data, 155–157, 164
On-line access, 117–118, 162, 181, 222–223
Operating systems, 184, 270, 271–272, 273
Operator control, 118
Operators, system, 195
Organizational controls, 163
Output controls, 163, 259
Owens Corning, 243

Palm print recognition, 185
Paper trail, 291
Parker, Donn, 12, 32, 123, 150
Passwords, 31, 117, 178, 188, 269
  administration, 21, 257–258
  vulnerability of, 199
Paton, Nancy, 234–235
PC Lock II, 265, 266
Personnel, 260. *See also* Employee(s)

controls, 15, 100, 115–117
curriculum for, 25–26
gap between computer and security, 27–33
records, 239
for risk analysis, 64–65
screening and monitoring of, 21
security, 189
of storage companies, 157
Personnel Management, Office of, 24
Physical access control, 221–232
  capabilities and considerations, 228–231
  cost of, 232
  programming method for, 227–228
  system reporting options, 231–232
  user code systems and methods, 223–228
Physical security, 5, 15, 99–100, 113, 254
  recovery of DP function and, 163
  technological advances and, 173
Planning, recovery, 164
Playpen view of computer systems, 124–125
Polak, Jack, 126
Practices, computing. *See* Technological advances
Predata processing validation, 119
President's Council on Integrity and Efficiency (PCIE), 11–12
Printers, 231
Privacy Act of 1974, 59, 161
Privacy systems, 193
Processing, distributed, 169
Processing controls, 162–163
Program library management, 259
Programmable-Read-Only Memory (PROM), 194
Programmers, 195
Programming controls, 118
Programming environment, 178
Programs. *See* Software/Programs
Project manager for risk analysis, 61
Property, software as, 47–48
Prosecution of computer-related crime, 46–47
Protect-CICS, 262, 263, 266
Protection
  of assets, 43–45
  default vs. declared, 256–257
  file, 31
  selective, 91, 93–95

Proximity of storage facilities, 156
"Public Key Cryptosystem," 176–177
Public relations department, 260
Pulping, 245, 248–249

Questioned document examiner, 287–292

Rabbit-4, 265, 266
RACF (Resource Access Control Facility), 262, 263, 266
Readers, 221–223, 227–229
Read Only Memory (ROM), 194
Recognition technology, 185. *See also* Readers
Record keeping function, 174
Records, personnel, 239
Recovery of DP function, 159–165
    data communications control and, 162–163
    EDP auditors and, 161–162
    physical protection and, 163
    plan for, 16–18, 22, 100
        cost of, 16–17
        maintenance of, 164
        outline for, 151–153
    *See also* Contingency planning
Recycling classified waste materials, 243, 248–249
Red Brigades, 128
Reference checks, 116
Remote batch processing, 169
Repair time, 67
Replacement costs and mode, 67
Research logs, 110
*Resolutions of the Strategic Directorate*, 128
Resource Access Control Facility (RACF), 188
Responsibility, 255
Ressin, Raymond, 127
Retailing industry, data security in, 113–119
Retinas, scanning of, 236
Ribicoff, Abraham, 49
Rifkin, Stanley, 125
Risk analysis, 15, 57–81, 100
    alternatives to, 85–86
    characteristics of, 83–84
    cost of, 84
    data collection for, 87–89
    documentation requirements and, 65
    establishing scope of, 61
    familiarity with EDP system and, 66–67
    flaws of, 84–85
    hidden risk of, 87–89
    identification of threats and vulnerabilities, 74–81
    management and, 66
    methodology, 59–61, 97–98
    outline of end product of, 65–66
    planning program of, 64
    project manager for, 61
    selection and training of team, 64–65
    systemic view of data processing center and, 58
    of theft, 150–153
    value of, 83–86
    value of EDP system and, 67–74
Rogers, G.R., 31
Routing function, 174
RPG, 25

SAC (Security Access Controller), 262, 263, 266
Scheduler, automated, 259
Schultz, John R., 143
Scrambling services, 190
Screening, personnel, 21
Search warrants, 141
Secrets, trade, 47
Secure Access Multiport, 265, 266
Secure Access Unit, 265, 266
Secure/CICS (security package), 262, 264, 266
Secure/IMS (security package), 262, 264, 266
Secure (security package), 262, 263–264, 266
Security department, 19–22
*Security Management* (magazine), xiii, xvi
Selective protection, 91, 93–95
Sensitive information, distribution of, 21
Service distribution systems, "in-the-floor," 211–213
Sets, momentum of, 30–31
"Shadow corporation," 127
Shannon, C.E., 193
Sheats, Jim, 243
Shredders, 241–243, 245
Single use restrictions, 230

Site selection, 215–220
SKK, Inc., 266
Smith, Gerald, 125
Smoke detectors, 206
Soapbox view of computer systems, 128
Sobol, Michael, 234
Software integrity, 6
Software/programs, 100, 270, 271, 273. *See also* Operating systems
  for access control, 36–37
  as balance sheet assets, 51–55
  call-back, 233, 234
  classification as property, 47–48
  security, 184–185, 188, 251
Sprinkler systems, 207–208
SRI International, 131
Staffing, 256. *See also* Employee(s); Personnel
Standard of care, 41
Standards, Bureau of, 83
*Statements on Auditing Standards* (SAS), 161–162
Statutes on computer-related crime, 10, 48–49
Storage of data/information, 102
  environment, 156
  off-site, 155–157, 164
Supervisory function, 173–174. *See also* Administration; Management
Support systems, computer, 219
Surveillance (security package), 262, 264, 266
Surveys, computer security, 148–150
System software. *See* Software/programs

Table control schemes, 199
Tables, "authorization," 162
Tamper alarms, 229
Tape management system, 258
Task force, security, 98–100
Team approach to security, 31–32
Technician, data, 181
Technological advances, 167–180. *See also* Accessories, security
  access management systems and, 174–175
  administration and, 176
  advantages of, 167–168
  encryption and, 176–177
  logical security and, 173–174

  in physical environment, 169–170
  physical security and, 173
  protective measures and, 179–180
  security considerations in, 178–179
  in user environment, 168–169
Technology
  for controlling computer-related crime, 14–15
  threat environment and, 28–29
Telecommunications, 170–173. *See also* Communications; Terminals
  dial-up access, 182–83, 278
Telegraphic messages, 103
Telephone traffic, 103
Television, closed-circuit (CCTV), 216–217
Temporary operations, 164
Terminals, 167, 169. *See also* Communications; Telecommunications
  at home, 107
  identification of, 178
  on-line, 117–118, 162
  proliferation of, 169–170, 173
Terminology, gap between computer personnel and security personnel due to, 27
Theft, computer, 47, 147–153. *See also* Crime, computer-related
  computer security surveys and, 148–150
  risk assessment of, 150–153
Threat(s)
  cryptography and, 194–195
  environment, 28–30
  identification of, 74–81, 148–149
  types of computer criminals and, 123–130
Threshold alarms, 255
Time-sharing systems. *See* Technological advances
Time zones, 227
Token recognition, 185
Toolbox view of computer systems, 129–130
Top Secret (security package), 262, 264, 266
Trade secrets, 47
Training, 20–21
  college courses, 24–25
  fire emergency, 209–210
Transaction logs, 118
Transmission, data, 102–103. *See also* Communications; Telecommunications

Travel, protecting information during, 106–107

"True" secrecy systems, 193

Trusted Computer System Evaluation Criteria, 271–272

*United States v. Jones*, 46–48

*United States v. Seidlitz*, 48

UPSU (User Profile Security Utility), 262, 264, 266

"User friendly," 12

User(s), 195. *See also* Access control
  authentication of ID of, 36, 175, 257–258, 268, 269
  authorization of, 36, 175, 257
  code systems and methods for, 223–228
  control, 118–119
  data security products and, 257–258
  environment, technological advances in, 168–169
  identification of, 36, 117, 175, 269
  management, 260
  restricted interface, 273
  screening, 275–285

Utility functions, 174

Vacations, mandatory, 116

Validation, predata processing, 119

Valuation of information assets, 51–55

Vendors, 164, 178–179
  dual, 98

Verification, user identity, 269

Visible alarms, 230–231

Voice-print recognition systems, 185

Vulnerability(ies)
  analysis of, 74–81, 148–149
  of communications, 104
  cost of risk analysis and, 84–85
  of passwords, 199
  in retailing, 113

*Ward v. Superior Court*, 47

Warrants, search, 141

War-zone view of computer systems, 127

Waste materials, classified, 247–249. *See also* Destruction technology

Water damage, 206–207

Water extinguishment, 218–219

Webb, Abe, 243

Whitaker, J.T., 245

Whiteside, Thomas, 128

Zones
  security, 216–217
  time, 227